With George Washington
in the Wilderness

ALSO BY PAUL R. MISENCIK AND SALLY E. MISENCIK
AND FROM McFARLAND

*American Indians of the Ohio Country
in the 18th Century* (2020)

ALSO BY PAUL R. MISENCIK
AND FROM McFARLAND

Sally Townsend, George Washington's Teenage Spy (2016)

*The Original American Spies: Seven Covert
Agents of the Revolutionary War* (2014)

*George Washington and the Half-King Chief Tanacharison:
An Alliance That Began the French and Indian War* (2014)

With George Washington in the Wilderness

The Frontier Life of Christopher Gist

PAUL R. MISENCIK *and*
SALLY E. MISENCIK

McFarland & Company, Inc., Publishers
Jefferson, North Carolina

Unless otherwise noted, photographs and maps
are from the authors' collection.

LIBRARY OF CONGRESS CATALOGUING-IN-PUBLICATION DATA

Names: Misencik, Paul R., 1940– author. | Misencik, Sally E., 1939– author.
Title: With George Washington in the wilderness : the frontier life
of Christopher Gist / Paul R. Misencik, and Sally E. Misencik.
Other titles: Frontier life of Christopher Gist
Description: Jefferson, North Carolina : McFarland & Company, Inc.,
Publishers, 2022. | Includes bibliographical references and index.
Identifiers: LCCN 2022009112 | ISBN 9781476688497 (paperback : acid free paper) ∞
ISBN 9781476645872 (ebook)
Subjects: LCSH: Gist, Christopher, -1759. | Ohio Company (1747-1779)—
History. | Soldiers—Virginia—Biography. | Washington, George, 1732-1799—
Friends and associates. | Scouts (Reconnaissance)—Ohio River Valley—
Biography. | Explorers—Ohio River Valley—Biography. | Northwest,
Old—Discovery and exploration. | United States—History—French and
Indian War, 1754-1763. | BISAC: HISTORY / United States / Revolutionary
Period (1775-1800) | HISTORY / Military / United States
Classification: LCC F517.G54 M67 2022 | DDC 977/.02092 [B]—dc23/eng/20220223
LC record available at https://lccn.loc.gov/2022009112

BRITISH LIBRARY CATALOGUING DATA ARE AVAILABLE

ISBN (print) 978-1-4766-8849-7
ISBN (ebook) 978-1-4766-4587-2

© 2022 Paul R. Misencik and Sally E. Misencik. All rights reserved

*No part of this book may be reproduced or transmitted in any form
or by any means, electronic or mechanical, including photocopying
or recording, or by any information storage and retrieval system,
without permission in writing from the publisher.*

Front cover: *Frontiersman with Pipe*, artwork by David Wright

Printed in the United States of America

McFarland & Company, Inc., Publishers
Box 611, Jefferson, North Carolina 28640
www.mcfarlandpub.com

To our intrepid pioneering ancestors and today's immigrants who exhibit much the same courage and resourcefulness of the earlier people who came to America and added to its greatness.

Table of Contents

Preface — 1

1. The Origin of a Frontiersman — 5
2. Christopher Gist and the Ohio Company of Virginia — 15
3. Gist's First Trek for the Ohio Company, 1750–1751 — 22
4. Toward the Falls of the Ohio — 45
5. Prelude to Another Journey for the Ohio Company — 50
6. Gist's Second Trek for the Ohio Company — 53
7. The Logstown Conference — 63
8. Gist's Move to Western Pennsylvania — 68
9. The French Invasion of Western Pennsylvania — 76
10. Mission to Evict the French — 84
11. The Perilous Return — 96
12. Fleur-de-Lis at the Forks — 109
13. The World on Fire — 117
14. Surrender on the Fourth of July — 127
15. Fort Cumberland at Will's Creek — 137
16. March to the Monongahela — 147
17. Death in the Forest — 151
18. Captain of Scouts and Indian Agent — 155
19. The Forbes Campaign against Fort Duquesne — 164
20. The Last Trail — 171

Epilogue — 175
Chapter Notes — 201
Bibliography — 211
Index — 215

Preface

"Gold is tried by fire, brave men by adversity."
—Seneca

The Seven Years' War, 1756–1763, is considered by most historians as the "real first world war," and that is not hyperbole. Despite its name, it lasted nine long years, and its battles were fought in South America, Europe, Africa, India, and as far as the Philippine Archipelago. Before it ended, it had claimed the lives of over one and a half million souls, one out of every 533 people on earth.[1] The war was historically significant and caused monumental changes, but most people don't realize that it was started as a result of a relatively minor land speculation venture concocted in 1748 by a group of wealthy Virginians who called themselves the Ohio Company of Virginia.

They wanted to develop and settle a tract of land in the area of the Forks of the Ohio, where the Allegheny and Monongahela rivers come together to form the Ohio River at present Pittsburgh, Pennsylvania. The land they sought to exploit was a 500,000-acre tract, which equated to 781.25 square miles or a block of land about twenty-eight miles square. The problem was that the land in question lay on the west side of the Allegheny Mountains, which despite the fact that it was populated by thousands of Shawnee, Lenni Lenape (Delaware), and Mingo Indians, was claimed by France and acknowledged as French territory by England in three separate treaties, the last of which was signed in 1748, that very same year.

In spite of the treaties, French ownership of the area was rejected by the Ohio Company, who made their own rather tenuous claim of English ownership. In 1750, the Ohio Company contracted Christopher Gist, who came from an aristocratic Maryland family, to explore the trans-Allegheny for the purpose of determining the best area to establish their speculative settlements. Gist completed two expeditions that covered present western Pennsylvania, Ohio, Kentucky, and

Preface

West Virginia, and was the first to describe those areas in his detailed journals. In addition to his explorations, Gist had the peripheral task of establishing and maintaining a friendly relationship with the Indians in the area.

In the winter of 1753, Gist became acquainted with twenty-one-year-old George Washington when he was asked to guide Washington through the Pennsylvania wilderness, and during that expedition, he saved young Washington's life on at least two occasions. From that time, Gist accompanied Washington on most of his earliest adventures, and the two formed a bond of friendship that lasted until Gist's death.

Christopher Gist was an intrepid explorer whose journals give us a marvelous glimpse at the wild, wonderful American wilderness before farms, towns, and highways. But Gist gives us more: a more personal look at humanness, greatness, and even the personality flaws of some of the more noteworthy people of American history, people like George Washington, Virginia Lieutenant-Governor Robert Dinwiddie, Generals Edward Braddock and John Forbes, Colonel Henry Bouquet, and a host of others with whom Gist worked closely.

Christopher Gist worked as a fur trader, ranger, explorer, guide, Indian agent, and army scout. His adventures during his relatively short life are exceptional, but it's even more extraordinary that in spite of his remarkable life and noteworthy accomplishments, he has in general been overlooked by historians. At most, some people know that Gist saved Washington from drowning in the freezing waters of the Allegheny River, but few are aware of their mission or its consequential ramifications. There are many books about Daniel Boone and his explorations of present Kentucky, but very few books mention the fact that Christopher Gist predated Boone's exploration of Kentucky by almost twenty years. The same can be said of many more of the famous frontiersmen of the Ohio territory. Frontier heroes like Simon Kenton and George Rogers Clark had not yet been born when Christopher Gist was exploring the area west and south of the Ohio River.

Why is that so? We suppose it might have something to do with the fact that Gist was not a swashbuckling Indian fighter. Instead, he was a peaceable man who tried to maintain congenial relations with those he met. The Indians respected and liked Christopher Gist and indeed often invited him to come and live among them, and when he died, they felt they had lost a person who dealt with them honestly and looked out for their interests.

In writing our manuscript, we found Gist's lack of fame or notoriety

Preface

presented some obstacles. There just wasn't very much information regarding his personal life. Gist's journals are very detailed, even to the point of listing distances and bearings traveled, but there are no written records regarding most facets of his life. For example, we don't know the details of his move to the Yadkin River of North Carolina, or even when or where his wife Sarah died, although we can deduce that she may have passed away about 1757.

Even so, doing the detective work in researching Christopher Gist's life and writing his history was fun for both of us, mostly because Gist was such an intriguing person. He had many strengths, and like every human, he had flaws, but in our opinion, he deserves a place in history alongside the other heroes of our American experience.

We have many people and organizations to thank for their assistance in writing this book. These include the Ohio History Connection, the Smithsonian Institution's National Museum of the American Indian and National Museum of American History, the U.S. Library of Congress, the French and Indian War Foundation, the National Library for the Study of George Washington, Fort Ligonier, and countless others including the many small community libraries and historical societies in Pennsylvania, Ohio, West Virginia, and Kentucky. We would especially like to thank Mr. Michael Hose of Oldtown, Maryland, for generously sharing his considerable knowledge of the colonial Cresap family.

1

The Origin of a Frontiersman

"Life is short, and the world is wide."
—Simon Raven

In the pantheon of American frontier heroes, Christopher Gist remains relatively unknown. Others like Daniel Boone, Davy Crockett, and Simon Kenton have received considerable deserved recognition for their exploits, yet Gist in many ways accomplished more at an earlier time than those more famous frontiersmen. For example, Gist was the first to provide a detailed description of the trans-Allegheny region, which we refer to as the Ohio territory, and his explorations of present Kentucky predated Daniel Boone by eighteen years.

There are no portraits or sketches of Christopher Gist that were made during his lifetime, but journals and other accounts from that period describe him as an impressive person. It was said that his son Nathaniel bore a remarkable resemblance to Christopher, and descriptions of Nathaniel survive. Based on those descriptions and other contemporary accounts, we know that Christopher Gist had a rather dark or swarthy complexion and stood over six feet, two inches tall, which was significantly taller than the average eighteenth-century man's height of five feet, eight inches.[1] He is also said to have had a husky, powerful physique, weighing more than fourteen stone[2] or roughly two hundred pounds, and he was capable of enduring considerable physical hardship.

Christopher came from a distinguished line of Englishmen, but it was his grandfather and namesake, Captain Christopher Gist (1655–1691), who along with his wife, the former Edith Cromwell (1663–1696), emigrated from England sometime before 1679 and settled in Baltimore County,[3] in the Province of Maryland. The colony had originally been established by the Roman Catholic Calverts as a refuge for England's Catholic population.

With George Washington in the Wilderness

George Calvert, 1st Lord Baltimore (1579–1632), sought a charter from King Charles I (1600–1649) to establish the colony called "Crescentia" (growing, or to grow) to be located between Massachusetts to the north and Virginia to the south, but George Calvert died in 1632 before the charter was granted. On Sunday, June 20, 1632, the king granted the charter to George's son Caecilius, or Cecil Calvert, 2nd Baron Baltimore (1605–1675), but rather than name the province Crescentia as Calvert proposed, the king preferred the name "Terra Mariae" or *Mary Land*, in honor of the king's wife Henrietta Maria of France (1609–1669).

Baltimore County, where the Gists settled, was established in 1659 and was named for Cecil, 2nd Baron Baltimore. Although Cecil was the proprietor of the colony, he never visited Maryland. Instead, in 1634, he appointed his next younger brother Leonard Calvert (1606–1647) as first proprietary governor Maryland, because Leonard was willing to come to Maryland and manage the colony as Cecil's surrogate. In essence, the title "proprietary governor" merely meant that Leonard was Cecil's resident manager. In 1647, Leonard Calvert died, and in his will he named his friend Thomas Greene as his successor, and Greene held that position from 1647 until 1649. Greene was followed as proprietary governor by William Stone, who managed the colony from 1649 to 1656; General Josias Fendall between the years 1657 and 1660; and Phillip Calvert, who was proprietary governor for one year until 1661.

In 1661, Charles Calvert, 3rd Baron Baltimore (1637–1715), arrived in the colony to become the first Calvert of the royal charter-holding family to govern Maryland in person. Charles later inherited the colony upon the death of his father Cecil in 1675.

Although Maryland was established as refuge for Roman Catholics, the Catholics were a minority consisting of only about 10 percent of the population, and there was continued unsettlement and strife between Anglicans, Catholics, Puritans, and Quakers. In 1684, Charles traveled to England for several years, and during his absence, Maryland was rocked by the Protestant Revolution of 1689, in which the Puritan revolutionaries took control of the colony. King William III, or William of Orange (1650–1702), withdrew the Calvert family's royal charter, and Maryland reverted to a Royal Colony.

Benedict Calvert, the 4th Baron Baltimore (1679–1715) and the son of Charles, realized that the loss of the family's charter was essentially due to their Catholic faith, so in 1713, he publicly converted to Anglicanism and petitioned King George I (1660–1727) for restoration of

1. The Origin of a Frontiersman

the family charter. In 1715, the charter was returned to the Calvert family. Notwithstanding the fact that Benedict's conversion to the Anglican faith brought about the restoration of the Colony to the Calvert family, Benedict's father Charles, a staunch Catholic, was so dismayed at his son's renunciation of Catholicism that he cut off all support for his son. Ironically, both father and son died within two months of each other in 1715.

It was during this time that Christopher Gist (1655–1691) and his wife Edith (1663–1694),[4] the grandparents of the frontiersman Christopher Gist, arrived in Maryland. In England, the Gist family was notable and distinguished, and the name has various spellings in records pertaining to the family. It is found as "Guest," "Gest," "Geyste," "Ghest," "le Gest," "le Gist," and "Gist" and is said to mean "the guest, or the received stranger."[5] Christopher's wife, Edith Cromwell Gist, was the daughter of Henry Cromwell, who claimed he was the first cousin of Oliver Cromwell (1599–1658), the Lord Protector and ruler of the British Isles from 1653 until his death in 1658.

Christopher Gist, the grandfather of the frontiersman, and his wife Edith established their residence in Baltimore County on the south side of the Patapsco River in what is now Anne Arundel County, Maryland. They were successful tobacco farmers, and records indicate that in 1682, Christopher Sr. was a member of the Baltimore County Grand Jury, and in 1689, he was one of the county justices.[6]

Christopher Sr. and Edith had one child, a son they named Richard (1684–1741). Young Richard learned to survey and was responsible for surveying much of the western shore of Maryland. He acquired extensive land holdings in addition to the land he inherited when his father died in 1691. In 1693, he purchased a 225-acre parcel of land he named "Gist's Rest." He then purchased in succession 200-acre "Turkey Cock Hall," 775-acre "Adventure," and 300-acre "Green Spring Traverse."

Richard married the former Zipporah Murray on Saturday, December 7, 1704, and the number of their children ranged from six to eleven, depending on which source is accessed. In most accounts, Christopher, who became the frontiersman, was the oldest, although there is some indication that a son Richard was born in 1704 and died at the age of six. There is also disagreement regarding the year of Christopher's birth, with some sources listing it as 1705 and others as 1706. As near as can be ascertained the children of Richard and Zipporah were Christopher (c. 1705–1759), Nathaniel (c. 1707–c. 1788), Edith (c. 1709–c. 1770), William (1711–1794), Thomas (1712–1787), Jemima (1714–c. 1748), Ruth

(1716–c. 1750), John (1722–1778), and Sarah (1724–c. 1770). Interestingly, the brothers Christopher, Nathaniel, and William married three sisters who were the daughters of neighbors Joshua and Joanna O'Carroll Howard.[7]

Christopher married Sarah Howard (1711–c. 1757) in 1728. He was twenty-three and she was seventeen, and most sources indicate they had six children, one of whom, Bell, died in infancy in 1734. Their five surviving children were Richard (1729–1780), Violetta (1731–1768), Nathaniel (1733–1796), Anne (1734–1795), and Thomas (1735–1788).[8] Anne was also referred to as "Nancy," which was a diminutive form for Anne, and Thomas in some sources is referred to as Benjamin. There may have been others, like Bell, who died in infancy, and their names were lost or not recorded. Also, Anne and Thomas being known by different names may give the impression that the Gists had additional children.

There are no existing records that describe the level of education that young Christopher received, but it's apparent from the quality of his writings, and his articulation of the principles of zoology, geography, and history show that he benefited from some formal schooling. Christopher learned the art of surveying from his father, which accounts for the accuracy and precision he exhibited during his explorations and mapping of the trans-Allegheny region.

Like his father and grandfather, young Christopher energetically worked to expand the Gist landholdings. In 1730, he purchased lot number 56 in Baltimore City.[9] The deed came with the stipulation that within eighteen months, Gist would complete a house on the property with a surface area of at least four hundred square feet.[10] The tract, called "Joshua's Lot," encompassed five hundred acres, and it was followed by other land purchases. Baltimore at the time was a small community, with around two dozen homes.

During that time, Maryland was experiencing Indian raids along its western frontier. Most of the Indian unrest had to do with the fact that the Calverts were not inclined to negotiate or deal fairly with the Indians for land purchases. Instead, they relied on the inexorable press of white settlements to force the Indians farther to the west. The Indians' animosity had its origins in the so-called Beaver Wars, or Iroquois Wars, which erupted in the mid-seventeenth century. Both the Europeans and the Indians enthusiastically engaged in the burgeoning fur trade. The Europeans could not get enough of the valuable furs, and the Indians quickly became addicted to European manufactured goods, such as metal pots, knives, beads, mirrors, cloth, and anything else the

1. The Origin of a Frontiersman

fur traders had to offer. In the past, the Indians trapped only enough to satisfy their family needs, but now, they scoured the woodlands and streams for every fur-bearing animal they could trap or hunt to trade for European merchandise.

Within a few years, the fur trade became very competitive, and the Iroquois grew increasingly aggressive in their quest to achieve and maintain a lion's share. They concluded that the way to monopolize the fur trade industry was through the simple expedient of eliminating the competition. That approach was similar to the methods used to eliminate the competition by bootlegger gangs in Chicago during the American Prohibition era some 270 years later.

The mighty Iroquois Confederation first attacked and dispersed or destroyed their nearest neighbors, the Wenro, Neutral, Mahican, Huron, and Erie nations, which caused the Calverts to look with alarm at the growing strength and aggressiveness of the Iroquois to the north. The powerful Susquehannock nation occupied the forests in Pennsylvania, and Charles Calvert entered into an alliance with the Susquehannock and provided them with arms so they would be a formidable buffer between Maryland and the rampaging Iroquois.

The Susquehannock were able to fight off the Iroquois for more than a decade, but in 1674, the Calverts grew apprehensive at the growing strength and belligerence of the neighboring Susquehannock. The threat of bellicose, battle-hardened, and well-armed Indians was bad enough, but more importantly, the Susquehannock were stifling the westward growth of the colony, and that was bad for business. Not only did the Calverts terminate their alliance with the Susquehannock, but they launched a war against them, sending Maryland militia forces to attack and destroy Susquehannock villages. Hundreds of Susquehannock men, women, and children as well as many prominent chiefs[11] were killed, and the survivors were driven farther into the hinterland.

Of course, the surviving Susquehannock were enraged at what they rightly considered a betrayal by the Marylanders. As a result, they, as well as other Indian nations, began to look upon English colonists in general as untrustworthy or hostile. The continued white encroachment into Indian lands to the west caused many of the affected tribes to strike back at frontier settlements.

In 1730, to counter Indian raids, Baltimore County formed a militia unit called the Maryland Rangers, and Christopher joined their ranks, reportedly as a lieutenant. As the name implies, the rangers carried out patrols along Maryland's western frontier in an effort to interdict incursions by Indian raiders. The experience educated Christopher about life and existence on the frontier and gave him a more intimate understanding of the various Indian cultures and a knowledge of the geography and topography of the lands to the west. In addition, it served to develop, toughen, and condition him so that he felt at home in the wilderness, and it instilled a desire to wander and explore the vastness of the great area beyond the Alleghenies.

While Christopher served as a ranger, he also started his own enterprise as a fur trader and associated himself as agent for the British Fur Company. He built a warehouse in Baltimore and apparently carried on his fur-trading enterprise with the Indians while he was on his ranger missions. One of his duties as a ranger was to ensure the maintenance of an old Indian trail that the whites called the Garrison Road, but in March 1742, he was placed on trial for not carrying out his duties. It appears that young Christopher was neglecting his ranger duties in favor of his fur trading. For some reason the charges were dropped, but Christopher was still required to pay the court costs.

When he was home in Baltimore County, Christopher served as the county coroner, while also being responsible for administering the family fortune. His father Richard died in 1741 and left no will, so it fell to Christopher as the eldest son to manage the Gist estates. Christopher's brother Nathaniel worked closely with him, and along with surveying and tobacco farming, they worked together in a mercantile business as well as the fur-trading enterprise. According to biographers Jean Muir Dorsey and Maxwell Jay Dorsey, "the Indians and traders who came to Baltimore to exchange their furs for supplies they needed, probably did considerable trading with him. In this way, he became acquainted with the different tribes of Indians, learned where they lived, and how to deal with them."[12]

While Christopher was energetic and desirous of expanding the family fortune, he apparently did not possess the keen head for business that his father and grandfather had. On Friday, April 26, 1745, Christopher purchased a sloop[13] of about forty-five tons[14] to transport their merchandise to settlements along the coastline and navigable rivers. Christopher named it *Two Brothers*, in reference to his partnership with his brother Nathaniel,[15] and he hired Richard Blakistone as its master. Unfortunately, Christopher's debts grew faster than his profits, and to make matters worse, he started off with a substantial liability. In 1732, Christopher's warehouse in Baltimore burned to the ground, destroying the furs stored within. The British Fur Company "pressed a claim for

1. The Origin of a Frontiersman

the amount of £10,000 sterling for the lost furs."[16] It was a crushing debt, and it left Gist broke.

To put the £10,000 into perspective, the cost of dinner in a London steakhouse that included beef, bread, and beer cost about one shilling (1s), and the monthly pay for a merchant seaman was about one pound fifteen shillings (£1 15s)[17] or about £21 a year, and a colonel in the army was paid about £430 a year. If you were a wealthy man about town in London, the cost of a grand night out, including dinner, wine and spirits, a bath, and the services of a fashionable courtesan, would cost you about £6.

"During the rest of his life, Christopher paid on this claim, but never to the legal satisfaction of the agents of the fur company."[18] Incidentally, Gist's father Richard had a similar experience when his fur warehouse burnt in 1718, but unlike Christopher, Richard was sufficiently capitalized to absorb the loss.

Between 1743 and 1745, the debts increased, and the Gists were sued by several creditors. In 1744, the two brothers were sued by Thomas Harrison and also by Benjamin Tasker, and to satisfy the judgment, Christopher was forced to sell his own lands and a large portion of the estate he had inherited. In May 1745, he sold to William Cromwell and Jacob Giles his "slaves, furniture, tools and stock, two riding horses, named Lott and Spark, at his dwelling plantation near the garrison, and other things at houses in Baltimore for 400 pounds sterling."[19] Then on July 2, 1745, he sold the sloop *Two Brothers* to William Cromwell for 200 pounds sterling, and that same month he sold to Cromwell and Giles the fifty-acre tract of land called Gist's Meadows and the fifty-acre tract called Elledges Folly. Also at this time, he sold a tract of one thousand acres to a Robert North. That land was located "at the head of Green Spring Valley, now within the present city of Baltimore."[20] Finally, in November 1745, he sold what was described in the *Baltimore Gazette* as "the estate of Christopher Gist of Baltimore County made up of two lots in Baltimore Town, lying on the water with a good brick Dwelling House and sundry other Outhouses, with a good garden."[21]

With his estate in shambles, Christopher packed up what he had left, and with his wife Sarah and children Richard, Violetta, Nathaniel, Anne or "Nancy," and Thomas, moved south into Virginia. It's not known exactly when he left Maryland, or how long he stayed in Virginia, but in 1750, he had relocated to what at the time was the extreme western part of North Carolina. The indication that Gist actually resided in Virginia is found in a record of conveyance for Gist's Limepits in Baltimore County.

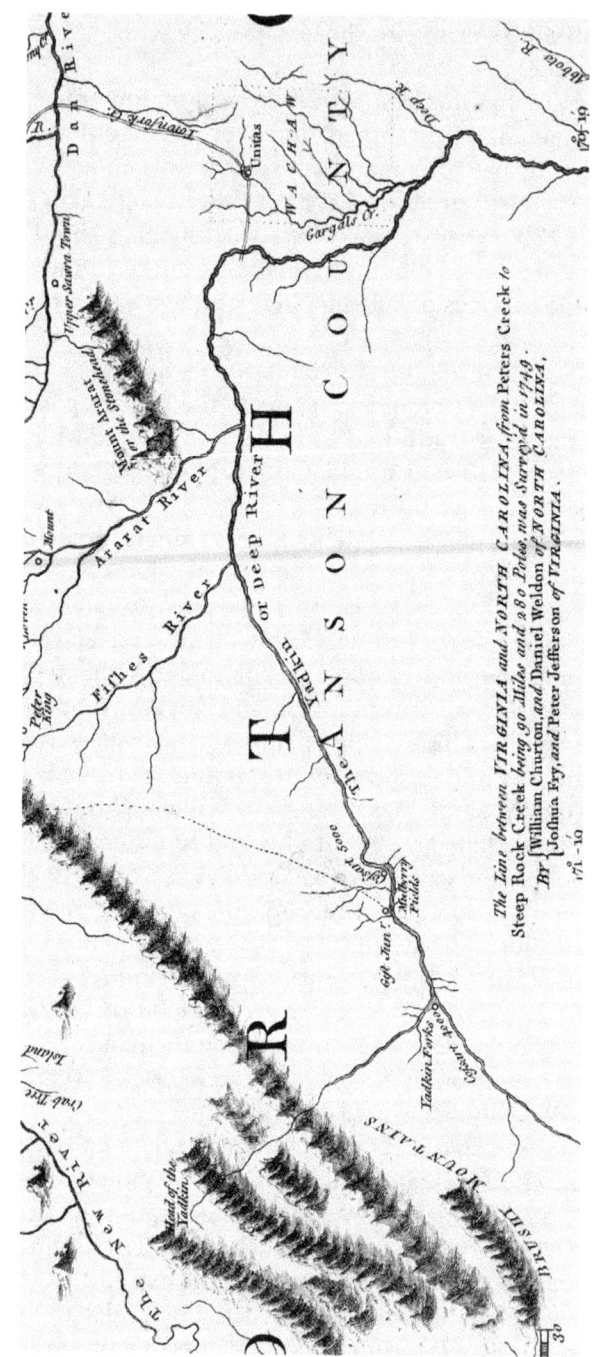

Portion of 1755 map by Joshua Fry and Peter Jefferson showing Gist Homestead (Gist Junr) (Library of Congress Geography and Map Division—74693089).

1. The Origin of a Frontiersman

In the document, Gist refers to himself as "late of Baltimore County ... but now in the Colony of Virginia."[22]

It's speculated that Gist's trek into Virginia and then to North Carolina was a gambit to escape extreme sanctions by his creditors, because Carolina, at that time, was a haven for those who wanted to escape debtor's prison.[23] In North Carolina, he and his family settled on the north side of the Yadkin River, near a little stream known as Saw Mill Creek, which was west of Reddies River at the site of present Wilkesboro, North Carolina.[24] His homestead was close to a major north-south Indian thoroughfare known as the Warriors Path or in some sources it was called the Great Indian Warpath. The Warriors Path was a network of trails east of the Appalachian Mountains that extended from north central Pennsylvania into Georgia. There was a branch that was an extension of the Scioto Trail in present Ohio that stretched from Sandusky Bay on Lake Erie to Lower Shawnee Town at present Portsmouth, Ohio. While the trail certainly conveyed Indian war parties, it was predominantly used for hunting, trade, and migration. Incidentally, Gist's home was not far from where eighteen-year-old Daniel Boone and his parents would establish their homestead around 1752.[25]

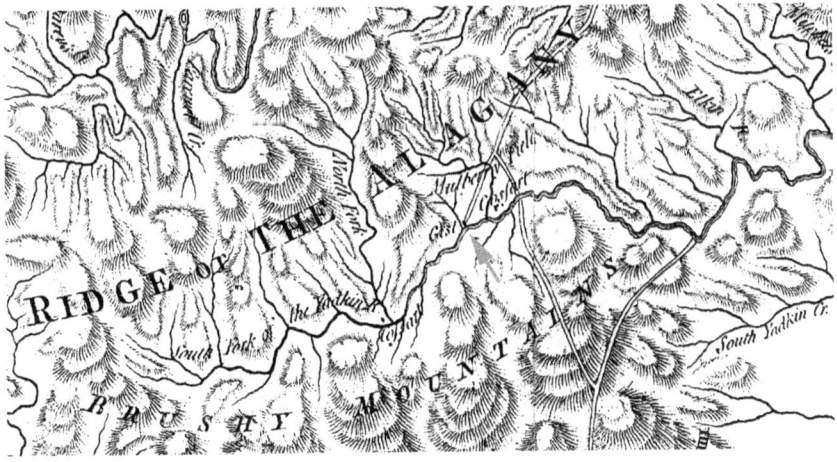

Portion of 1755 Henry Mouzon map with arrow pointing to Gist homestead in center of map labeled "Gist." Note: The area to the north of Gist was called "Mulberry Field" after the many mulberry trees in the area. There were two Cosfort family settlements, one east and one southwest of Gist's. The Cosfort homestead to the east of Gist's is at the present site of Wilkesboro, North Carolina (Library of Congress Geography and Map Division—gm71002153).

With George Washington in the Wilderness

Christopher immediately began trading with the Catawbas to the east and the Cherokees to the west. Within a short time, Gist's presence was known to the extent that his home was depicted on several maps including Fry[26] and Jefferson's[27] maps of 1751 and 1755 and Mouzon's[28] map of 1775.

It must have been quite a cultural shock for Christopher's family to move from a life of relative gentility and ease to a hardscrabble existence on the wild fringes of the North Carolina frontier.

2

Christopher Gist and the Ohio Company of Virginia

"From nowhere we came, into nowhere we go.
What is life? It is the flash of a firefly in the night,
It is the breath of a buffalo in the wintertime,
It is a little shadow which runs across the grass,
And loses itself in the sunset."
—Crowfoot

Christopher was about forty years of age when he moved his family to the Yadkin River, his wife Sarah was thirty-four, and his children ranged in age from ten to sixteen. Life on the frontier required children to grow up quickly and work hard, not only to thrive, but merely to survive. When they arrived at their new homesite, their priorities were to build a home, clear the land, and plant crops for sustenance during the coming winter. As soon as they had a roof over their heads, Christopher and his sons devoted time to hunting, fishing, and fur trapping as well as expanding and growing their garden. Being so close to the Warriors Path provided Christopher the opportunity to continue his fur trading and mercantile enterprises. However, before long, Gist was soon on the move, but this time without his family.

A land speculation company was established in 1748 by a group of wealthy Virginians who petitioned for a grant of a vast tract of land between the Monongahela River and the Kanawha River including the area around the Forks of the Ohio at present Pittsburgh. The scheme was the brainchild of Thomas Lee (c. 1690–1750), a leading figure in colonial Virginia. In the autumn of 1747, Lee and other influential Virginians presented their petition to Virginia Royal Lieutenant-Governor William Gooch (1681–1751), who did not receive it favorably. Gooch publicly stated his concern that the French might take offense at English

With George Washington in the Wilderness

expansion into New France at a time when England had hopes of maintaining a general peace between the two nations.

Lieutenant-Governor Gooch was certainly aware of the quite strong claim the French had to the trans-Allegheny region, which was based on the right of discovery and exploration by French explorers beginning early in the seventeenth century. Those explorers included Jacques Cartier, Samuel Champlain, Father Pierre François Xavier de Charlevois, Louis Joliet, Pierre Gaultier de la Vérendrye, Father Jacques Marquette, Jean Nicollet, and Pierre-Esprit Radisson. Even more concrete was the acknowledgment of French ownership of the area by three treaties signed by the British government, the last of which was concluded in 1748, that very same year that the Ohio Company was formed. They were the treaties of Ryswick[1] (*Rijswijk*) (1697) and Utrecht[2] (1713) and the Treaty of Aix-la-Chapelle[3] (1748), which recognized French ownership of the territory west of the Allegheny Mountains.[4]

In spite of the treaties they had signed, the British maintained a claim to the Ohio country based on rather tenuous logic. They reasoned that John Cabot[5] (c. 1450–c. 1500), who was commissioned by King Henry VII of England, reached the coast of North America in 1497, before anyone else, which made the English the legitimate owners of the continent by right of discovery. They also reasoned that in a previous treaty, the French recognized British dominion over the Iroquois, and since the Iroquois conquered the Erie in Ohio, British jurisdiction extended to those lands by right of conquest.

Needless to say, the French considered British logic regarding ownership of the region as spurious and let it be known that they were willing to defend their claim by force. Those were the signs that Lieutenant-Governor Gooch was interpreting and likely his reason for rejection of Thomas Lee and the Ohio Company's petition for a land grant in an area controlled by the French.

As a result of Gooch's nonsupport, and notwithstanding the risk of precipitating yet another war with France, Lee and the other members of the Ohio Company changed tack and resorted to a rather Byzantine way of going around Gooch. They used the names of powerful and influential people as shareholders in the Ohio Company, even though several of those who lent their names to the venture stated that they had no interest in investing in the company. Then, Lee and his fellow board members directed their appeal to the king by first sending their petition to the Commissioners for Trade and Plantations.[6] They reckoned the commissioners would be more receptive to the idea of lucrative business

2. Christopher Gist and the Ohio Company of Virginia

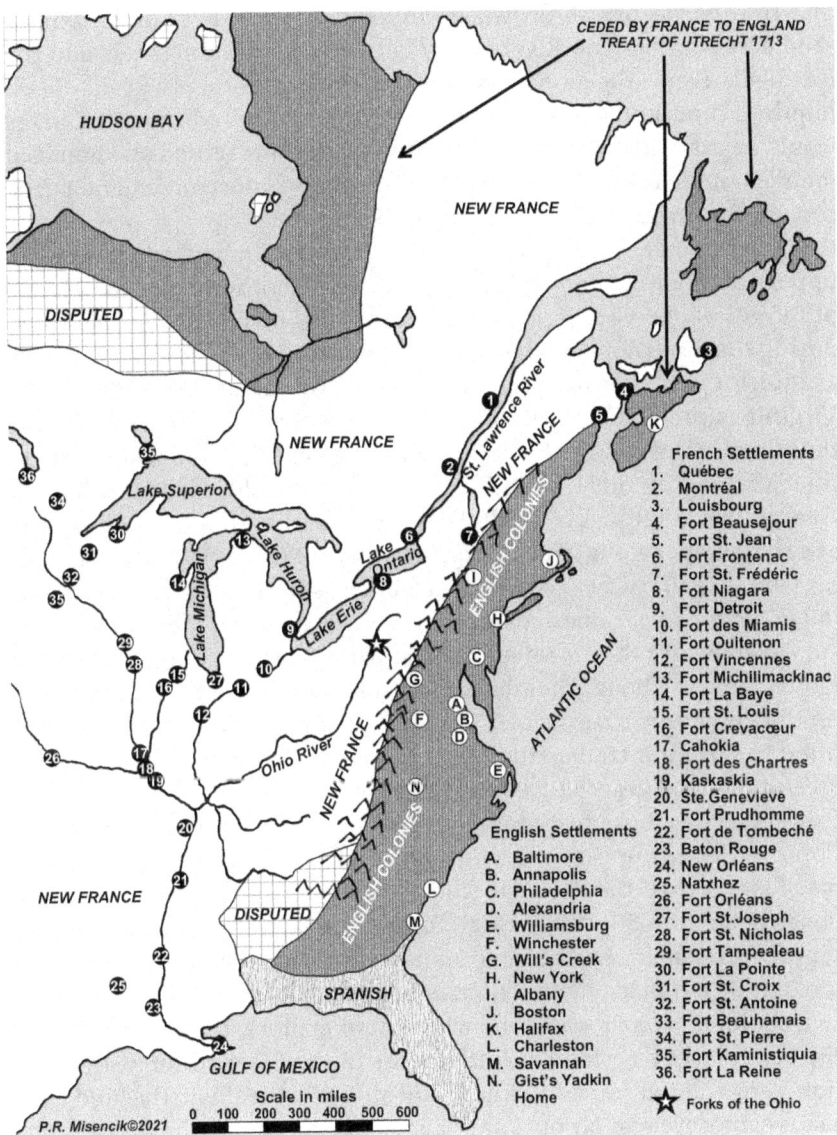

New France and the English Colonies in 1750.

opportunities in the trans-Allegheny region and convey their support for the venture to the king. In 1748, as Lee and the others anticipated, the Commissioners for Trade and Plantations recommended approval to the king's Privy Council.[7]

With George Washington in the Wilderness

In 1749, the British Crown granted the company five hundred thousand acres in the Ohio River Valley between the Monongahela and the Kanawha rivers. The grant was in two parts; the first was a grant of two hundred thousand acres, and the other three hundred thousand acres would be granted if the Ohio Company successfully settled one hundred families in the area within seven years and also constructed and garrisoned a fort in the area at the company's expense.

Thomas Lee was a member of the Virginia Council, which was the upper chamber of the Virginia legislature, the other being the House of Burgesses. Lee was a powerful figure in his own right. At one time, during the governor's absence, Lee as president of the Council filled in as interim governor of Virginia. He was also one of the judges of the Virginia Supreme Court. Among the other noteworthy shareholders of the Ohio Company were Lawrence Washington (1718–1752) and Augustine Washington, Jr. (1720–1762), who were the older half-brothers of George Washington (1732–1799). George Washington was later added as a shareholder along with George Mason (1725–1792). Robert Dinwiddie (1692–1770) succeeded William Gooch as royal lieutenant-governor in 1751 and also became a major shareholder in the company.

Even before they received official word from London, Lee and the Ohio Company board members moved forward with their enterprise. At the recommendation of Thomas Cresap (c. 1702–c. 1790), they hired the frontier trader Hugh Parker (?–1751) to map and explore the area of the land grant and construct a storehouse to be used for trade. Parker constructed a two-story log trading post on the south side of the Potomac River opposite the confluence of Will's Creek and the Potomac River, across the Potomac from where Fort Cumberland[8] would be constructed in 1755. While Hugh Parker was likely an able and competent frontiersman, Lee became somewhat disillusioned with him and looked for a replacement. Thomas Lee and the other Ohio Company shareholders wanted someone who would explore, map, and evaluate the best places to establish settlements in the Ohio country. In addition, they wanted someone who could study and evaluate the land with a surveyor's eye and lay out roads and trails to connect the future frontier settlements. Once again, Lee approached Thomas Cresap for a recommendation.

Cresap was an English-born settler and trader who arrived in the Province of Maryland about 1717. In 1734, he enlisted as a captain in the Maryland militia and in 1736 established his home near a Shawnee Indian village on the Maryland side of the Potomac River

2. Christopher Gist and the Ohio Company of Virginia

at present Oldtown, Maryland. The Shawnee village was variously known as Opessa's Town, Shawnee Old Town, or simply Old Town. The village was established by the Shawnee chief Straight Tail Meaurroway Opessa (c. 1630–c. 1709), who some historians claim was the great-great-grandfather of the celebrated Shawnee war chief Tecumseh (1768–1813). By the time Cresap settled at Old Town, Chief Opessa was long gone, but some Shawnee still lived in the area, and the name Opessa's Town was still frequently used as the location's name.

Author Sally E. Misencik at home of Michael Cresap, built c. 1764 at Oldtown, Maryland. He was the son of Thomas Cresap, whose post is believed to have been a short distance to the south.

With George Washington in the Wilderness

While Thomas Cresap and his family were notable frontier figures, they were not generally considered to possess ethical or virtuous qualities. In fact, they were abrasive, roughnecks who were considered shady dealers by the Indians. The Indians called Thomas Cresap "Big Spoon," supposedly because of the pot of soup that he kept ready in his trading post. Other accounts claim he was called Big Spoon because of his large size; however, the English referred to him as a "rascal" and a "rattlesnake colonel."

Since Cresap was an officer in the Maryland militia, he was familiar with Christopher Gist from Gist's service with the Maryland Rangers. He knew Gist as a talented surveyor as well as a capable frontiersman, so when Thomas Lee asked for someone to replace Hugh Parker, Cresap recommended Christopher Gist. However, Gist was no longer in the area but had recently relocated to the North Carolina frontier, which was more than 260 miles west-southwest of Williamsburg.

That apparently was not an obstacle, because sometime in 1750, Lee made contact with Gist. Then on Tuesday, September 11, 1750, Thomas Lee and his son Richard Henry Lee (1732–1794),[9] along with Nathaniel Chapman (1709–1760),[10] the Reverend James Scott (c. 1715–c. 1781), and George Mason, acting as the Committee of the Ohio Company, met with Christopher Gist at Stafford Court House.[11] They offered Gist a job with the following written instructions:

> You are to go out as soon as possible to the Westward of the great Mountains, and carry with you such a Number of Men, as You think necessary in Order to search out and discover the Lands upon the River Ohio, & other adjoining Branches of the Mississippi down as low as the great Falls[12] thereof: You are particularly to observe the Ways & Passes thro all the Mountains you cross, & take an exact Account of the Soil, Quality, & Product of the Land, and the Wideness and Deepness of the Rivers, & the several Falls belonging to them, together with the Courses & Bearings of the Rivers & Mountains as near as you conveniently can: You are, also to observe what Nations of Indians inhabit there, their Strength & Numbers, who they trade with, & in what Commodities they deal.
>
> When you find a large Quantity of good, level Land, such as you think will suit the Company, You are to measure the Breadth of it, in three or four different Places, & take the Courses of the River and Mountains on which it binds in Order to judge the Quantity: You are to fix the Beginning & Bounds in such a Manner that they may be easily found again by your Description, the nearer in the Land lies, the better, provided it be good & level, but we had rather go quite down the Mississippi than take mean broken Land. After finding a large Body of good level Land, you are not to stop, but proceed farther, as low as the Falls of the Ohio, that We may be informed of that

2. Christopher Gist and the Ohio Company of Virginia

Navigation; And You are to take an exact Account of all the large Bodies of good level Land, in the same Manner as above directed, that the Company may the better judge where it will be most convenient for them to take their Land.

You are to note all the Bodies of good Land as you go along, tho there is not a sufficient Quantity for the Company's Grant, but You need not be so particular in the Mensuration[13] of that, as in the larger Bodies of Land.

You are to draw as good a Plan as you can of the Country You pass thro: You are to take an exact and particular Journal of all your Proceedings, and make a true Report thereof to the Ohio Company.[14]

In addition to the above instructions, Gist agreed to recruit 150 or more families who would settle on the Ohio Company's lands within two years. The settlers would be obligated to pay the Ohio Company four pounds sterling (£4) for every hundred acres at the time they settled on the land.

Gist signed on for the sum of £150, and the council authorized the treasurer, Nathaniel Chapman, to advance Gist £30 and instructed Hugh Parker, who was given the job of factor,[15] to supply Gist with arms, ammunition, and whatever else Gist would need for his expedition.[16]

3

Gist's First Trek for the Ohio Company, 1750–1751

"We learn who we are by how we handle adversity."
—Anonymous

It's likely that Christopher Gist returned to his home and family on the Yadkin River before starting out on his expedition. However, to do so required him to travel about 350 miles back to his North Carolina home and then another 370 or so miles to Thomas Cresap's post at Old Town. At any rate, Gist's first journal entry, on Wednesday, October 31, 1750, states, "Set out from Col Thomas Cresap's at the old Town on Potomack River in Maryland, and went along an old Indian Path N 30 E about 11 Miles."[1] Gist wouldn't return home for another seven months, and one wonders how his wife Sarah and their young family coped on the frontier during Gist's absence, but unfortunately, there is no surviving account.

From Cresap's post, Gist would have used the trail called the Warriors Path to the Juniata River near present Bedford, Pennsylvania. On his way to the Juniata, Gist had not progressed far before he took ill and was forced to spend two days recuperating. Apparently, he was not fully recovered when he started off again, because on Friday, November 2, 1750, he wrote in his journal, "N 30 E 6M, here I was so bad that I was not able to proceed any farther that Night, but grew better in the Morning."[2] The unknown ailment continued to plague him for most of the month of November, causing him to progress very slowly, and in some cases he was unable to travel at all. When he was on the move again, he covered less than fifty miles in four days, likely due to his illness, and he reached the Juniata River on Saturday, November 3.

From the Juniata, Gist turned west and followed the well-used trail leading to the Forks of the Ohio[3] (present Pittsburgh, Pennsylvania). That trail, which ran from Paxtang (present Harrisburg, Pennsylvania)

3. Gist's First Trek for the Ohio Company, 1750–1751

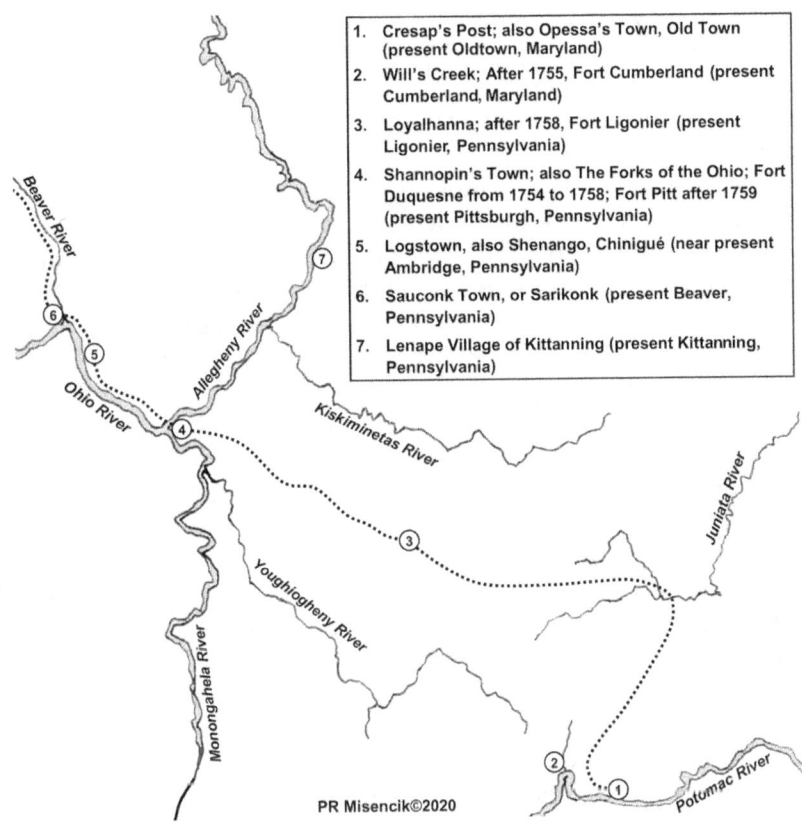

First stage of Christopher Gist's travels in western Pennsylvania beginning at Thomas Cresap's post at Old Town on Wednesday, October 30, 1750, then entering the present state of Ohio on approximately Saturday, December 1, 1750.

to the Forks of the Ohio, was known as the northern branch of the Allegheny Path, and after John Ray set up his trading post in 1751 at Ray's Town (present Bedford, Pennsylvania), the trail became known as the Rays Town Path or Raystown Path.[4]

Along with his lingering illness, a run of bad weather also inhibited Gist's travels. His journal entry for Tuesday, November 6, through Thursday, November 8, 1750, was "Had Snow and such bad Weather that we could not travel for three days; but I killed a young bear so that we had Provisions enough."[5] That entry in which he uses the pronoun "we" piques one's curiosity. From Gist's journal, we know that he had a young fellow helper traveling most of the way with him, but he doesn't mention him by name or how or where the lad had joined Gist. Apparently the "boy," as Gist simply refers to him, was with Gist throughout the entire trek, except for a short time when he may have left the lad at Lower Shawnee Town to care for their horses while Gist ventured to Pickawillany. A few sources state that the lad was a seventeen-year-old slave boy, but we could find nothing to authenticate that fact. The first time Gist mentions a companion by name was in his journal entry for Monday, November 26, 1750: "met one Barny Curran a Trader for the Ohio Company, and we continued together as far as Muskingum."[6]

Gist followed the Rays Town Path to the Lenape[7] village of Loyalhanna (present Ligonier, Pennsylvania), which he reached on Wednesday, November 14, 1750. Gist had no way of knowing, but on that day, Thomas Lee, the driving force of the Ohio Company, died, and the leadership fell to Lawrence Washington, thirty-two-year-old elder half-brother of George Washington. Unfortunately, Lawrence was afflicted with consumption or tuberculosis, and he would only live slightly less than two more years.

At Loyalhanna, Gist encountered an Indian who spoke good English. The Indian directed him to Shannopin's Town at the Forks of the Ohio, which he said was about sixty miles away.[8] It should be pointed out that while Christopher Gist was intelligent and in general a quick study, he was not gifted with the ability to learn other languages easily. He never did achieve the ability to hold a conversation in an Indian dialect and was dependent on translators. If none were available, he was forced to communicate on a very basic level using a few words and gestures.

Along the way, Gist's illness flared up, and on Sunday, November 18, 1750, he came to an old Indian camp and wrote, "I was very sick, and sweated myself according to Indian Custom in a Sweat-House,[9] which gave Me Ease, and my Fever abated."[10]

On Monday, November 19, 1750, Gist wrote that he traveled hard for about twenty miles and came to a small Delaware (Lenape) town called Shannopin's Town located at the Forks of the Ohio. Once again, his illness resurfaced, and he wrote, "Tuesday 20, Wednesday 21, Thursday 21, and Friday 23 [November 1750].—I was unwell and stayed in this Town to recover myself; While I was here I took an Opportunity to set my Compass privately & took the Distance across the River, for I understand it was dangerous to let a Compass be seen among these Indians."[11] Ever since the French expedition of Céloron de Blaineville in 1749, during which Céloron buried lead plates and nailed the French coat of

3. Gist's First Trek for the Ohio Company, 1750–1751

arms to trees proclaiming the land to be the property of the French king, the Indians were suspicious of anyone who appeared to be measuring or writing about their land, taking it as an indication that they planned to appropriate it.

Even so, Gist surreptitiously appraised the town and the area, and wrote his description of Shannopin's Town: "The River Ohio is 76 Poles wide[12] (approximately 418 yards or 382 meters) at Shannopin Town: There are about twenty Families in this Town: The Land in general from Potomack to this Place is mean stony and broken, here and there good Spots upon the Creeks and Branches but no Body of it."[13]

On Saturday, November 24, 1750, Gist departed Shannopin's Town and used the plural pronoun "our" when he wrote, "Set out from Shannopin's Town, and swam our horses across the River Ohio."[14] Gist likely forded the Allegheny River from Shannopin's Town and was possibly following the French custom of referring to the Allegheny as the "Upper Ohio" or simply the "Ohio." The French did not consider the Allegheny to be a separate river but rather an extension of La Belle Rivière, or "the Beautiful River," which was their name for the Ohio.

In his journal, Gist described the land along the Ohio as good land for farming, although the bottom land was not broad. Also, it was covered with small red and white oaks, and the river and streams were suitable for mills.

On Sunday, November 25, 1750, Gist reached the Indian village known as Logstown, or sometimes *Chiningué* or *Shenango*, on the north bank of the Ohio River, about eighteen miles downstream of the Forks of the Ohio. Logstown was originally established by the Lenape, but soon became unique as a cosmopolitan village composed of Lenape, Shawnee, and Mingo expatriates who migrated into the area.[15] When Gist entered the town, many of the chiefs and Indians were out hunting, and he was greeted coldly and regarded with some suspicion. He described his greeters as "a Parcel of reprobate Indian Traders." He learned that the Pennsylvania trader George Croghan (c. 1718–1782) and Andrew Montour (c. 1720–1772) had been there about a week prior.

Croghan was an Irish-born fur trader who traveled deep into the Ohio country and was known as "King of the Pennsylvania traders." He was so successful as a fur trader that many French traders were unable to compete with him, and his impact on the French fur trade in Ohio caused the French authorities to place a bounty on his head. It was never collected. Andrew Montour, also known as *Sattrelihu*, and *Eghnisara*, was a Métis, or of mixed French, Oneida, and Algonquin ancestry. Like

With George Washington in the Wilderness

Author Paul R. Misencik at the site of Logstown.

his mother, Madame Montour (c. 1667–1753), he was an extremely intelligent interpreter and negotiator who spoke several Indian dialects along with French and English. Croghan and Montour had been sent out as representatives of Pennsylvania to promote trade with the Indians. Both Montour and Croghan were well respected and held in high regard by the Indians in western Pennsylvania and in the Ohio country. Gist was sorry he missed the two at Logstown because they would have vouched for him and given their endorsement, lessening the friction between Gist and the Indians.

It was apparent that Gist was not there to trade, which immediately raised the suspicions of the Indians, especially when he appeared to be appraising the area. Quite naturally, they began to question him about his reason for being there as well as his motives. Gist was savvy enough not to admit he was exploring and surveying the area on behalf of the Ohio Company. However, being able to converse only in English

3. Gist's First Trek for the Ohio Company, 1750–1751

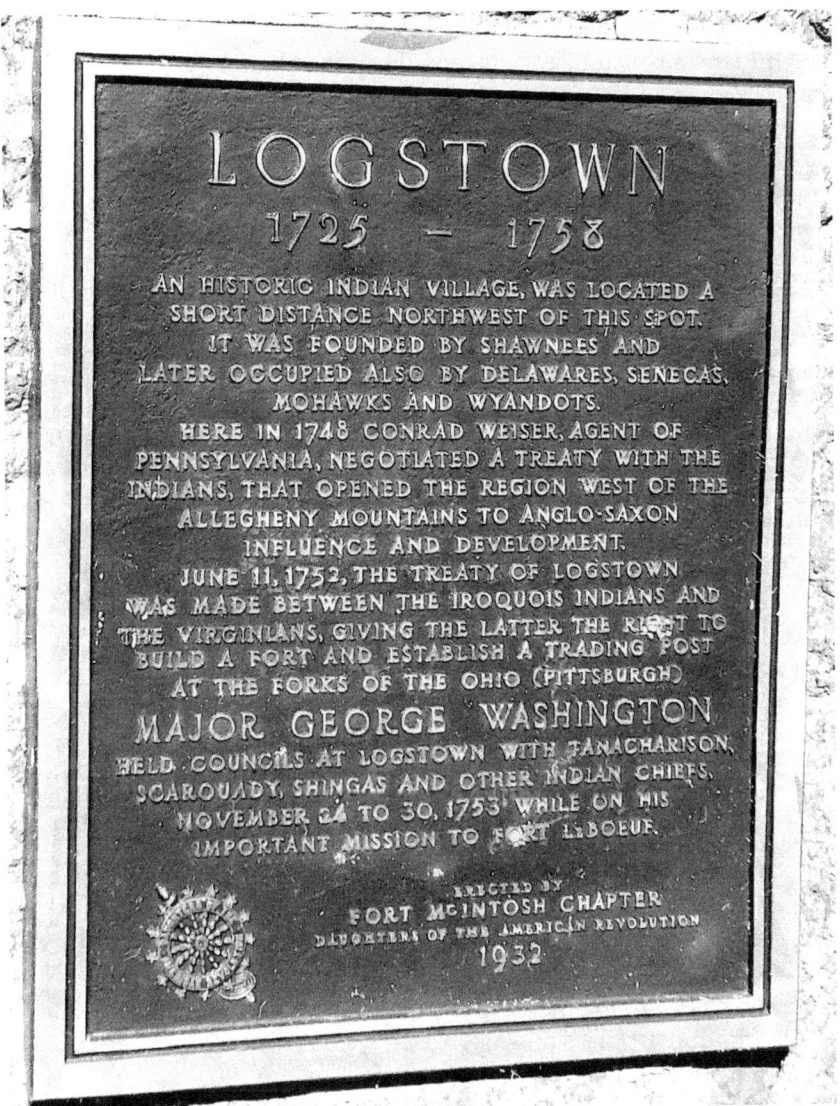

Plaque on Logstown marker.

put him at a disadvantage, and even then, he offered vague and ambiguous answers, which made the Indians even more suspicious. Gist was astutely aware that the Indians were becoming increasingly incensed, and it looked like it might end badly for him. Finally, he told them he was looking for George Croghan and Andrew Montour and had come on behalf of the "President of Virginia" to deliver a message from the king. The Indians' suspicions eased when they heard that Gist was acquainted with Croghan and Montour, and that he was essentially on a diplomatic mission. Gist's Journal captures the tenseness of those interactions.

> Sunday, Nov. 25, [1750]—Down the River W 3 M [miles], NW 5 M to Loggs Town; ... The People in this Town, began to enquire my Business, and because I did not readily inform them, they began to suspect me, and said, I was come to settle the Indian's Lands and they knew I should never go Home again safe; I found this discourse was like to be of ill Consequence to me, so I pretended to speak very slightingly of what they had said to me, and enquired for Croghan (who is a meer idol among his Countrymen and Irish Traders) and Andrew Montour the interpreter for Pennsylvania, and told them I had a Message to deliver the Indians from the King, by Order of the President of Virginia, & for that Reason wanted to see M Montour: This made them all pretty easy (being afraid to interrupt the King's Message) and obtained me Quiet and Respect among them, otherwise I doubt not they would have contrived some Evil against me.[16]

Apparently, the experience unnerved Gist to a certain extent, and even though he was still ailing, he was eager to leave Logstown. The very next day, Monday, November 26, 1750, he wrote, "Tho I was unwell, I preferred the Woods to such Company, & set out from the Loggs Town."[17] That same day, he traveled about six miles downstream from Logstown to the Lenape village of Sauconk (present Beaver, Pennsylvania) on the west side of the Beaver River where it joined the Ohio. There Gist encountered Barney Curran, an Ohio Company fur trader, and several colleagues. From there they accompanied Gist into the Ohio country, which was Gist's first mention of an identifiable traveling companion in his journal. A later entry on Tuesday, December 4, 1750, indicated that Curran and his associates were nine in number, because it read, "Set out late S 45 W about 4 M here I killed three fine fat deer, so that tho we were eleven in Company, We had great Plenty of Provision."[18]

According to Gist's journal, his party consisted of the young traveling companion and, most recently, Barney Curran and eight other men. They followed the west bank of the Beaver River north to the vicinity of the Mingo[19] village of Kuskusky,[20] near present New Castle, Pennsylvania, where they turned west and followed the Great Trail. They passed the Mingo village of Painted Post, at present Dungannon, Ohio, and continued west until they came to the Tuscarawas River, which Gist called Elk's Eye Creek. The Tuscarawas River joins the Walhonding River at present Coshocton, Ohio, to form the Muskingum River. The name "Muskingum" in Lenape means "the eye of the elk," and most

3. Gist's First Trek for the Ohio Company, 1750–1751

native Americans considered the Tuscarawas not to be a separate river but rather the upper reaches of the Muskingum, hence, "eye of the elk" or "elk's eye creek."

Christopher Gist was still diligently taking notes of the land as part of his report for the Ohio Company of Virginia. On Saturday, December 1, 1750, he wrote in his journal, "Land high and tolerable good." The next

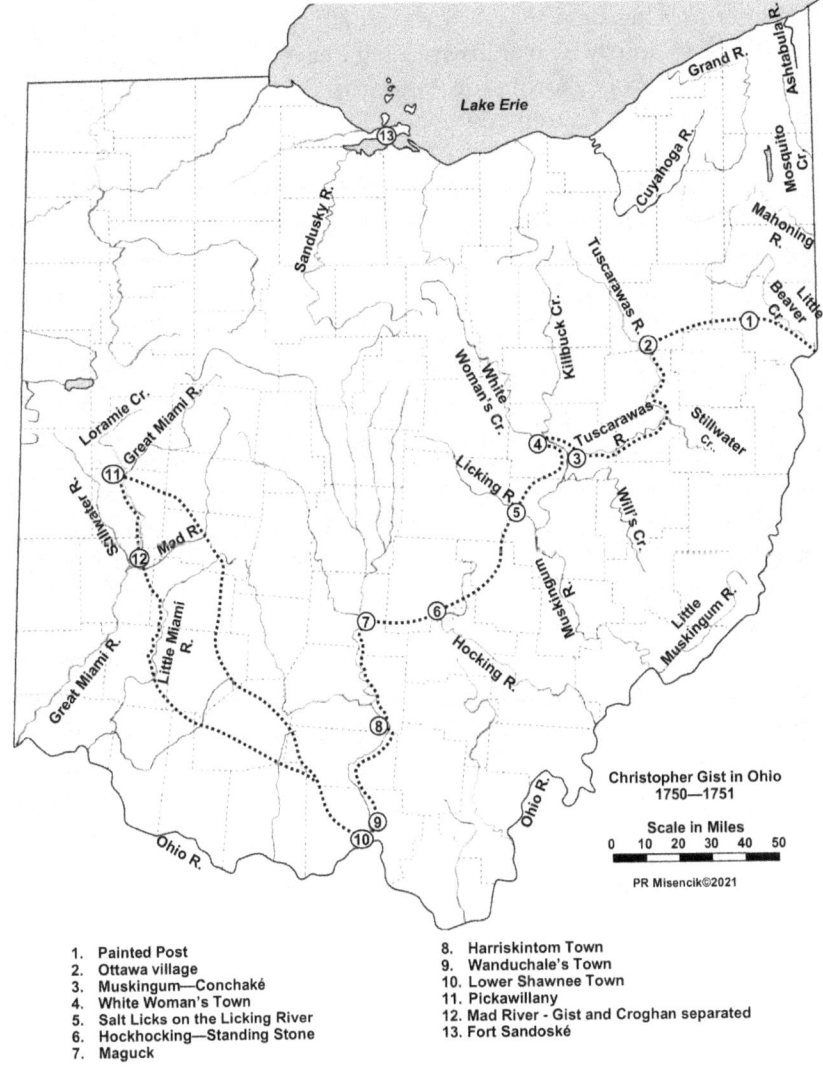

1. Painted Post
2. Ottawa village
3. Muskingum—Conchaké
4. White Woman's Town
5. Salt Licks on the Licking River
6. Hockhocking—Standing Stone
7. Maguck
8. Harriskintom Town
9. Wanduchale's Town
10. Lower Shawnee Town
11. Pickawillany
12. Mad River - Gist and Croghan separated
13. Fort Sandoské

Christopher Gist in Ohio, 1750–1751.

With George Washington in the Wilderness

day, he wrote, "the same sort of Land, but near the Creeks bushy and full of thorns." On Wednesday, December 5, 1750, his entry was "Set out down the side of a Creek called Elk's Eye Creek S 70 W 6 M, good Land, but void of Timber. Meadows upon the Creek, fine runs for Mills."[21] At that time, Gist and his party were descending the Tuscarawas River in the vicinity of present Bolivar, Ohio, where six years later the Lenape Chief Shingas (fl. 1740–c. 1764), and his brother Tamaqua, also known as Beaver or King Beaver (c. 1710–c. 1770), would establish their village, called variously Beaver Town, King Beaver Town, Shingas's Town, and the Tuscarawas. During the American Revolutionary War, Bolivar was the site of Fort Laurens,[22] the only Revolutionary War fort in present Ohio.

On Friday, December 7, 1750, while in the vicinity of Bolivar near the junction of Sandy Creek and the Tuscarawas River, they came to an Indian camp, which Gist described as "a Town of Ottoways, a Nation of French Indians." The Ottawa or *Odawa* Indians were members of the Three Fires Confederacy made up of Ottawa (*Odawa*), Ojibwe or Chippewa, and Potawatomie (*Bodowdomi*) whose homelands were centered in present Michigan and Manitoulin Island in Ontario, Canada.[23] Gist added, "an old French Man (named Mark Coonce) who had married an Indian Woman of the Six Nations [Iroquois Confederacy] lived here; the Indians were all out a hunting; the old Man was very civil to me, but after I was gone to my Camp, upon his understanding I came from Virginia, he called me Big Knife. There are not above six or eight Families belonging to this Town."

Other than Gist's mention of Mark Coonce, there is no biographical information regarding that individual. If Mark Coonce had a wife who was a member of the Six Nations, which refers to the Iroquois Confederacy, it's not known how she came to be residing in an Ottawa village. It's interesting to note that Mark Coonce called Gist "Big Knife" after he learned Gist came from Virginia. Most Lenape Indians referred to Europeans as *Wapsid Lenape* (white people), however members of the Virginia militia often carried swords, so the Lenape referred to Virginians as *Mechanschican* (long knives) to distinguish them from other white people;[24] however, the Ottawa did not necessarily follow that custom.

Gist spent the night in the town, and on Sunday, December 9, 1750, he and his party departed and continued down the Tuscarawas River. That day, they crossed a stream Gist called Margaret's Creek, which some sources claim was named for Margaret Montour, the daughter of Madame Montour. There is no evidence that Madame Montour or her

3. Gist's First Trek for the Ohio Company, 1750–1751

daughter ever visited the Ohio territory, so it's more likely the stream was named after another unknown Margaret. At any rate, the stream is now called Sugar Creek.

On Friday, December 14, 1750, they arrived at a town Gist referred to as "Muskingum," at the junction where the Tuscarawas and Walhonding rivers join to form the Muskingum River at present Coshocton, Ohio. There, he caught up with George Croghan and Andrew Montour. His journal entry reads:

> Set out W 5 M to Muskingum a Town of the Wyendotts [Wyandot]. The Land upon Elk's Eye Creek is in general very broken, the Bottoms narrow. The Wyendotts or little Mingoes[25] are divided between the French and the English, one half of them adhere to the first, and the other half are firmly attached to the latter. The Town of Muskingum consists of about one hundred Families. When We came within Sight of the Town, We perceived English Colours hoisted on the King's House, and at George Croghan's; upon enquiring the Reason I was informed that the French had lately taken several English Traders, and that Mr Croghan had ordered all White Men to come into this Town, and had sent Expresses to the English Traders of the lower Towns, and among the Pickweylinees[26]; and the Indians had sent to their People to come to Council about it.[27]

Gist was correct is identifying the town's inhabitants as primarily Wyandots. In 1747, the charismatic Wyandot chief Nicholas Orontony (c. 1695–c. 1750) rebelled against French restrictions that prevented the Wyandots from engaging in the more lucrative trade with the English. To escape the constraints of an enforced French monopoly, Orontony rebelled, and open war with the French broke out in what became known as the Conspiracy of Nicholas or Orontony's Rebellion.[28] The French responded with overwhelming military force, and rather than fight a bloody and hopeless war, Orontony abandoned his villages in early 1748 and moved his people from the south shore of Sandusky Bay to the head of the Muskingum. The town he established was called Conchaké (where the waters come together), although some sources also list the town as Wyandot Old Town and, as Gist referred to it, "Muskingum." Orontony died of smallpox in late 1750 or in 1751, and since Gist does not mention the chief of Muskingum or Conshaké by name, it's not known if Orontony or his successor was there to greet Gist at the time.

Gist and his party spent a full month at Conchaké, living among the Wyandot and alongside George Croghan, Andrew Montour, and an assortment of other white fur traders who came to do business with the Indians. Croghan had built a fine log house as his residence, and also a large storehouse and trading post he called the "King's House."

With George Washington in the Wilderness

While there on Monday, December 17, 1750, two of Croghan's fur traders returned to the town and said that French military patrols from Fort Detroit were doing all they could to interdict English trade in the Ohio Country. They said a patrol of about forty Frenchmen and twenty Indians had captured two of Croghan's men along with seven horse loads of furs and took them to a new fort they were constructing on the south shore of Lake Erie. They were likely referring to Fort Sandoské or Sandoski,[29] which was begun about 1749 on the southern terminus of the DeLery Portage[30] on Sandusky Bay, due south of present Port Clinton, Ohio.

On Tuesday, December 18, 1750, Gist wrote, "I acquainted Mr Croghan and Andrew Montour with my Business with the Indians, & talked much of a Regulation of Trade with which they were much pleased, and treated me kindly." Apparently, Croghan felt that British control of the area, whenever it came, would be good for business, and considerably less perilous, in light of the French bounty placed on his head.

On Christmas Day, Tuesday, December 25, 1750, Gist offered to read prayers in honor of the day, but he received a negative reaction from some of the white men who being of different religious persuasions, refused to take part. However, a white blacksmith named Thomas Burney, who was living among the Indians at Conchaké, convinced several of the white traders to listen to Gist, and Andrew Montour likewise convinced several of the Indians to do the same. The Indians apparently were impressed with Gist's prayer reading and homily, and he wrote in his journal, "The Indians seemed well pleased, and came up to Me and returned Me their Thanks; and invited Me to live among Them, and gave me a Name in their Language *Annosanah*: the Interpreter told Me this was a Name of a good Man[31] that had formerly lived among them."[32]

The day after Christmas, Wednesday, December 26, 1750, Christopher Gist recorded the brutal killing of a woman captive who had been recaptured a couple days before after attempting to escape. His journal entry graphically records the event.

> This Day a Woman, who had been a long Time a Prisoner, and had deserted, & been retaken, and brought into the Town of Christmas Eve, was put to Death in the following manner: They carried her without the Town & let her loose, and when she attempted to run away, the Persons appointed for that Purpose pursued her, & struck her on the Ear, on the right Side of her Head, which beat her Face on the Ground; they then struck her several Times, thro the Back with a Dart, to the Heart, scalped Her, & threw the Scalp in the Air,

3. Gist's First Trek for the Ohio Company, 1750–1751

and another cut off her Head: There the dismal Spectacle lay til the Evening, & then Barny Curran desired Leave to bury Her, which He, and his Men, and some Indians did just at Dark.[33]

Between Saturday, January 12, and Monday, January 14, 1751, Gist along with Croghan and Montour met with Indians who arrived from as far away as Pickawillany. Croghan presented the chiefs with strings of wampum and said that the great King George had sent a large present of goods for the Indians, which was being held for them in Virginia, and invited the chiefs to travel to Virginia for a council and to receive their presents. The Indians, however, thanked the Governor of Virginia for the invitation but said they couldn't commit to attend the council until they all met in council, which would not be until the next spring. With no further reason to stay at Conchaké, Gist prepared to leave the following morning to continue his mission for the Ohio Company.

On Tuesday, January 15, 1751, Gist wrote, "We left Muskingum [Conshaké], and went W 5 M to the White Woman's Creek."[34] At the time, the Walhonding was shown on French maps as *Rivière des Blanches Femmes*, and English maps as White Woman's Creek. Mary Harris, the "white woman," had been captured during the combined French and Indian raid on the small Massachusetts village of Deerfield on Friday, February 29, 1704, during Queen Anne's War (1702–1713). Mary, who was about nine years old at the time, was taken back to Canada where she was adopted by the Indians. Little is known about her early life, but as she grew into womanhood, she became the wife of a Lenape warrior and bore him several children.[35] Mary and her Indian family were still in Canada in 1744, because Joseph Kellogg of Suffield, Connecticut, who was also a captive, encountered her family at that time. Kellogg wrote, "Two young men, Mary Harrises children, have been with me twice, which have lodged at my house. One of them is a very inteligable man about thirty years of age, and from them indeavored to critically examine them about the affairs of Canada."[36] That must have been shortly before Mary and her family moved to Ohio, because a French map dated 1746 shows the Walhonding River as *Rivière des Blanches Femmes*, which referred to her. Walhonding is derived from the Lenape word *Walhandi*, which means "ditch" or "trench," and refers to the relatively high banks of the river. There is some suggestion that it comes from the Lenape verb *Walheu*, meaning "he is digging a hole," because the Lenape people seasonally dug for roots along the stream.

Gist recorded his visit with Mary Harris at her town, which was located just south of the confluence of Killbuck Creek and the

With George Washington in the Wilderness

Walhonding River, about five miles west of Conshaké. "Tuesday, [January] 15, [1751]—We left Muskingum [Conshaké], and went W 5 M to the White Woman's Creek, on which is a small Town; this White Woman was taken away from New England, when she was not above ten Years old, by the French Indians; She is now upwards of fifty, and has a Indian Husband and several Children—Her name is Mary Harris, she still remembers they used to be very religious in New England, and wonders how the White Men can be so wicked as she has seen them in these Woods."[37]

According to Coshocton, Ohio, researcher Scot Butler, Mary Harris and her family returned to Canada during the French and Indian War, likely around 1755, because in 1756 she is reported to have provided care and comfort to English prisoners in Canada. At that time, she identified herself to a prisoner of war from Pennsylvania and told him she was Mary Harris and had been taken captive as a child from Deerfield, New England. She also said that one of her sons was an important war leader.[38] It's not known what became of Mary Harris after that time.[39]

Gist departed White Woman's Town on Wednesday, January 16, 1751, and doubled back toward the Muskingum River and intercepted the trail that led southwest from Conchaké at the Forks of the Muskingum, and then followed the Coshocton Trail to the Indian towns along the Scioto River.

It should be mentioned that the Indians didn't really name their trails the way we now name roads, streets, and highways. The Indians would generally refer to a path or trail according to their destination at the time. Thus, someone traveling south on what we call the Scioto Trail[40] to the Mingo village of Salt Lick Town at present Columbus, Ohio, would likely refer to the path he was traveling on as "the Salt Lick Town trail." If he was taking the same route north to Junqueindundeh (present Fremont, Ohio), he would refer to it as the "Junqueindundeh Trail." The names on trails we use now are those given them by non-Indians and historians, and generally reflect their origin, route, or connecting points. Even so, not all sources agree on a trail's name or even the specific route. The trail names used in this book are the names most commonly used.

Following the Coshocton Trail along the west side of the Muskingum River, Gist passed present Dresden, Ohio. There was not a settlement there at the time, but from 1758 to 1774, it became the site of a fairly large Mekoche Shawnee[41] village called *Wakatomika*.

The trail then left the Muskingum River and veered toward the

3. Gist's First Trek for the Ohio Company, 1750–1751

southwest crossing the Licking River about five miles northwest of present Zanesville, Ohio. At the time, the area contained salt springs and salt licks, which gave the river its name, and was where the Indians hunted and made salt through evaporation. Gist wrote, "The land from Muskingum [Conchaké] to this Place rich but broken—Upon the N Side of Licking Creek about 6 M from the Mouth, are several Salt Licks, or Ponds, formed by the little Streams or Dreins of Water, clear but a blueish Colour, & salt Taste the Traders and Indians boil their Meat in this Water, which (if proper Care be not taken) will sometimes make it too salt to eat."[42]

Gist made camp there, and the following day, Thursday, January 17, 1751, continued southwest along the trail to what he referred to as "a Great Swamp," which according to the *Ohio History Connection* was referred to by Indians as "Big Swamp," or "Big Pond."[43] The swamp overlapped the corners of present Licking, Fairfield, and Perry counties, Ohio. Gist camped there for the night and then spent two days traveling the twenty-five or so miles to the Hockhocking River at present Lancaster, Ohio. The weather likely affected Gist's rate of travel, because he later mentioned that "the snow began to grow thin."

The name of the Hockhocking River is now called the Hocking River. At present Lancaster, Ohio, he came upon a small Lenape village he called "Hockhockin." The most striking geographical feature is a 250-foot-high sandstone bluff now known as Mount Pleasant, which towers over the present city. At the time, the hill was called "Standing Stone," and several Indian villages were located along the Hockhocking River in fairly close proximity to Standing Stone. It was an important location, situated at or near the junction of several major Indian trails, including the Coshocton Trail, Ohio-Standing Stone Trail, and Belpre Trail.[44]

At Standing Stone, Gist described the Lenape villages as "a small Town with only four or five Delaware [Lenape] Families."[45] Although Gist does not mention his traveling companions at this point, it's quite probable that he was traveling with a group that included George Croghan and Andrew Montour, since he mentions them by name on Wednesday, January 30, 1761, while visiting Lower Shawnee Town at the mouth of the Scioto River.

Gist departed Standing Stone on Sunday, January 20, 1751, writing, "The Snow began to grow thin, and the Weather warmer; Set out from Hockhockin S 5 M, then W 5 M, then SW 5 M, to Maguck a little Delaware [Lenape] Town of about ten Families by the N Side of a plain or

Standing Stone (now Mount Pleasant, Lancaster, Ohio).

clear Field about 5 M in Length NE & SW & 2 M broad, with a small Rising in the Middle, which gives a fine Prospect over the whole Plain, and a large Creek on the N Side of it called Sciodoe Creek [Scioto River]."

Maguck was another town whose importance was greater than its

3. Gist's First Trek for the Ohio Company, 1750–1751

size implied. It was strategically located on the Scioto Trail, which along with the very navigable Scioto River, were two of the most significant north-south thoroughfares in Ohio. In addition, three other major trails joined or crossed the Scioto Trail at Maguck. Those included the Belpre Trail, the Kanawha Trail, and the Shawnee-Miami Trail.[46]

The town sat in what was known as the Pickaway Plains, about three and a half miles south of present Circleville, Ohio, and the small hill nearby that Gist mentioned was known by the natives as "Black Mountain."[47] Gist described the land between the Licking River and Maguck as being fine and rich, with large spacious meadows and timbered areas of large walnut, hickory, poplar, cherry, and sugar maple trees. For whatever reason, Gist stayed at Maguck three days, from Monday, January 21 until Wednesday, January 23, 1751.

Gist departed Maguck on Thursday, January 24, 1751, and wrote that he traveled south about fifteen miles to a small village called Harrickintoms Town. This is likely the village shown on a 1755 map by British mapmaker Lewis Evans as "Hurricane Tom's Town" on the west side of the Scioto River approximately opposite the mouth of Salt Creek. Another British mapmaker named John Mitchell shows an Indian village called "Harriskintom" on the east side of the Scioto River in the vicinity of Salt Creek. On Evans's map, "Hurricane Tom" is likely a corruption of "Harriskintom" or "Harickintoms," as Gist spelled it. According to Gist's journal entry, the town only consisted of about five or six Delaware (Lenape) Families on the southwest side of the Scioto. Gist had to cross the Scioto to get to the town, which required a detour of several miles because of the high water and ice floes on the river.

Leaving Harriskintom's Town on Saturday, January 26, 1751, Gist continued down the Scioto River to what he described as "a small Delaware [Lenape] Town of about twenty Families."[48] He was invited to lodge in the house of the chief, who Gist referred to as *Windaughala*, and according to Gist, favored the English over the French. The town was undoubtedly the village of the Lenape chief *Wanduchale*,[49] which was at the time the westernmost of the Lenape villages. While there, Gist and his entourage went into council with the Indians who affirmed their loyalty to the British and agreed to come to Logstown in the spring for a conference with representatives of the Pennsylvania governor. Apparently, Croghan was still traveling with Gist at this point, because Croghan generally acted in the interests of Pennsylvania, while Gist was representing the Ohio Company of Virginia. Depending on the good will of the Indians, which Croghan and Montour could facilitate, Gist

With George Washington in the Wilderness

likely was not inclined to demonstrate more political bias toward Virginia over Pennsylvania.

On Tuesday, January 29, 1751, Gist and his party moved down the east side of the Scioto River to its confluence with the Ohio River at present Portsmouth, Ohio. On the west bank of the Scioto stood the large Shawnee village generally known as Lower Shawnee Town.[50] The town was established about 1734 and was so large that some of it extended across the Ohio River to the opposite shore. Gist and his party were on the east side of the Scioto, so to cross, they fired their guns to alert the residents of the Shawnee town, and some fur traders canoed over to ferry them across. Gist described the town as a considerable settlement containing about three hundred warriors, and the town had about one hundred houses on the north side of the Ohio, with about forty houses on the south side. It's estimated that the population of the town was between 1,200 and 1,500 residents. The town had a large council house, which Gist called a "Kind of State-House" that was about ninety-feet-long and covered with bark.

The following day, on Wednesday, January 30, 1751, they met in council with the Indians, and George Croghan once again delivered speeches on behalf of the governor of Pennsylvania, warning the Shawnee of the perfidy of the French and extolling the friendship of the English. Andrew Montour interpreted for Gist, who was unable to converse in the Shawnee language. Gist's message was that the king had sent a large present of goods, which were under the care of the governor of Virginia, and he invited the Indians to come and see him the next summer. The chief of the Shawnee, who Gist identified as "Big Hannaona," thanked Gist and said he would come to Logstown in the spring. The principal chief at the time at Lower Shawnee Town was called *Neucheconneh*, and two of his influential leaders were *Coyacolline* and *Layparewah*. Gist likely was referring to *Neucheconneh* when he wrote Big Hannaona.

The location of Lower Shawnee Town was at the confluence of two major navigable waterways, the Scioto and the Ohio rivers, and the junction of four major Indian trails. These were the Scioto Trail, the Kanawha Trail, the Pickawillany Trail, and the Warriors Path leading south to Catawba country. As such, it quickly became a major rendezvous point and trading hub for both English and French fur traders.

It should be mentioned that the village was sometimes referred to as *Chillicothe*, which in the Shawnee language meant "principal town of the Chalahgawatha." The Chalahgawatha was one of the five septs, or

3. Gist's First Trek for the Ohio Company, 1750–1751

branches, of the Shawnee nation, and there were in fact several Chalahgawatha villages called "Chillicothe." Lower Shawnee Town some was sometimes referred to as "Chillicothe on the Ohio."

Gist wrote that they stayed at Lower Shawnee Town until Monday, February 11, 1751, and while there he witnessed what he described as a very extraordinary kind of festival:

> In the evening a proper officer made a public proclamation that all the Indian marriages were dissolved, and a public feast was to be held for the three succeeding days, in which the women, as their custom was, were to choose again their husbands. The next morning early the Indians breakfasted and after, spent the day dancing until the evening; when a plentiful feast was prepared. After feasting they spent the night in dancing. The same way they spent the two next days until the evening. The men dancing by themselves, and then the women in turns, around fires, and dancing in their manner and in the Form of the figure eight, about sixty or seventy of them at a time. The women, the whole time they danced, sung a song in their language, the chorus of which was, "I am not afraid of my husband, I will choose what man I please."
>
> The third day, in the evening, the men, being about one hundred in number, danced in a long string, following one another, sometimes at length, at other times in the figure of eight, quite around the fort, and in and out of the long house where they held their council, the women standing together as the men danced by them, and as any of the women liked a man passing by, she stepped in and joined the dance, taking hold of the man's shroud or blanket, whom she chose, and then continued in the dance until the rest of the women stepped in and made their choice in the same manner, after which the dance ended, and they all retired to consummate.[51]

On Tuesday, February 12, 1751, Gist set out from Lower Shawnee Town to visit the Indians in the west who had revolted against the French. These were a band of Miami Indians whose chief was named *Memeskia*. The French for some reason referred to him as La Demoiselle or "young lady" or "damselfly," while the English called him "Old Briton" because of his staunch loyalty to the British. Memeskia and his band of Piankashaw Miami moved into present western Ohio from their homeland around present Fort Wayne, Indiana.

The Miami Indians referred to themselves as *Mihtohseeniaki* (the people), and the name *Miami* derives from *Myaamia* (downstream people). Other tribes and some whites called them *Twightwee* (sandhill crane), but it was not a name they used for themselves. *Quiskakon*, their principal town, was also referred to as *Kekionga* (blackberry bush). The Miami Indians whom Gist wanted to contact were a breakaway band of

With George Washington in the Wilderness

Piankashaw Miami, who wanted to take advantage of the more advantageous trade with the fur traders from the British colonies. For several reasons, including the advanced English Industrial Revolution and the shorter distance required to transport their trade merchandise, English goods were considerably less expensive, more plentiful, and of better quality than what the French traders had to offer.[52] Indians, like people everywhere, were attracted to a bargain, so they preferred to trade with the British traders like George Croghan. The French, however, were not willing to have their business eroded by what they considered English trespassers. The French admonished the Indians not to trade with the English, and they also sent out patrols to capture English fur traders, confiscate their goods, and in many cases, imprison the traders themselves. Captured English traders were taken to Fort Detroit, Montréal, Québec City, and some were transported as far as Paris to face trial and punishment. Also, to keep the Miami Indians in compliance, the French constructed Fort St. Phillipe, adjacent to the Miami principal city of Quiskakon. The fort was more commonly called Fort des Miamis.

When Memeskia and his band learned of the Wyandot chief Orontony's move to the southern shore of Lake Erie to escape the French monopoly, the chief decided to likewise move his band. Memeskia relocated his village approximately eighty miles southwest of Quiskakon to the west bank of the Great Miami River where he established his village of Pickawillany near present Piqua, Ohio. As with Orontony's Wyandots, the French viewed Memeskia's move to Ohio as a defection to the British, and they began to exert pressure on both Orontony's Wyandot and Memeskia's Miami to return to the fold.

Both Orontony and Memeskia rebelled and open warfare broke out, and in 1747, a combined force of Wyandot and Miami burned Fort des Miamis to the ground. While the French regrouped and rebuilt Fort des Miamis, Old Briton's town of Pickawillany became one of the most important trading centers in present Ohio. English traders came all the way across the Alleghenies from the mid–Atlantic colonies and also up from the Carolinas to do business at Pickawillany.

Faced with expanding rebelliousness of the breakaway Indians and fearful of more tribes joining the rebellion, the French began to pour troops into Fort Detroit to subjugate and punish the breakaway tribes. Orontony realized the French military might would soon be sent against him and his Wyandot, so rather than continue a suicidal battle against overwhelming odds, he decided to relocate. Orontony abandoned his villages on Sandusky Bay and moved most of his people ninety or so

3. Gist's First Trek for the Ohio Company, 1750–1751

miles southwest, establishing the town of Conchaké at the Forks of the Muskingum. Not all of Orontony's Wyandot moved with him, but some instead moved south along the Sandusky River to establish the towns of Upper Sandusky and Junqueindundeh at present Fremont.

Orontony's Wyandot may have moved beyond the reach of the vindictive French, but not so for the Miami Indians at Pickawillany. In a little more than two years, the French would strike a blow at Old Briton and his village of Pickawillany, and the savagery of their attack would be a grim lesson to any other Indians who were considering breaking away from the French.

The British authorities were well aware of the conflict between the French and the Indians, and part of Gist's mission was to befriend the Indians in the west, especially those who had rebelled against the French. Gist was also told to discover the strength and numbers of those who were inclined toward the English and deliver messages of encouragement and support from Virginia Lieutenant-Governor Dinwiddie.

Gist planned to return to Lower Shawnee Town after visiting the Miami Indians at Pickawillany, so he left a boy to take care of some of his horses and equipment until he returned. It's not known who the boy was, but quite possibly it was the young assistant who accompanied Gist from the very beginning of his trek, or he may have hired a young Shawnee to look after his horses. When Gist rode out of Lower Shawnee Town on February 12, he noted that he was traveling with what he called "my old Company, viz George Croghan, Andrew Montour, Robert Kallandar,[53] and a servant to carry the provisions etc."

It was about 150 miles to Pickawillany from Lower Shawnee Town, and Gist's party followed the Pickawillany Trail from Lower Shawnee Town northwest to Pickawillany. According to Gist's journal, they traveled about thirty-five miles the first day and camped near present Cynthiana, Ohio, in the northwest corner of present Pike County. They likely did not pass any permanent villages along the route that first day, because the nearest Indian towns at that time were clustered along the Scioto River to the east.

The following day, Thursday, February 14, 1751, Gist noted in his journal that they traveled about another thirty miles to present Clinton County, but again did not encounter anyone. The following day, however, on Friday, February 15, 1751, they traveled about fifteen miles and were in present Greene County where they met nine Shawnee Indians who were returning from a council with the Miami at Pickawillany. They said that fifteen more Shawnee remained at Pickawillany to meet a party

With George Washington in the Wilderness

of Miami Indians who were delivering a captive Shawnee woman and her child to them. The Shawnee said the woman and child were captured by the Miami the previous fall, and that incident had very nearly precipitated a war between the two nations. Now, the Miami claimed the two had been captured by mistake and were returning them to the Shawnee.

The remainder of their journey to Pickawillany was uneventful, but Gist dutifully described the land in his journal for the Ohio Company.

> All the way from the Shannoah Town [Lower Shawnee Town] to this Place (except the first 20 M, which is broken) is fine, rich, level Land, well timbered with large Walnut, Ash, Sugar Trees, Cherry Trees &c, it is well watered with a great Number of little Streams or Rivulets, and full of beautiful natural Meadows, covered with wild Rye, blue Grass and Clover, and abounds with Turkeys, Deer, Elks, and most Sorts of Game particularly Buffaloes, thirty or forty of which are frequently seen in one Meadow: In short it wants Nothing but Cultivation to make it a most delightful Country—The Ohio and all the large Branches are said to be full of fine Fish of several kinds, particularly a Sort of Cat Fish of a prodigious Size; but as I was not there at the proper Season, I had not an opportunity of seeing any of them.[54]

They arrived at the Great Miami River opposite Pickawillany on Sunday, February 17, 1751, and because the river was high, they constructed a raft to carry their saddles, equipment, and goods, and then swam their horses across. Gist commented that the white traders told him the distance from Lower Shawnee Town to Pickawillany was about two hundred miles, but he more accurately computed it as closer to 150 miles.

When they arrived in the town, they were greeted enthusiastically by both Indians and fur traders with a lot of celebratory gunfire, and the chief Memeskia invited them into his own lodge, which flew the English flag above it. Gist estimated the town had a population of about four hundred families, which was increasing daily, and he commented that it was perhaps the "strongest" Indian town on this part of the continent. Memeskia or Old Briton told Gist that when the French traded with the Miami, they furnished only a few trifles at exorbitant prices, and that Memeskia's Indians left their former habitation near Quiskakon and Fort des Miamis to be able to trade with the English.

Gist and his entourage stayed at Pickawillany the rest of February, during which time they regularly met in council and presents were exchanged. On Saturday, February 23, 1751, an alarm was spread warning that four Indians in the company of four hundred French troops were on the march in their direction, but then the messenger said that only four French Indians were coming to the town. On Sunday, February

3. Gist's First Trek for the Ohio Company, 1750–1751

24, 1751, the four French Indians arrived carrying the French flag, and were received kindly by the residents of Pickawillany. The French colors were raised over the council house along with the English colors, and a council was held. The French Indians presented the Pickawillany Miami with four kegs of brandy, which held about seven quarts each, and they were also given about ten pounds of tobacco. After they presented their gifts, the French Indians told Memeskia that he and his Pickawillany Miami should return to Quiskakon. They had been missed and would be welcomed back, and "their French father would forget all the little differences that had been between them."[55]

The Pickawillany Miami chief Memeskia said he would consider what the French Indians had said and would give them his answer in another council meeting. That meeting took place on Tuesday, February 26, 1751, and the Pickawillany Indians made their decision clear. Gist recorded what Memeskia said to the French Indians: "You have often desired We should go Home to You, but I tell You it is not our home." He continued, "As you threaten us with War in the Spring, We tell You if You are angry We are ready to receive You; And resolve to die here before We will go to You; And that You may know this is our Mind, We send You this String of black Wampum."[56] On Wednesday, February 27, 1751, The French colors were taken down, and the four French Indians were dismissed and set off on their return to Quiskakon.

The next day, Friday, March 1, 1751, Memeskia met with Gist and his party, and thanked them for coming to visit him., and he asked them to arrange for a blacksmith to come and live among them to repair their guns and hatchets. He also told them that they would come to meet at Logstown, as soon as the women planted the corn in the spring and after they met with other Indians who were expected.

Gist, Croghan, Montour, and their party prepared to leave Pickawillany, and before leaving, Gist wrote, "The Land upon the great Miamee River is very rich level and well timbered, some of the finest Meadows that can be: The Indians and Traders assure Me that the Land holds as good and if possible better, to the Westward as far as the Obache [Wabash] which is accounted 100 Miles, and quite up to the Head of the Miamee River, which is 60 Miles above the Twigtwee Town [Pickawillany]. And down the said River quite to the Ohio which is reckoned 150 Miles—The Grass here grows to a great Height in the clear Fields, of which there are a great Number, & the Bottoms are full of white Clover. Wild Rye, and blue Grass."[57]

They departed Pickawillany on Saturday, March 2, 1751, and

traveled together for about thirty-five miles to the Mad River, where they separated. Croghan, Montour, and their party continued eastward toward Standing Stone on the Hockhocking River, while Gist continued south and then followed the Little Miami River to near present Oregonia, in Warren County, Ohio. From there he continued southeast until rejoining the Pickawillany Trail back to Lower Shawnee Town.

Along the way, Gist was worried that the French Indians who were rebuffed at Pickawillany would pursue him, so he avoided any of the major trails until he was most of the way to Lower Shawnee Town. On Monday, March 4, 1751, he heard several guns firing and wrote that he was afraid to find out who fired them lest it was the French Indians. That evening just before nightfall, he killed a buffalo cow and took only the tongue and some of the best meat. He also wrote, "The Land still level rich and well timbered with Oak, Walnut, Ash, Locust, and Sugar Trees."[58] On Wednesday, March 5, 1751, Gist wrote that he killed a fat bear and loaded his horse with the bear meat. On Thursday, March 7, 1751, he met a young fur trader, and they camped together. The next night, Friday, March 8, 1751, after traveling about thirty miles, Gist arrived at Lower Shawnee Town.

Gist wrote an explanation in his journal for the Ohio Company, saying, "In my Return from the Twigtwee [Pickawillany] to the Shannoah [Lower Shawnee] Town, I did not keep an exact Account of Course or Distance; for as the Land thereabouts was everywhere much the same, and the Situation of the Country was sufficiently described in my journey to the Twigtwee Town."[59]

On Saturday, March 9, 1751, in Lower Shawnee Town, Gist met a Mingo chief who had just returned from the Falls of the Ohio (present Louisville, Kentucky). The Mingo said that he had encountered a party of French Indians hunting in the vicinity of the falls and warned Gist that the Indians would either kill him or take him to the French as a prisoner. That was a concern, but Gist's orders from the Ohio Company were to proceed as far as the Falls of the Ohio, so he decided to venture as far as he could in that direction.

4

Toward the Falls of the Ohio

"We travel not to escape life, but for life not to escape us."
—Anonymous

After breakfast on Tuesday, March 12, 1751, Gist and his boy servant were ferried across the Ohio. He wrote that the river was smooth, about three-quarters-of-a-mile wide and very deep at that point. They spent the night on the south side of the river, and on Wednesday, March 13, 1751, they started west following the south side of the Ohio River for about eight miles and then headed south. They had traveled about eighteen miles when they met two white traders, one of whom was called Hugh Crawford, an associate of another trader named Robert Smith, whom Gist had met at Pickawillany.

The two men had in their possession several large mammoth teeth, which they had salvaged from a salt lick spring about thirty miles south of the mouth of the Great Miami River, southwest of present Cincinnati, Ohio.[1] Crawford told Gist they had seen rib bones there that were eleven feet long, and the largest skull bone they found was six feet wide across the forehead. There were also several teeth, some of which they called horns, that were upwards of five feet long and difficult for one man to carry. Crawford gave Gist two of the teeth, one of which Gist described as "a Jaw Tooth of better than four Pounds Weight; it appeared to be the furthest Tooth in the Jaw, and looked like fine ivory when the outside was scraped off."[2] Later on that same day, Gist encountered four Shawnee Indians who were canoeing up the North Fork of the Licking River. They warned Gist about sixty French Indians that were camped at the Falls of the Ohio.

Gist followed the North Branch of the Licking River south for about fifteen miles, then he turned west. The next day, Friday, March 15, 1751, Gist came arrived at a stream where the water was so high, they couldn't

With George Washington in the Wilderness

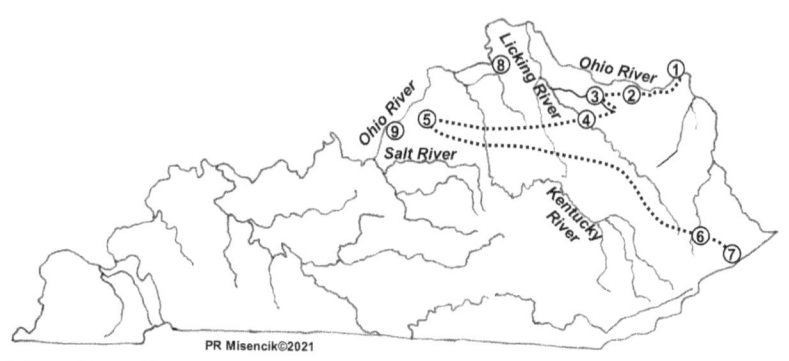

1. Lower Shawnee Town
2. Met traders with mammoth teeth - March 13, 1751
3. Met Four Indians on North Fork of the Licking
4. High water on Licking River - March 15, 1751
5. Farthest point west - March 18, 1751
6. Found brass-like stones and coal - March 21, 1751
7. Found coal - March 27-28, 1751
8. Big Bone Lick
9. Falls of the Ohio

Gist in Kentucky, 1751.

get across until the following morning. It was likely the main branch of the Licking River near the present Blue Licks Battlefield State Park.

On Monday, March 18, 1751, Gist wrote, "N 45 W 5 M then SW 20 M, to the lower Salt Lick Creek, which Robert Smith and the Indians told Us was about 15 M above the Falls of the Ohio."[3] That was likely at or near present Floydsburg, Kentucky, on Floyd's Fork, a tributary of the Salt River.[4] They were probably less that twenty miles from the Falls of the Ohio, and now recalling the warnings regarding French-allied Indians in the vicinity of the Falls, Gist became more vigilant. He grew even more cautious when he heard the sounds of gunfire and found some newly set traps around which he saw numerous Indian moccasin prints that were no more than a day old. His orders plainly stated that he was to proceed as far as the Falls of the Ohio, but now he was concerned that he would be unable to comply because of the danger posed by hostile Indians.

He considered leaving the servant boy along with the horses and proceeding stealthily alone on foot to the Falls, but then he wrote, "The Boy being a poor Hunter, was afraid he would starve if I were long from him."[5] He also considered that the enemy Indians might come upon the boy and the horses while he was gone, so Gist decided to forego the Falls. He wrote his justification in his journal: "I had seen good Land enough, [and] I thought perhaps I might be blamed for venturing so far, in such dangerous Times, so I concluded not to go to the Falls."[6]

46

4. Toward the Falls of the Ohio

Gist and the boy turned away toward the southeast, and on Tuesday, March 19, 1751, they crossed over what he called the "little Cuttaway River" (Kentucky River), near present Frankfort, Kentucky. From there, Gist appeared to have used an Indian trail that led in a southeasterly direction past present Lexington and Winchester, Kentucky, arriving near the confluence of the Kentucky and the Red River on Thursday, March 21, 1751. Gist wrote in his journal, "Here I found a Place where the Stones shined like high-coloured Brass, the Heat of the Sun drew out of them a Kind of Borax or Salt Petre only something sweeter; some of which I brought in to the Ohio Company, tho I believe it was Nothing but a Sort of Sulphur."[7]

On Friday, March 22, 1751, Gist wrote that he killed a fat bear, and later that night he became ill. The next day, he decided to construct a sweat lodge and wrote that he sweated himself in the Indian fashion. By Sunday, March 24, 1751, he felt fit enough to travel, and by his reckoning covered another twenty-two miles before making camp. Gist wrote that they only had poor food for their horses, which, along with Gist and his companion, were "much wearied." The traveling that day was difficult because of the steep riverbanks and almost impassible terrain. The following day, Monday, March 25, 1751, Gist killed a buck elk, and the following day he killed two buffalo, taking their tongues for food. The going was very difficult, and on Wednesday, March 27, 1751, they and their horses were so fatigued they were forced to spend the day resting. Gist wrote about the abundance of coal in the area and carried some of it back for the Ohio Company.

About Monday, April 1, 1751, Gist crossed into Virginia in the vicinity of present Conway, Virginia, in Buchanan County. There he found what he called blocks of coal that were about eight to ten inches square laying upon the surface of the ground. A few miles into Virginia, on Wednesday, April 3, 1751, Gist came upon a recently abandoned Indian camp large enough to have contained seventy or eighty warriors. One tree had a painted pictograph of a crane, which Gist interpreted as the Indian leader's name. They stayed at the camp for two days, until Saturday, April 6, 1751, in order to rest their horses and wait out the rain. Gist wrote that they joined the Warriors Path, but the journey was no easier, and in fact, it was the worst traveling he had ever experienced. On Sunday April 14, 1751, the going was so rough that two of the horses were injured in falls. Gist scouted ahead on foot and found that the mountainous terrain was so severe that they had to rest the horses before continuing.

With George Washington in the Wilderness

On Monday, April 15, 1751, while cutting a trail up the mountain through thick laurel to make it more passable for the horses, Gist was injured. He wrote, "We cut a passage through the Laurels better than 2 M, as I was climbing up the Rocks, I got a Fall which hurted Me pretty much."[8] While the injury was severe enough to mention, he was still able to kill a bear that same day and start off again through a thunderstorm the following day.

The going was very slow, and Gist and his companion struggled eastward through the mountains. On Wednesday, May 1, 1751, they were in the southern portion of present West Virginia where they came upon what is now known as Pinnacle Rock.[9] Gist's entry in his journal recorded the event. "Went up a very high Mountain, upon the Top of which was a Rock 60 or 70 feet high, & a Cavity in the Middle, into which I went, and found there was a Passage thro it which gradually ascended to the Top, with several Holes in the Rock, which let in the Light, when I got to the Top of this Rock, I could see a prodigious Distance, and could plainly discover where the big Conhaway [Kanawha][10] broke the next high Mountain."[11]

They pressed onward to the east, and on Tuesday, May 7, 1751, endeavored to cross the New River somewhere east of present Blacksburg, Virginia. However, the water was so high, because it had been raining steadily, that they were only able to cross the river part way to a large island in the middle. They completed the crossing the following morning, but since there are several islands in that stretch of the river, their precise crossing point is difficult to determine.

On Saturday, May 11, 1751, Gist wrote that he went up "a very high Mountain up on the Top of which was a Lake or Pond about ¾ of a Mile long NE and SW, & ¼ of a Mile wide the Water fresh and clear, and a clean gravelly Shore about 10 Yards wide with a fine Meadow and six fine Springs in it."[12] Gist was referring to Mountain Lake,[13] in present Giles County, near Newport, Virginia, which along with Lake Drummond in the Great Dismal Swamp are the only two natural lakes in Virginia. Gist stayed an extra day near the lake to rest their horses and dry some of the meat they had killed.

Leaving Mountain Lake on Monday, May 13, 1751, they reached the home of one Richard Hall, who Gist described as "one of the farthest Settlers to the Westward upon the New River."[14] From Gist's bearings and distances, Richard Hall's homestead was likely at or near present Radford, Virginia. They stayed with Hall for two nights, and while there, Gist wrote a message informing the president of the Ohio Company that

4. Toward the Falls of the Ohio

he could meet with the company by Tuesday, June 15, 1751. Gist was not yet aware that Thomas Lee had died the previous November 14, 1750, and Lawrence Washington now directed the Company.

Gist departed the homestead of Richard Hall on Wednesday, May 15, 1751, and generally followed branches of the Warriors Path south, and on Friday, May 17, 1751, he reached the border of Virginia and North Carolina. They camped for the night and completed the final leg of the journey to Gist's home on Saturday, May 18, 1751.

After an absence of over seven months, Gist arrived at his home on the Yadkin River only to find it empty. An old man who lived nearby told Gist that an Indian war party had swept through the area the previous winter killing five people. The raid had frightened Sarah Gist and her children, so they gathered up what they could and fled east toward "Roanoke." His journal entry was "Set out S 20 M to my own House on the Yadkin River, when I came there I found all my Family gone, for the Indians had killed five People in the Winter near that Place, which frightened my Wife and Family away to Roanoke about 35 M nearer in among the Inhabitants, which I was informed of by an old Man I met near the Place."[15]

Christopher Gist and his companion rested one night at Gist's home before setting off to find his family. He wrote in his journal, "Saturday, [May] 19, [1751]—Set out for Roanoke, and as We had now a Path, We got there the same Night where I found all my Family Well."[16]

Where exactly Gist's family had fled is questionable. Gist's journal mentions "Roanoke," but it's unlikely he meant Roanoke, Virginia, since it was more than 105 miles to the northeast and at the time it was called "Big Lick." The name wasn't changed to Roanoke until 1882. Most likely, Sarah and her children fled eastward toward the frontier settlements near present Salisbury in Rowan County, North Carolina. Salisbury, which was officially designated Salisbury Township in 1755, is the oldest continuously populated town in the western region of North Carolina. It was located at the intersection of three major trading routes, one of which was the Great Wagon Road that ran from Pennsylvania to Georgia. It's altogether likely that Sarah Gist and her children headed east for safety, and Gist simply confused the word Rowan and Roanoke, or perhaps he was thinking of the old Roanoke Colony on the North Carolina coast that was first established by Sir Walter Raleigh between 1585, and inexplicably disappeared between 1587 and 1590.

5

Prelude to Another Journey for the Ohio Company

"Life is either a daring adventure, or nothing at all."
—Anonymous

Gist had written the board members that he could meet with the company by Saturday, June 15, 1751. Now that he was back home on the Yadkin River, he was faced with the tasks of planting crops for the coming year and otherwise getting his house in order. As a result, he was a month late for his meeting with the Ohio Company in Williamsburg, Virginia, but apparently the members of the company took the delay in stride. For the first time, Gist learned of the death of Thomas Lee the previous November and that Lawrence Washington was now head of the committee. The meeting at the residence of the Reverend James Scott was composed of Lawrence Washington, the Reverend James Scott, and George Mason.[1]

Gist delivered his journal along with his maps and sketches and presented the committee with the various exhibits he brought back from his expedition, during which he discussed the details. When they questioned him about the most suitable places to establish settlements, they were surprised when Gist recommended the area between the Great Miami and the Little Miami rivers south of Pickawillany in present western Ohio. The committee disregarded those suggestions because the area was far beyond where they hoped to establish their settlements, and also because it was too near the French military posts at Fort Detroit and Fort des Miamis. Since the committee was not satisfied with Gist's recommendations, they decided to send him out on a second expedition to explore the large area between what they called the "Monongeyela and the Big Conhaway Rivers," or the Monongahela and the Kanawha rivers.

While the committee wanted Gist's detailed report on the territory

5. Prelude to Another Journey for the Ohio Company

south of the Ohio River as far as the Kanawha, they also saw the necessity of cultivating and maintaining a friendship with the Indians in that area. For that purpose, they proposed a commission for Gist to invite the Indians to a grand council at Logstown in August 1751. At that council, the Indians would be promised gifts from the king of England through the governor of Virginia, and Andrew Montour would serve as the interpreter during the conference.

The council gave Gist written instructions dated Tuesday, July 16, 1751, which read:

> After you have returned from Williamsburg, and have executed the Commission of the President & Council, if they shall think it proper to give You One, otherwise as soon as You can conveniently You are to apply to Col. Cresap for such of the Company's Horses, as You shall want for the Use of yourself and such other Person or Persons You shall think necessary to carry with You; and You are to look out & observe the nearest & most convenient Road you can find from the Company's Store at Will's Creek to a Landing at Monongeyela [Monongahela]; from thence you are to proceed down the Ohio on the South Side thereof, as low as the Big Conhaway [Kanawha], and up the same as far as You judge proper, and find good Land—You are all the Way to keep an exact Diary & Journal & therein note every Parcel of good Land, with the Quantity as near as You can by any Means compute the same, with the Breadth, Depth, Course, and Length of the several Branches falling into the Ohio, & the different Branches any of Them are forked into, laying the same as exactly down in a Plan thereof as You can; observing also the Produce, the several Kinds of Timber and Trees, observing where there is Plenty and where the timber is scarce; and You are not to omit proper Observations on the mountainous, barren, or broken Land, that We may on your Return judge what Quantity of good land is contained within the Compass of your Journey, for we would not have you omit taking notice of any quantity of good land, tho not exceeding 4 or 500 Acres provided the same lies upon the River Ohio & may be convenient for our building Store Houses & other Houses for the better carrying on a Trade and Correspondence down that River.[2]

Whether or not Gist received the commission to convene a council with the Ohio Indians is unknown because the council failed to take place that August at Logstown. It may have been too short notice to convene the tribal leaders, or it might also have been machinations by rival land speculators or opponents of the Ohio Company that caused the failure of having a council with the Indians in 1751. Instead, Gist prepared for his second expedition on behalf of the Ohio Company of Virginia, which would begin on Monday, November 4, 1751.

One might ask why Gist left so late in the season for his treks across

With George Washington in the Wilderness

the wilderness, which would be conducted in the harshest of the winter weather. Quite likely, Gist wanted to spend some time with his family after having been absent for over seven months, and he wanted to ensure that his family was well supplied and provisioned as much as possible during his second absence. Also, by taking the trip after the trees were bare of leaves, he would better be able to view the distant terrain than during the summer months.

6

Gist's Second Trek for the Ohio Company

> *"When you are in doubt, be still and wait:*
> *When doubt no longer exists for you,*
> *Then go forward with courage."*
> —White Eagle

Christopher Gist set off again on Monday, November 4, 1751, this time accompanied by one of his sons and at least one other unnamed person, who was probably an interpreter since Gist was not able to speak any of the Indian dialects. Interestingly, Gist doesn't mention the name of the son who accompanied him, but sources indicate it likely was Nathaniel,[1] who would have been about eighteen years of age. His other sons, Richard and Thomas, were about twenty-two and sixteen years old respectively at the time. It appears that Nathaniel, more than his brothers, shared his father's wanderlust and sense of adventure as well as his strength and hardiness. It's also quite possible that Christopher wanted his older son to remain at home to help Sarah and the other children during the coming winter. Some sources state that before Gist's second mission, he relocated his family to Virginia where they would be safer from Indian attacks,[2] but Ohio Company records indicate Gist began his move from the Yadkin in October 1752, after his second expedition.

According to Gist's journal, he and his son started from the Ohio Company storehouse on the Potomac River opposite the mouth of Will's Creek, and opposite to where Fort Cumberland was later built in 1755. The storehouse was a two-story log structure constructed in 1750 by Hugh Parker, the Ohio Company factor.[3] Gist does not mention when he and his son left their home on the Yadkin, but it likely was at least ten days earlier in order to cover the more than 360 miles to the Will's Creek storehouse.

With George Washington in the Wilderness

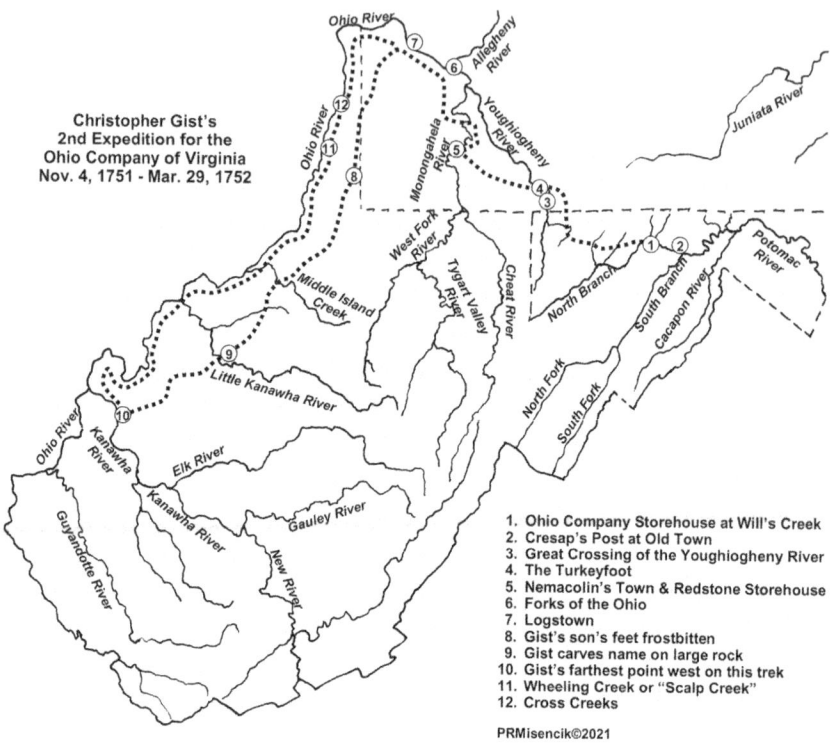

Gist's second expedition for the Ohio Company in present West Virginia.

Starting the trek, Gist crossed the Potomac and followed the so-called Nemacolin Path. That trail had been laid out by Thomas Cresap and the Lenape chief Nemacolin the previous year as the best route between Will's Creek and the Ohio Company storehouse at the confluence of Redstone Creek[4] and the Monongahela at present Brownsville, Pennsylvania. For much of the route as far as Chestnut Ridge, the old Nemacolin Path overlays US 40, or the National Road.

On their second day, Tuesday, November 5, 1751, Gist's small group traveled about as far as the present town of Frostburg, Maryland, but because of the heavy rain they were unable to continue any farther. Gist wrote, "It rained and obliged us to stop."[5] They traveled only about three miles on Wednesday, November 6, 1751, and the following day, Thursday, November 7, it rained so hard that Gist and his son were unable to travel at all.

On Friday, November 8, 1751, Gist wrote, "Set out the same Courses

6. Gist's Second Trek for the Ohio Company

N 80 W 3M here We encamped, and turned to see where the Branches lead to & found they descended into the middle Fork of Yaughaugaine [Youghiogheny]—We hunted all the Ground for 10 M or more and killed several Deer, & Bears, and one large Elk."[6] It makes one wonder why it was necessary to kill such a large amount of game for a small party of men. Gist also dutifully wrote a description of the land for the Ohio Company: "The Bottoms upon the Branches are but narrow with some Indian Fields about 2000 Acres of good high Land about a Mile from the largest Branch."[7] William Darlington (1815–1889), who collected, compiled, and annotated Gist's journals, estimates this area was on the west side of Little Meadow Mountain, near the Casselman River, near present Grantsville, Maryland. They spent ten days, from Saturday, November 9 to Tuesday, November 19, 1751, looking over and documenting the area.

On Wednesday, November 20, 1751, they set out in a westerly direction and by Thursday, November 21, 1751, crossed Negro Mountain and were less than five miles from the Great Crossing of the Youghiogheny River. That was a major fording point of the river, near present Addison, Pennsylvania. For some reason, Gist veered north of the Nemacolin Path to join the Turkeyfoot Path, which was about six miles to the north. On Sunday, November 24, 1751, they crossed the Youghiogheny River at the Turkeyfoot,[8] at present Confluence, Pennsylvania, and camped on the west side.

Their camp was about a mile or so from what Gist described as a small Lenape hunting town, and Gist purchased some corn from the Indians and invited them to Logstown for a conference that would begin at the time of the full moon in May.[9] Gist added, "They treated Me very civilly, but after I went from that Place, my man informed me that they threatened to take away our Guns and not let Us travel."[10]

It shouldn't be a surprise that the Lenape would be suspicious of a white party in western Pennsylvania who were obviously not fur traders. The Lenape had been victimized by Pennsylvanians with the aid of the Iroquois ever since the death of William Penn in 1718.

Prior to his death, Penn insisted that like whites, Indians were children of God, entitled to love and respect, and should be treated equally and fairly. He also insisted that in dealing with Indians, they were entitled to the same quality of goods as white people, and there should be no attempt to deceive them. If anyone violated those principles, they would be subject to the same penalty under the law as if they had wronged a white person. Penn called this his "holy experiment," but not everyone found it palatable. Most Europeans considered the Indians to be on a par with the animal and birds living in the forest, and not entitled to recourse of the law.

All that changed after Penn's death. His second wife, Hannah Callowhill (1671–1721) managed Penn's affairs until her death, and his three sons, Thomas, William and John, became joint proprietors of the colony. They did not share the elder Penn's ethical philosophy and were more than willing to appropriate Indian lands in the most expedient manner.

For example, in 1736, the Penns desired a large tract of the Lenape homeland that abutted the Maryland border, which the Lenape refused to sell. Undaunted, the Penns used their agent Conrad Weiser (1696–1760), to negotiate the land purchase from the Iroquois who had no claim to it. When the Lenape protested, they were threatened by both the Pennsylvanians and the Iroquois and were forced to cede the land to the Penns.

The following year 1737, the Penns wanted another large tract of Lenape land on the upper Delaware River. In that case, they claimed to have found a "lost" treaty from 1686, that ceded a tract between the fork of the Delaware and Lehigh rivers as far as a man could walk in one-and-a-half days. That was generally recognized as about forty miles. Again, with the threat of force from both the Iroquois and Pennsylvanians, the Lenape were forced to agree to the "Walking Purchase," as it was called. In preparation for the "walk," the Penns had a carefully cleared and graded path constructed that lay in a direct line through the forest, and then they hired the three fastest long-distance runners they could find. In addition, they offered a handsome prize to whichever one of their runners would cover the greatest distance. As a result of the infamous swindle, the Lenape were forced to give up about twelve hundred square miles of their homeland.

Because of the loss of their land, the Lenape were forced to continue relocating farther and farther to the west. When they encountered Gist and his party near the Youghiogheny River, it's little wonder they were suspicious of the white men and considered sending them packing.

Gist and his party continued their journey, and between Monday, November 25 and Friday, December 6, 1751, Gist diligently examined the lands along the Youghiogheny River. Initially he wrote that it was rocky and mountainous, but once west of the last ridge of mountains in the vicinity of present Uniontown and Connellsville, Pennsylvania, and the nearby Monongahela River, he wrote that "the foot of the Mountains to the River Mohongaly the first 5 M of which E & W is good

6. Gist's Second Trek for the Ohio Company

level farming Land, with fine Meadows, the Timber white Oak and Hiccory—the same Body of Land holds to 10 M, S, to the upper Forks of the Mohongaly, and about 10 M, N, towards the Mouth of the Yaughyaughgaine—The Land nearer the River for about 8 or 9 M wide, and the same Length is much richer & better timbered, with Walnut, Locust, Poplars and Sugar-Trees, but is in some Places very hilly, the Bottoms upon the River 1 M, and in some Places near 2 M wide."[11] The area must have appealed greatly to Christopher Gist, because that is where he would establish his home the following year.

On Saturday, December 7, 1751, they arrived at a Lenape Indian town on the Monongahela River, at present Brownsville, Pennsylvania. The village chief was Nemacolin, the same Indian who along with Thomas Cresap in 1749 and 1750 plotted the Nemacolin Path. The trail, of course, predated Cresap and Nemacolin, but at the behest of the Ohio Company, the two improved the trail, which was the best route between Will's Creek and the Ohio Company storehouse at Redstone Creek. The Redstone storehouse was a short distance from Nemacolin's village.

A white trader by the name of Charles Poke happened to be in Nemacolin's village, so with Poke and his own interpreter, Gist and the Lenape chief had an interesting discussion. When Gist invited Nemacolin to come to the Logstown Council the following May, the chief responded with a complaint. He asked that since Gist could bring word from the king to invite Nemacolin to a council to receive presents, why couldn't Gist deliver a message to the king from Nemacolin? The chief explained that the proprietor of Pennsylvania, William Penn, had granted Nemacolin's father, Checochinican, a large tract of land on Brandywine Creek, west of Philadelphia. But subsequently, white people moved onto those lands and would neither pay Checochinican for them nor even let the Indians live on them. Nemacolin asked Gist to tell the Virginia governor to inform the king, who would either make the white people give the land back to Checochinican or pay him for it. Gist did not record how he answered the chief, but apparently, he appeared sympathetic in order to maintain a friendly relationship with Nemacolin. His journal entry simply states, "This I was obliged to insert in my journal to please the Indian."[12]

While in the area, Gist moved north along the east side of the Monongahela and examined the surrounding area, which he described as having "fine Bottoms a Mile wide and the Hills above them are extraordinarily rich and well timbered."[13] It snowed on Saturday, December 14, 1751, and the following day Gist and his party crossed the Monongahela near present McKeesport, Pennsylvania, and he described the river as being "53 Poles wide," which equals about 875 feet across.

By Tuesday, December 17, 1751, Gist had passed the Forks of the Ohio, and came upon a small Lenape hunting camp under the leadership of a man called Oppaymolleah. There was also another Lenape there by the name of Joshua, whom Gist had previously met and who spoke very good English. Gist didn't say where he had met Joshua before, but it may have been during his previous expedition, or perhaps when he was a ranger or fur trader.

Joshua said he was glad to see Gist again, but according to Gist, the Indian asked "where I was going so far in those woods."[14] Gist wisely did not tell the Indian that he was looking for land for the Ohio Company upon which to establish white settlements. Instead, he said he had come to invite all the "great Men of the Indians to a Treaty to be held at Loggs Town." He added that the council would begin at the full moon in May, and the king of Great Britain had sent a great parcel of goods which the president of Virginia would distribute to the Indians. The reference to the president of Virginia referred to the president of the Ohio Company of Virginia.

Joshua translated Gist's invitation to Oppaymolleah and the other Indians and was told that Gist should also extend that invitation to Tamaqua (Beaver) at his town at Sauconk[15] at the mouth of the Beaver River. Gist instead wrote out the invitation to the Logstown Council and gave it to Joshua to deliver to Tamaqua. Joshua said he would deliver the message, and a white trader at Sauconk would read it to Tamaqua.

They stayed in the Lenape camp until Friday, December 20, 1751, and then traveled along the south side of the Ohio River, paralleling it by as much as eighteen or twenty miles. The weather turned bad with a great amount of snowfall and the temperature dropped well below freezing. South of present Moundsville, West Virginia, Gist wrote that his son's feet became frostbitten, so they made camp and remained there until Wednesday, January 8, 1752. That morning they started out again, but after traveling only about eight miles, Gist's son's feet were still too tender to travel, so they stopped and camped until Sunday, January 19, 1752. Their camp was comfortable, and Gist wrote, "We killed Plenty of Bear, Deer & Elk, so that We lived very well."[16]

On Monday, January 20, 1752, they were again stopped by heavy snow after traveling only about five miles. Darlington estimates that their camp was at the head of Fish Creek in present Marshall County,

6. Gist's Second Trek for the Ohio Company

West Virginia. They remained in camp through January 21 and set out again on Wednesday, January 22, 1752. After traveling about twelve miles, they were east of present New Martinsville, West Virginia, and Gist wrote, "We scared a Panther from under a Rock where there was Room enough for Us, in it We encamped & had good shelter."[17]

Because of the heavy snow, they stayed there until Saturday, February 1, 1752, when they set off again across the rugged terrain. They had veered east, paralleling the Ohio River, and Gist wrote, "The Land was very hilly and rocky, yet here and there good Spots on the Hills."[18] However, on Monday, February 2, 1752, they were again stopped by the heavy snow in the vicinity of present Middlebourne, West Virginia. The snow was so heavy that they were unable to leave their camp until Monday, February 10, 1752. Even then, traveling was difficult. Gist wrote, "The Snow hard upon the Top & bad traveling."[19]

By Friday, February 14, 1752, they were near present Elizabeth, West Virginia, which is on the Little Kanawha River about twenty miles east of the Ohio River. Gist's camp was in the fork of a creek, which Darlington figured was the junction of the Standingstone Creek and Parish Fork. Gist wrote,

> We found a large Stone about 3 Feet Square on the Top, and about 6 or 7 Feet high; it was all covered with green Moss except on the SE Side which was smooth and white as if plaistered [sic] with Lime. On this Side I cut with a cold Chizzel in large Letters,
>
> THE OHIO COMPANY
> FEB^Y 1751
> BY CHRISTOPHER GIST[20]

Gist did not leave a clue as to why he used the previous year instead of the current year in his rock engraving. Some historians believe he simply erred or may have somehow confused the old-style Julian calendar with the new Gregorian calendar, which England and its colonies adopted in stages beginning on Wednesday, January 1, 1752. According to the Julian calendar, the new year began on March 25, while the new year in the Gregorian calendar began on January 1. When the British completed the switch from the Julian to the Gregorian calendar and synchronized them, they would simply eliminate eleven days in September 1752. That meant that Wednesday, September 2, 1752, would be followed by Thursday, September 14, 1752. It's difficult to think Gist carved the date on the rock in accordance with the Julian calendar year when his journal was accurately kept according to the new Gregorian calendar. Quite possibly, Gist intended to show the date his expedition began on behalf of the Ohio Company, which indeed was 1751.

Between Saturday, February 15, 1752, and Wednesday, February 19, 1752, they passed through present Wirth, Jackson, and Mason counties, West Virginia, and reached the Kanawha River in the vicinity of present Leon, West Virginia. During the trek, Gist dutifully recorded his impressions of the surrounding countryside with these notations: "Land but hilly. Very rich bottoms up the Creek but not above 200 yards wide"; "Thro rich Land, the Bottoms about ¼ of a Mile wide upon the Creek"; "Over a Creek upon which was fine Land, the Bottoms about a Mile wide"; and "To the Top of a high Ridge, from whence We could see over the Conhaway [Kanawha] River—Here we encamped, the Land mixed with Pine and not very good."[21]

When they reached the Kanawha River, they turned north toward the Ohio River and began to follow it northeast. On Monday, February 24, 1752, Gist wrote, "Up the River all fine Land the Bottoms about 1½ Miles wide, full of lofty Timber." Then crossing what he called Smith's Creek, he added, "The Land here is level & good, but the Bottoms upon the River are not above ½ a Mile wide."[22]

On Sunday, March 1 and Monday, March 2, 1752, Gist remarked that they were camped on a creek called *Nawmissipia*, or Fishing Creek. His son went hunting, and when he returned, he mentioned that about six miles in a straight-line distance, he had come upon the same large stone that Gist had carved his name and date upon the previous month. Gist also wrote that where they were camped "the Bottoms upon the Creek are very narrow, the high Land hilly, but very rich and well timbered."[23]

On Saturday, March 7, 1752, they passed over Wheeling Creek, which Gist wrote as "Wealin or Scalp Creek." That reportedly comes from the Lenape phrase *Whee-lunk*, or "place of the skull." Supposedly, the Indians placed the head of a slain enemy on a pole overlooking the river, as a warning to their enemies.

On Monday, March 9, 1752, Gist and his party were at Cross Creeks, just north of present Wellsburg, West Virginia. Cross Creeks are two creeks directly opposite each other on the Ohio River and were a landmark for whites during the eighteenth century. The Indian village of Mingo Town (present Mingo Junction, Ohio) was on the west side of the Ohio, just north of Cross Creeks. Gist examined the area around Cross Creeks in detail, and then continued north. On Wednesday, March 11, 1752, he reached their previous camp where they camped

6. Gist's Second Trek for the Ohio Company

from December 21 to January 8 to care for young Gist's frostbitten feet. Since they were now backtracking over their outbound route, Gist refrained from making an exact account of the remainder of their journey. He wrote, "After We had got to this Place in our old Tract, I did not keep any exact Account of Course and Distance, as I thought the Rivers & Creeks sufficiently described by my Courses as I came down."[24]

On Thursday, March 12, 1752, Gist diverged from his previous outbound track to return by a more direct route. He modified his previous statement, by writing, "I set out for Mohongaly [Monongahela] crossed it upon a Raft of Logs from whence I made the best of my Way to Potomack—I did not keep exactly my old Tract but went more to the Eastward & and found a much nearer Way Home."[25]

While on his return journey along the Monongahela River, Gist mentioned another interesting encounter with a Lenape Indian who queried him about the white man's claims of land ownership. Gist described the conversation in his journal. The Indian said that

> their great Men the Beaver [*Tamaqua*][26] and Captain Oppamylucah[27] (these are two Chiefs of the Delawares) [Lenape] desired to know where the Indians Land lay, for that the French claimed all the Land on one side of the River Ohio & the English on the other side; and that Oppamylucah asked me the same question when I was at his camp in my Way down, to which I had made him no Answer.—I very well remembered that Oppamylucah had asked me such a Question, and that I was at a loss to answer Him as I now also was: But after some Consideration 'my Friend' said I, 'We are all one King's People and the different Colour of our Skins makes no Difference in the King's Subjects; You are his People as well as We, if you will take Land & pay the King's Rights You will have the same Privileges as the White People have, and to hunt You have Liberty every where so that you don't kill the White Peoples Cattle & Hogs.[28]

The Indian asked Gist to remain in his camp for two days, after which the Indian returned and said, "The great Men bid Him tell Me I was very safe that I might come and live upon that River where I pleased—that I had answered Them very true for We were all one King's People sure enough & for his Part he would come to see Me at Will's Creek in a Month."[29] The conversation with the Indian, and the assurance by the Lenape chiefs that Gist was welcome to settle and live in the area, undoubtedly played some role in his decision later that year to move his family up from the Yadkin River to a new homestead west of the Alleghenies between the Youghiogheny and the Monongahela rivers.

On Thursday, March 12, 1752, Gist was less than one hundred miles in a direct line from Will's Creek, yet it took him seventeen days to cover that distance. He commented in his journal, "We were traveling from Mohongaly to Potomack for as We had a good many Skins to carry & the Weather was bad We traveled but slow."[30] They arrived at the Ohio Company storehouse opposite the mouth of Will's Creek on Sunday, March 29, 1752.

When Gist presented his journal to the Ohio Company directors, he attested to the accuracy of his observations but qualified the accuracy of the mileages mentioned in his report. He said he "did not actually measure and therefore cannot be certain of Them, but computed Them in the most exact Manner he could & according to the best of his Knowledge."[31]

7

The Logstown Conference

"The ground on which we stand is sacred ground. It is the blood of our ancestors."
—Plenty Coups

Upon his return from his second expedition for the Ohio Company, Gist had a lot to accomplish. There is no surviving documentation that describes the specifics of what Gist did between the return from his trek at the end of March and the beginning of the Logstown Conference, but it can be assumed that he rushed home to the Yadkin to prepare his family for their move to a new homestead in western Pennsylvania. While the move was in accordance with his agreement to lead new settlers to Ohio Company land grant, Gist was also motivated by his recent exploration of the land, and also by the friendly invitation of the Indians to settle in the area.

The Logstown Council was sponsored by Lieutenant-Governor Robert Dinwiddie of Virginia, who was a major stockholder in the Ohio Company. The reason for the Logstown Conference was to obtain the Indians' agreement to the provisions of the earlier 1744 Treaty of Lancaster in which the Iroquois sold their claim to the Shenandoah Valley for £200 in gold and £200 worth of goods. The wording at the time specified "the King's right to all the lands that are or shall be, by his Majesty's Appointment in the Colony of Virginia."[1] The Virginians believed that when the Indians signed the 1744 Lancaster Treaty, they agreed that the boundaries of the Virginia Colony were in accordance with the original 1609 Virginia Charter, meaning the colony's western limit was the Pacific Ocean. The Iroquois on the other hand, maintained that they had sold land only as far as the "setting sun," which to them logically meant the crest of the Allegheny Mountains, behind which the sun set every day.

The Logstown Conference was scheduled to begin at the full moon of May 1752, and the full moon that month occurred on Saturday, May

With George Washington in the Wilderness

16, 1752. However, due to the late arrival of the Iroquois half-king[2] Tanacharison, the council was delayed until Monday, June 1, 1752. Tanacharison in effect was the representative of the Iroquois at the Logstown Conference, but as a mere resident supervisor or half-king, he was not authorized to sign treaties or make policy on behalf of the Six Nations. That put him in an uncomfortable position, since he was recognized as the Iroquois representative, and as such was the object of the Ohio Company's main lobbying efforts.

Also represented at the conference were the Shawnee, Lenape, and Wyandot. Dinwiddie and the Virginia Council appointed James Patton[3] (c. 1692–1755) and Joshua Fry[4] (1699–1754) as the commissioners to negotiate a treaty with the Indians. Gist's role at the conference was more as a lobbyist for the Ohio Company, but Dinwiddie and the council added the proviso that if Fry declined to take part, Christopher Gist would take his place as commissioner. On Saturday, April 4, 1752, Lunsford Lomax[5] (1705–1772) was appointed as the third commissioner, and Thomas Cresap was deputized to arrange for the transportation of the Indians' gifts to Logstown.

Patton, Fry, and Lomax, with the assistance of Christopher Gist, were instructed by Dinwiddie to strengthen the chain of friendship with the Indians and also emphasize the value of the gifts they were receiving. They were additionally directed to correct any impression the Indians may have that the 1744 Treaty of Lancaster was unfair to them and remind them of their treaty obligations. In addition, the commissioners were told to convince the Indians of the perfidy of the French, and that it was in the Indians' best interest to align themselves with Great Britain. The overriding goal, however, was to persuade the Indians to agree to the English interpretation of the Treaty of Lancaster and "secure a quiet and peaceable Possession to his Majesty's Subjects of this Colony [Virginia] of all lands recognized by the said Treaty [Lancaster, 1744], particularly those on the Ohio [River]."[6] Andrew Montour was chosen to be the interpreter at the conference, with Christopher Gist as his assistant.

On Tuesday, April 28, 1752, Gist met with the Ohio Company Committee and was given instructions regarding the Logstown Conference. Publicly, he was to acquaint the Indians with the establishment of the Ohio Company of Virginia and inform them of the company's benefits. Those benefits would include an Ohio Company storehouse, which would be built near the Ohio River, and would provide cheaper and more plentiful trade goods to the Indians.

Gist was given another document with secret directives, which

7. The Logstown Conference

specified that if the Virginia commissioners were unable to secure a general agreement with the Indians on the items previously mentioned, or if it transpired that their agreement should contain "doubtful or ambiguous expressions, which may be prejudicial to the Ohio Company," Gist was authorized to obtain a horse and a supply of wampum from the Ohio Company storehouse, and was given full authority to purchase from the Indians "the land on the east side of the river Ohio and Allagany [Allegheny River] as low as the great Canhaway [Kanawha River], providing the same can be done at a reasonable rate, and to obtain a deed or written agreement from the Indians mentioning the land boundaries as specifically as possible."[7] In addition, Gist was instructed to ensure that an adequate road was cleared for wagon traffic between Will's Creek and the Forks of the Ohio. Finally, Gist was told that if the Indians did not agree to the company proposals, he was ordered to immediately return and report that fact to the Ohio Company directors.

While the planning for the Logstown conference was underway, Lieutenant-Governor Dinwiddie received word that French forces were planning to move an army across the Niagara portage and seal off the Ohio region with a chain of forts along the Allegheny and the Ohio rivers. That news, of course, caused some panic among the Ohio Company commissioners who would lose their considerable investments in the company and, more importantly, their anticipated profit if their land speculation venture did not come to fruition.

As a result of the Virginians' desire to finalize an agreement with the Indians, the Logstown Conference that began on Monday, June 1, 1752, was a rather hurried affair. Traditionally, most Indian conferences were conducted with rounds of toasting, banqueting, exchanging of gifts, and flowery orations. However, the Logstown Conference's ritual was quite abbreviated. The Virginians immediately got down to business, pressing for confirmation of the 1744 Treaty of Lancaster and recognition of Virginia's claim to the territory.

The half-king Chief Tanacharison who represented the Iroquois Council as an overseer of the Ohio tribes was recognized by the Virginians as the most powerful chief at the conference, but in reality, he didn't have much power at all. Iroquois policy was that all formal councils required full Iroquois Council involvement, which certainly was not the case at Logstown. Tanacharison was smart enough to insist that he could not speak for the Iroquois Council but could only speak for himself. Even so, Andrew Montour was able to get Tanacharison to sign a document stating his personal agreement with the Treaty of Lancaster.

With George Washington in the Wilderness

When the Virginians got the document that Tanacharison signed, they considered they had achieved their main goal, which was Indian recognition of their claim to the Ohio territory. The problem was that virtually everyone present at the Logstown Conference was aware that Tanacharison's signed document would not be considered binding by the Iroquois Council. Even so, Patton, Fry, and Lomax decided among themselves that they had achieved their main objective.

Dinwiddie and the other Ohio Company commissioners, however, were reticent to accept Tanacharison's signed document as a valid treaty. They were fully aware that at best it stated the half-king's personal opinion, and they were not willing to risk inciting the Iroquois into a full-blown war on the flimsy basis of a minor chief's agreement in principle. So, since the so-called Logstown Treaty was not sanctioned or had any standing whatsoever with the Iroquois Grand Council, the Logstown Conference was not really worth the effort or expense. Dinwiddie invited the Iroquois to another conference at Winchester, but they declined, and the Ohio Indians who attended the Logstown Conference refused to discuss land transactions or land sales with the Virginians.

As an aside, Memeskia's Miami at Pickawillany were invited to the conference but were notably absent, so William Trent (c. 1715-c. 1787)[8] was ordered to deliver their share of the gifts to Pickawillany. While en route, he learned that on Sunday, June 21, 1752, Pickawillany was attacked and destroyed as a trading hub by a force of 240 French and Indians under the leadership of Charles Michel de Langlade and the Ottawa Chief Pontiac. Memeskia and several others were killed outright, and the chief known as Old Briton was ritually boiled and eaten. The survivors scattered, with some returning to the Fort des Miamis area, and the rest fled into the interior of Ohio. Trent distributed the gifts to whatever survivors he could locate before returning to Virginia.

Regardless of their failure to secure an agreement with the Indians, the Ohio Company pressed on with their land speculation venture. The company went through the formality of applying to Lieutenant-Governor Dinwiddie and the Council of Virginia for permission to survey and plat out the first two hundred thousand acres of their land grant. Dinwiddie, who had a vested interest in the Ohio Company, certainly would have approved, but the council denied the company's request. At the same time, the company asked the College of William and Mary to grant Christopher Gist a formal surveyor's commission, which would have added gravitas to their survey, but the college refused

7. The Logstown Conference

to confer Gist's commission. Undaunted, the company went ahead with their survey, while Dinwiddie and the other influential Ohio Company commissioners pressured William and Mary, which paid off in the summer of 1753 when William and Mary granted Gist a formal surveyor's commission.[9]

After the Logstown Conference, Gist was told to proceed as per his written instructions of Tuesday, September 11, 1750, and begin settlement on the Ohio Company lands in what is now western Pennsylvania. He was urged to contact those people who agreed to settle on Ohio Company lands and inform them to do so as soon as possible. Gist reported to the Ohio Company Committee that the settlers would begin occupying their new tracts that fall or the following spring. However, he told the committee that he did not think it was logistically prudent to have all the settlers move onto the land grant at the same time, since it would initially be difficult to furnish them with necessary supplies and provisions.

Lawrence Washington, who had been ailing with consumption (tuberculosis) for some time, died on Sunday July 26, 1752, creating yet another leadership vacuum in the Ohio Company, and the leadership now fell to Lieutenant-Governor Dinwiddie, George Mercer, and George Mason. The Ohio Company Committee urged Gist to hasten the survey and settlement of Ohio Company lands, which he attended to, even though he was in the midst of relocating his own family to the Monongahela area. In October 1752, after giving his maps and journals to the Ohio Company Committee in Williamsburg, he went back to the Yadkin and packed up his family to move to the area he had previously selected between the Youghiogheny and the Monongahela rivers on the western side of the Alleghenies.

8

Gist's Move to Western Pennsylvania

"Regard heaven as your father, Earth as your mother, and all that lives as your brother and sister."
—Anonymous

Christopher Gist and his family resettled between present Uniontown and Connellsville, Pennsylvania, on very large piece of rich, level farmland with fine stands of timber.[1] While he was in Williamsburg, Gist, along with Thomas Cresap and Andrew Montour, petitioned Virginia Lieutenant-Governor Dinwiddie for eighty thousand acres of land separate from that of the Ohio Company's tract, but it was refused. Quite possibly, Dinwiddie, who was a major stakeholder in the Ohio Company, was aware of competing land speculation ventures that were forming, so he did whatever he could to forestall any other land grants in the Ohio region until the Ohio Company's venture was well under way.

Disappointed by his failure to secure land for his own speculative enterprise, Gist went ahead with the Ohio Company's planned settlement by relocating his family to the Monongahela area along with several other families who had been recruited as settlers on Ohio Company land. Christopher's family included his wife Sarah; two of their sons, Richard and Thomas; their daughters, Anne (or Nancy, as she was called) and Violetta; and Violetta's husband, William Cromwell. Twenty-year-old Nathaniel opted to conduct business as a trader living among the Overhill Cherokee[2] at their town Chota,[3] near present Vonore, Tennessee. Nathaniel and his business partner, Richard Pearis, traded among the Cherokee but had a falling out over a parcel of land that both men wanted for their own. The argument would resurface a few years later and have a negative impact on both Nathaniel and Christopher.

8. Gist's Move to Western Pennsylvania

Gist's daughter Violetta and son-in-law William Cromwell established their home on 318 acres adjacent to the Youghiogheny River about five miles from Gist's new home site. However, Violetta soon grew fearful of being in a remote area of what she considered the wilderness, so she and her husband left their homesite and built another home much nearer to her parents.

There were other families who joined Gist in western Pennsylvania, but their identities and numbers depend on which source is being accessed. Ensign Edward Ward (c. 1726–c. 1793), who was George Croghan's half-brother, visited Gist's homesite in 1753 and recorded that "only four or five families who had lately settled there."[4] However, in July of 1753, one Richard Peters (1704–1776) said, "There are at this time, actually fifteen families at Monongila [sic]."[5] There are other estimates of the number of families at Gist's settlement, but the Ohio Company likely had the most accurate figure. An Ohio Company report written sometime later stated, "He [Gist] in that fall [1752], and the next spring not only removed his own family, but procured William Cromwell, his son in law, and eleven other families to settle between Yaughyaughgane [sic] and Monongahela."[6] Sources indicate that William Crawford (1722–1782), a future associate and friend of George Washington, and who in 1782 was horribly tortured and burned to death by Indians in Ohio, was for a time one of the residents at Gist's Monongahela settlement.[7] However, Crawford may have been a later settler in the area. In 1770, Washington visited the area, and according to Washington's diary, spent time with Christopher's son Thomas and also several days with "Captn. Crawford."

Aside from the Gists, most of the settlers were German Protestants from Pennsylvania who were enticed by the Ohio Company's guarantees of religious liberty under the 1689 Acts of Toleration:[8] the promise of civil rights, moderate Virginia taxes, and the absence of ecclesiastical courts. They were also promised ten years freedom from all taxes, the use of Ohio Company warehouses, the ability to purchase goods at wholesale prices, and credit for two years at 5 percent interest. In addition, the Ohio Company described the area as teeming with fish and game and having good land and roads, and also promised regular shipments of goods to a number of planned storehouses that would be conveniently located to the settlers. The Ohio Company also promised to lay out a two-hundred-acre site for a town, which would contain one-half acre lots for development and residences. Lots would be set aside for a church, other public buildings, and a school, which would

With George Washington in the Wilderness

also educate Indian children. The Ohio Company stipulated that every person who takes a lot must build upon it within three years, and their annual fee would be one ear of Indian corn and the requirement to furnish one able-bodied man to work sixty days on the adjoining fortification.[9] Any tradesman who established a business in the new town would have title to the land forever, and after three years, pay only one farthing quit-rent[10] per year thereafter.[11]

Those settlers who followed Gist across the Alleghenies to his settlement, and indeed Gist himself, believed the area was part of Virginia. Virginia considered the Ohio Company lands to be the western part of Augusta County, Virginia, and on Friday, August 17, 1753, Christopher Gist was appointed by the Virginia legislature as one of the justices of Augusta County. However, that area was also claimed by Pennsylvania, which disputed the Virginia claim, and the issue would not be resolved in favor of Pennsylvania until some thirty years later in the 1780s.

While Gist and the other families at his settlement were confident they were settling on Ohio Company land, the Ohio Company was having a difficult time finalizing its land grant and obtaining legal title to the land. Not only were other land speculation companies trying to obtain land grants in the same area, but individual Virginians collectively drew up petitions demanding individual small land grants on which to build homesteads that would be free from quit rents for at least ten years. Some Virginia legislators, and also the Board of Trade, were sympathetic to the requests by the prospective settlers, and legislation was passed granting small parcels to individual families.

Those small families, however, were not the biggest concern for the Ohio Company. It was the other large, influential land speculators who caused the company the most distress. Four of them in particular were the most troublesome; they were William Winstone, who acquired a fifty-thousand-acre grant; Maquis Calmes with sixty thousand acres; Richard George with thirty thousand acres; and the company of John Blair, William Russell, and Andrew Lewis, who had a grant of one hundred thousand acres.

Blair's company posed the biggest threat because its members wielded as much political influence as that of the Ohio Company. To make matters worse, Blair joined forces with Maquis Calmes against the Ohio Company. Their surveyors conducted a survey of the lands granted to their companies which indicated that many of Gist's settlers who believed they were on Ohio Company lands were in fact on the Blair and Calmes tracts. In addition, the Blair and Calmes tracts came so close

8. Gist's Move to Western Pennsylvania

to Gist and his son-in-law William Cromwell's tracts that it negatively impacted the value of their settlements. Worse yet, the land ownership dispute caused considerable reluctance on the part of many prospective settlers, including those who had previously agreed to settle on Ohio Company lands. In an attempt to resolve the matter, both competing factions submitted petitions to the Crown, but the French army moving down the Allegheny River made those arguments moot.

Even so, Gist's settlement was becoming somewhat of a prominent frontier outpost and landmark along the trail into the Ohio Country. On the map showing General Braddock's 1755 ill-fated march to the Monongahela, Gist's homestead is shown as "Guests." Gist's is also depicted on the 1755 map by Peter Jefferson and Joshua Fry. It's depicted on Lewis Evans's 1755 map and also on the 1756 map by Thomas Kitchin.

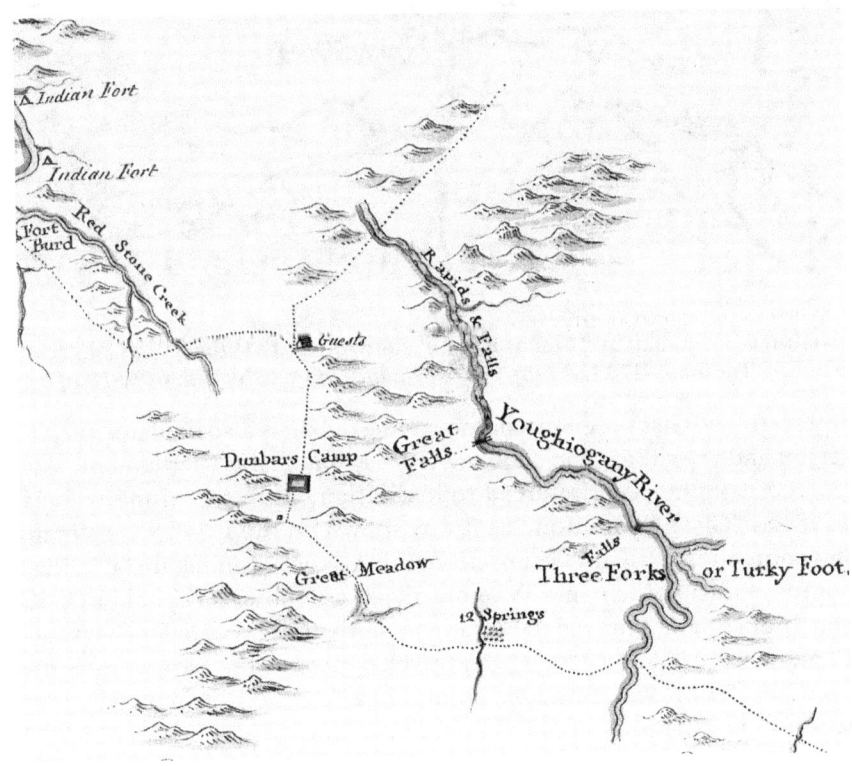

Portion of map of Braddock's 1755 march, showing Christopher Gist's homestead as "Guests" (Library of Congress, *Braddock's route, Fort Cumberland to Fort Pitt. 71002325*).

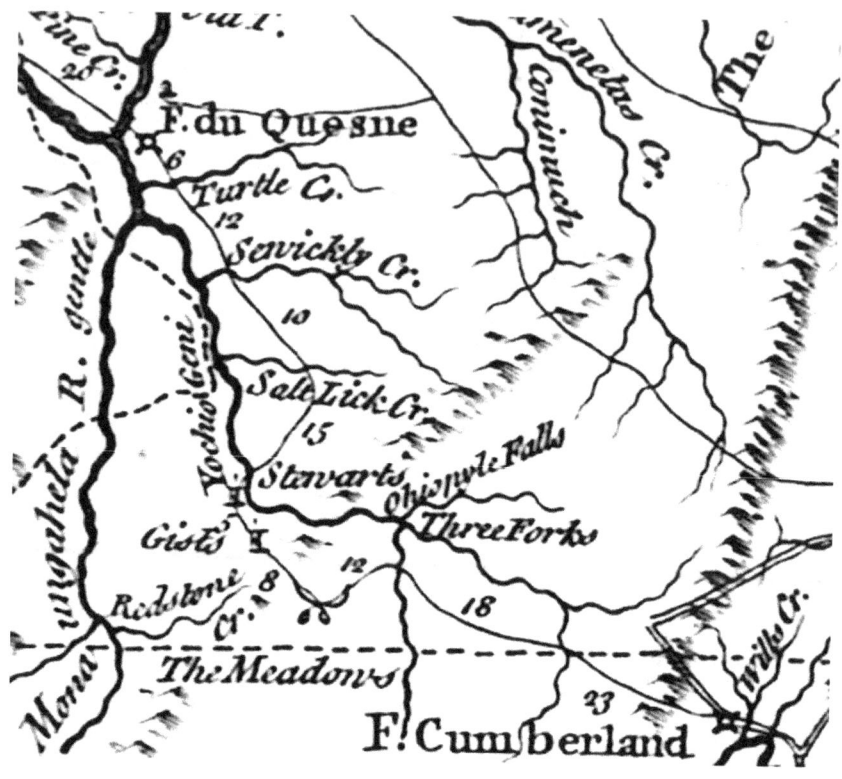

Portion of 1756 map by Thomas Kitchin showing Gist's (Library of Congress, Kitchin, Thomas—1784, *A map of the province of Pensilvania. 00561200*).

Interestingly, Gist's previous home on the Yadkin is also depicted on Jefferson and Fry's 1755 map showing Gist's Monongahela settlement.

Christopher Gist referred to his settlement in the Monongahela valley as "Gist's Plantation," as it was shown on the Lewis Evans map, but some sources claim Gist preferred the name "Monongahela." Other sources indicate the name "Monongahela" was how Christopher Gist's son Thomas later referred to his father's settlement. Whatever Gist's settlement was called by people who traveled through the area, there is little doubt that it was a notable landmark along the Nemacolin Path in western Pennsylvania.

Gist was busily occupied with establishing his own home while also helping other families settle on Ohio Company lands, yet, at the same time, the Ohio Company was trying to solidify its hold on those lands. With the threats of French troops moving across the southern shore of

8. Gist's Move to Western Pennsylvania

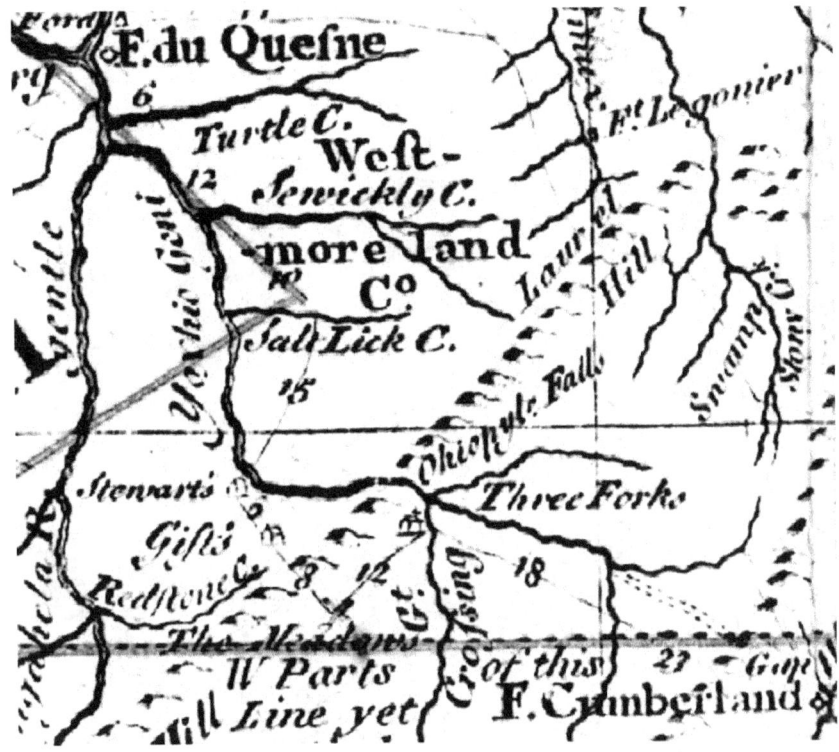

Portion of 1755 map by Lewis Evans showing Gist's settlement simply as Gist's (Library of Congress, Evans, Lewis, *A general map of the middle British colonies, in America. 71005449*).

Lake Erie to fortify the Allegheny River, and the encroachment of rival land companies, the Ohio Company committee decided to construct a fort to protect their investment.

They had originally promised the Indians they would build a fortified trading post near the Forks of the Ohio, but for some reason, they backed away from that promise at the Logstown Conference. Their excuse was that since the French and the English were at peace, there was no need for a fort. Now with rumors of a French invasion of the Allegheny and the Ohio rivers region, and the intrusion of competing land companies, the Ohio Company had a change of heart. Interestingly, the planned Ohio Company fort would not be at the actual Forks of the Ohio but almost three miles beyond the Forks at the site of present McKee's Rocks, Pennsylvania. No explanation can be found as to why that site was chosen.

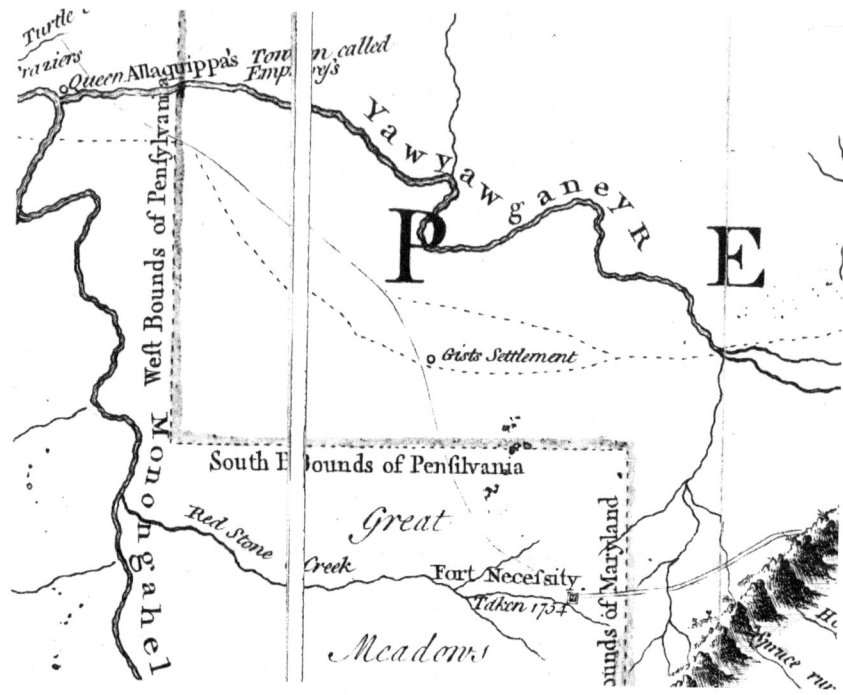

Portion of 1755 map by Fry and Jefferson showing Gist' settlement (Fry, Joshua, Peter Jefferson. *A map of the most inhabited part of Virginia containing the whole province of Maryland: with part of Pensilvania, New Jersey and North Carolina.* 74693089).

The location of the fort would be "on a hill just below Shertees Creek [Chartiers Creek] upon the South East side [of] the River Ohio, that the Walls of the said Fort shall be twelve feet high to be built of Sawed or hewn Loggs and to inclose a piece of Ground Ninety feet Square, besides the floor for Bastions at the Corners of sixteen feet square each, with houses in the middle for Stores Magazines &c."[12] The company appointed Gist, Thomas Cresap, and William Trent to recruit the "Labourers, Carpenters and other Workmen to build and compleat [sic] the same as soon as possible, and employ Hunters to supply them with Provisions and agree with some honest Industrious Man to overlook the Workmen and Labourers as Overseer, and that they be supplied with Flower, [sic] Salt, and all other Necessaries at the Company's Expense."[13]

Through the early part of 1753, Ohio Company agents were engaged in London pressing the company's petition for clear title of their land

8. Gist's Move to Western Pennsylvania

grant, and at the same time they hired William Trent to continue negotiations with the Indians and push for recognition of the Treaty of Lancaster. The company also told Gist that since he held a surveying commission from the College of William and Mary, he should obtain a measuring wheel[14] and measure the road from Will's Creek to the Fork of the Monongahela, to determine the exact place where the competing companies surveyed their land. In addition, Gist was told to have the Ohio Company settlers attest in writing that they settled on Ohio Company land and not on other companies' land.

Even so, despite the company's efforts to fortify their investment, the influx of settlers onto Ohio Company lands in western Pennsylvania came to a standstill when all eyes were turned toward the upper Allegheny River and the activities of the French army.

9

The French Invasion of Western Pennsylvania

"The earth was trembling from the multitude of French who were at Rivière au Bœuf."
—Anonymous Indian observer

Prior to February 1753, neither Lieutenant-Governor Dinwiddie nor the other members of the Ohio Company of Virginia were concerned or felt threatened by the French military. The only recent overt activities by the French were the punitive destruction of Pickawillany by French militia and Indians the year before, and Céloron de Bienville's expedition four years prior. Certainly, Céloron's burying of lead plates and posting proclamations proclaiming French sovereignty along with the destruction of Pickawillany were indicators of French resolve, but the French presence in the area was still minimal. The French outposts nearest to the Forks of the Ohio were Fort Niagara, 200 miles north, Fort Detroit, 205 miles northwest, and Fort des Miamis, 275 miles west, all too far to be much of a concern to the Virginians.

As far as Dinwiddie and the Ohio Company were concerned, the status quo existed, which greatly favored them and led them to believe that the land along the Monongahela and the Ohio rivers was theirs for the taking. To support that attitude, English traders were still reaping the benefits of the fur trade in New France despite French efforts to keep the Indians from dealing with English traders. As mentioned, the Ohio Company was more concerned with the difficulties of obtaining a clear title to their land grant west of the Alleghenies and the increased competition from the other land speculation companies then they were of the French army.

As a result, it came as a severe shock to Dinwiddie and the other committee members when they received word of an overwhelming French Force on the upper Allegheny River. While Christopher Gist was

9. The French Invasion of Western Pennsylvania

busily establishing his Ohio Company settlement in the Monongahela valley west of the Allegheny Mountains, the French army came ashore at present Erie, Pennsylvania, and built Fort de la Presqu' Île, more commonly called Fort Presque Isle. That was the first of a line of forts that would stretch from Presque Isle in the north, south to the Allegheny River and even beyond the Forks of the Ohio.

The French government was signaling in no uncertain terms that it was their intention to fortify and defend the territories west of the Allegheny Mountains, and to repel any and all English traders, settlers, and military intrusions. If the French were able to enforce their claim to the area and prevent the Ohio Company from retaining their land grant, Dinwiddie and his fellow investors faced the real threat of the collapse of their business venture along with the loss of their investments and future profits.

To be sure, it was a real threat posed by a massive professional army the likes of which had never been seen on the frontier. At a time when a large war party might consist of fifty combatants, the more than two thousand troops under Captain Paul Marin de la Malgue (1693–1753) seemed immense. One Indian reported that "the earth was trembling from the multitude of French who were at Rivière au Bœuf, and beside that ... [t]hey are holding hands from Presquisle to La Chine."[1, 2]

Previous Governors-General of New France like Jacques-Pierre de Taffanel de la Jonquière (1685–1752) and Roland-Michel Barrin de la Galissonière (1693–1756) had unsuccessfully used threats and force to coerce the Indians to remain loyal. But now their successors, Charles Le Moyne de Longueuil (1697–1755) and particularly Michel-Ange Duquesne de Menneville, Marquis Duquesne (c. 1700–1778) decided to take action to preserve French authority by interdicting British incursions. That's exactly what a chain of French forts along the frontier was meant to accomplish. Even before Fort Presque Isle was completed, Marin moved his men south to Rivière au Bœuf (La Bœuf Creek) where they started to build Fort de la Rivière au Bœuf, or more commonly, Fort la Bœuf.

The Iroquois were also taken by surprise when Marin's army landed at Presque Isle. The area had long been within the domain of the Six Nations, and now it was invaded by the French army. However, the Iroquois council tried to avoid a situation that might be considered confrontational by sending a delegation of women to question the French commander regarding the reason for a military incursion into their territory. They also asked if the French came with hatchets uplifted as in

With George Washington in the Wilderness

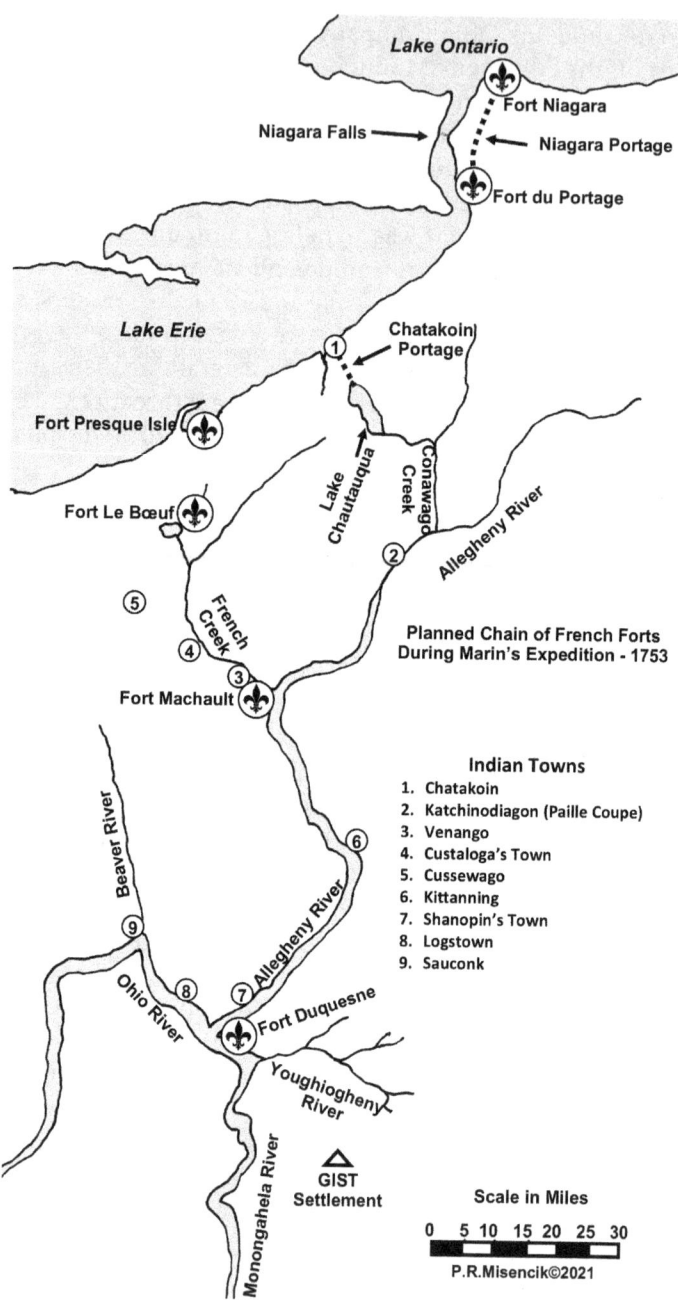

Planned chain of French forts from Lake Erie to the Forks of the Ohio.

9. The French Invasion of Western Pennsylvania

war or if they come in peace to establish tranquility. That was the Six Nations' polite way of expressing Iroquois displeasure with the French incursion.

Marin understood the diplomatic significance of the matriarchal delegation, yet his response was anything but diplomatic. He bluntly told the astonished women that "when he marched with the hatchet, he bore it aloft, in order that no person should be ignorant of the fact."[3] The Iroquois were justifiably alarmed by Marin's breech of diplomatic etiquette, but they did not resort to war. Instead, they presented Marin with three ritual protests, each stronger than the previous, which were the strongest measures the Iroquois could take short of war.

The first protest warned the French not to proceed any farther, which Marin bluntly and summarily rebuffed. By the time the Iroquois sent the second message, Marin's force was in the process of constructing the third fort near the Lenape village of Venango at the junction of French Creek and the Allegheny River. Tanacharison delivered that second message on behalf of the Iroquois:

> Your children on Ohio are alarmed to hear your coming so far this way. We at first heard that you came to destroy us. Our women left off planting, and our warriors prepared for war. We have since heard that you come to visit us as friends without design to hurt us, but then we wondered why you came with so strong a body. If you had any cause of complaint, you might have spoken to Onas [Proprietary Governor Horatio Sharpe of Maryland] or Corlear [Royal Governor George Clinton of New York], and not come to disturb us here. We have a [council] Fire at Logstown, where are the Delawares and Shawonese, and Brother Onas; you might have sent deputies there and said openly what you came about, if you had thought amiss of the English being there, and we invite you to do it now, before you proceed any further.[4]

Marin, already frustrated by the innumerable vexing problems that were delaying his expedition, was rapidly losing patience with the constant complaints and demands of the Indians. He was barely able to keep his temper in check when he bluntly told the Indian emissaries that he had no intention of attending a council at Logstown to obtain permission to proceed into the area. He said his authority came directly from the king of France, who commanded him to occupy the Ohio territory and build forts at Presque Isle, Le Bœuf, Venango, the Forks of the Ohio, and Logstown, and on Beaver Creek. The stunned Iroquois, who were initially frustrated by Marin's disregard for their concerns or his lack of a reasonably diplomatic response to their protests, were now alarmed by his declaration that the French army intended to enter their territory

With George Washington in the Wilderness

uninvited and build a chain of forts along the Ohio Valley. The Iroquois hurriedly held another conference and sent Tanacharison with a third, more strident notice that lacked the customary diplomatic tenor. The Iroquois message bluntly forbade the French from progressing any farther and directed them to turn back and return to Canada. Tanacharison's speech was unequivocal and was in essence an ultimatum to a declaration of war.

> Now Fathers, it is you who are the Disturbers in this Land, by coming and building your Towns; and taking it away unknown to us, and by Force.
>
> Fathers, We kindled a Fire a long Time ago, at a Place called Montréal, where we desired you to stay, and not come and intrude upon our Land. I now desire you may dispatch to that Place; for be it known to you, Fathers, that this is our Land, and not yours.
>
> Fathers, I desire you may hear me in Civilness; if not, we must handle that Rod which was laid down for the Use of the obstreperous. If you had come in a peaceable Manner, like our Brothers the English, we should not have been against your trading with us, as they do; BUT TO COME, FATHERS, AND BUILD HOUSES UPON OUR LAND, AND TO TAKE IT BY FORCE, IS WHAT WE CANNOT SUBMIT TO.
>
> Fathers, Both you and the English are white, we live in a Country between; therefore the Land belongs to neither one nor t'other: But the Great Being above allow'd it to be a Place of Residence for us; so Fathers, I desire you to withdraw, as I have done our Brothers the English: For I will keep you at Arms length. I lay this down as a Trial for both, to see which have the greatest Regard to it, and that Side we will stand by, and make equal shares with us. Our Brothers the English have heard this, and I come now to tell it to you; for I am not afraid to discharge you off this Land.[5]

For the irritable and cantankerous French commander, this was too much. Marin completely lost his temper and threw Tanacharison's proffered goodwill wampum belt to the ground, shouting that he despised all the stupid things the chief had said. He added that he was not afraid of flies or mosquitoes, which he likened the Indians to, and that he had sufficient numbers to crush any opposition and tread under his feet anyone who would oppose him. He insultingly added that the Indians foolishly claim that it is their land, but they don't even own land equal to the dirt under Marin's fingernails.

Marin was by nature a blunt, curmudgeonly officer, but his outrageous outburst was likely more the result of the stress, fatigue, sickness and deaths afflicting his troops, and indeed afflicting himself as he worked to complete his mission.

Meanwhile, the English were also trying to decide how to

9. The French Invasion of Western Pennsylvania

appropriately react to the French invasion. Governor-General Duquesne knew the English would learn of Marin's fort-building expedition, but he would have been surprised at the swiftness the news traveled across the frontier. The landing of Marin's army of over two thousand troops and more than two hundred Canadian Indians was such an extraordinary event that word flashed among the Indians from village to village with incredible speed. Within a few days of the French landing at Presque Isle, Indian runners informed Sir William Johnson (1715–1774) at his estate named "Fort Johnson,"[6] more than three hundred miles away. Johnson had very close ties with the Iroquois, particularly the Mohawk nation. Indeed, all of the Six Nations held Johnson in very high regard, and Johnson and the Iroquois were fiercely loyal to each other. Johnson spoke the Mohawk language fluently, was intimately familiar with Iroquois customs, and was recognized by the Iroquois as someone who would always act in the interests of the Six Nations.

After the death of his first wife, Catherine Weisenberg, in 1749, Johnson's next two wives were Mohawk women. The first was Caroline Hendrick, the daughter of the Mohawk Chief Abraham and niece of the famous Mohawk Chief Tiyanoga, who was called King Hendrick by the British. Caroline died around 1752, and Johnson next took Molly Brandt as his wife. Molly was the sister of the renowned Mohawk war chief and political leader Thayendanegea (1743–1807), who was also known as Joseph Brandt. Interestingly, there is no documentation to show that Johnson ever formally wed any of the women with whom he lived and who bore him children.

When Johnson heard of the French expedition in Pennsylvania, he immediately sent word to Pennsylvania Lieutenant-Governor James Hamilton (1710–1783), who was over 220 miles south, and Hamilton in turn relayed the message to Maryland Provincial Governor Horatio Sharpe (1710–1790) and Lieutenant-Governor Robert Dinwiddie of Virginia. Hamilton also sent messengers to the traders on the Allegheny and the Ohio rivers about 270 miles away, warning them of the French military force heading their way.

The traders, however, had already received word from their own network of friendly Indians who had been observing the French activities and passing the news along from one to the other. In this way, word of the French invasion spread very quickly. For example, the first French detachment came ashore at Presque Isle on Thursday, May 3, 1753, and by Monday, May 7, 1753, word reached George Croghan 115 miles away at his storehouse near present Etna, Pennsylvania. Croghan had received the message by Indian runner from another trader, John Fraser (1721–1773), who was at the Indian village of Venango at present Franklin, Pennsylvania.

The system of Indian runners to disseminate information was obviously very effective. By comparison, Lieutenant-Governor Hamilton's dispatch riders did not reach George Croghan until Saturday, May 12, 1753, a full five days after Indian runners had given Croghan the same information.

Other than Gist's small settlement, there were very few other English colonists living west of the Alleghenies, and those were individual fur traders. The most active were George Croghan and John Fraser. When word of a massive French army on the march in western Pennsylvania reached whatever Englishmen were in the trans-Allegheny area, they began to plan for their best course of action. Croghan had trading posts in western Pennsylvania and in the Ohio country, and John Fraser regularly visited the Indian towns along the Allegheny River from his post at the junction of Turtle Creek and the Monongahela River. Both men viewed the approaching French army with trepidation and began to plan on withdrawing from the area.

Christopher Gist and his fellow settlers at Gist's Plantation undoubtedly received the news of the French advance as quickly as Croghan and Fraser, but apparently Gist had no plans to abandon his plantation. He likely figured that his small settlement at the very edge of New France was an insignificant threat to French sovereignty, and as long as he and his fellow settlers kept a low profile and did not arouse the ire of either the French or the English, they should be able to coexist with both sides. Neutrality seemed like a decent plan, but events in the final months of 1753 and the first half of 1754 made that concept virtually impossible for Gist and the others at his plantation. As the Iroquois Chief Scarouady once sagely commented, "You can't live in the woods and be neutral."[7]

Meanwhile the French fort-building campaign in western Pennsylvania continued with the French commander Captain Marin mercilessly driving his troops to accomplish the back-breaking work of clearing a road, transporting men and equipment, and building the outposts in the depths of the rugged wilderness. They had begun construction of Fort Presque Isle at present Erie, Pennsylvania, on Sunday, April 15, 1753, and then started work on Fort LeBœuf at present Waterford, Pennsylvania, on Thursday, July 12, 1753. Next was Fort Machault near the Lenape village of Venango at the junction of French Creek and the Allegheny

9. The French Invasion of Western Pennsylvania

River at present Franklin, Pennsylvania. However, the incredibly difficult working conditions resulted in a terrible attrition. Marin started out with two thousand troops, but by the time they reached Venango, the French force consisted of less than eight hundred men. Over four hundred had perished from overwork, exhaustion, bad food, and sickness. A full 20 percent of the original force was dead, and another eight hundred were incapacitated by fatigue, injuries, and sicknesses, ranging from broken bones, fever, bloody flux,[8] pneumonia, spitting blood, lung diseases, and hemorrhaging. Most were scarcely able to walk, much less work.

Somehow, they completed Fort Machault, but it was virtually impossible for them to push on any farther. Marin left minimal garrisons at the three new forts, and then sent the remainder of his force back to Montréal for rest and recuperation. When the pitiful troops staggered into the city, they were reviewed by Governor-General Duquesne, who was horrified by their deplorable state. Ironically, only that June, Duquesne had written to Marin regarding rumors that Marin was "living as magnificently as a Marshal of France in command of an army."[9] Nothing could have been further from the truth. Marin shared the same sparse diet as his men and drove himself every bit as mercilessly. Back at Fort LeBœuf, Marin became bedridden from illness, and although he was ordered to return to Montréal to recuperate, he refused, preferring to die in the field like a soldier. He got his wish, dying on Monday, October 29, 1753, at the age of sixty-one.

Ironically, in September, the month before he died, Marin was awarded the Royal and Military Order of Saint Louis, but word of the honor did not reach Fort LeBœuf until after Marin's death. The Military Order of Saint Louis was an order for chivalry founded on April 5, 1693, by King Louis XIV and was the predecessor of the French Ordre national de la Légion d'honneur (National Order of the Legion of Honor). Marin was buried in the Fort LeBœuf graveyard. When Duquesne received word of Marin's death, he wrote: "the King loses an excellent subject who was made for war. I had formed the highest opinion of that officer."

10

Mission to Evict the French

"If we had no winter, the spring would not be so pleasant."
—Anne Bradstreet

During the autumn of 1753, Christopher Gist and his family were preparing for the winter at Gist's Plantation in western Pennsylvania. Supplies of meat and vegetables along with everything it would take to live with a modicum of comfort during the winter were being addressed. Certainly, Sarah Gist was looking forward to having her husband home during the long dreary winter months, which was something she missed the previous two years. Unfortunately, she would once again be disappointed.

When Tanacharison, on behalf of the Iroquois, warned the French not to proceed into the Ohio territory, he expected support from the English. Unfortunately, the English like the Iroquois were caught off guard and had no practical idea on how to respond. Lieutenant-Governor Dinwiddie and the Ohio Company Committee realized there was no way they could stand militarily against the French army, so Dinwiddie rushed a letter to King George II hoping he would send an army powerful enough to challenge the French. However, the response from London was certainly less than Dinwiddie desired.

The reply dated Tuesday, August 28, 1753, and addressed to all the colonial governors was written by Secretary of State Robert Darcy, 4th Earl of Holderness. It specified that before any hostilities could be initiated, the French must be formally requested to withdraw from the area, and if they refused, the colonies were given a rather vague authorization to use force. In addition, the letter stipulated that any action taken against the French could be undertaken only in areas that were unquestionably within the king's dominion. That was the rub. The French claim to all the land west of the mountains was agreed to by the British in the 1697 Treaty of Ryswick, the 1713 Treaty of Utrecht, and only five years previous in the 1748 Treaty of Aix-la-Chappelle. So, in effect, the king's

10. Mission to Evict the French

permission to use force was an ambiguous authorization. How could Dinwiddie use force against the French in an area that the British government agreed belonged to the French?

That meant that Dinwiddie and the Virginia Company were where they were before Dinwiddie sent his letter. No British troops were on the way, and indeed, the king did not seem to have any intention of sending an army to expel the French. Worse yet, it was apparent that Virginia would not get help from the other colonies, so the Virginians would have to do the best they could on their own. The Pennsylvanians were not inclined to help the Virginians because they believed the land Virginia was claiming belonged to Pennsylvania. Likewise, the Maryland colonial legislature was apathetic about supporting claims of wealthy Virginia land speculators, and New York's royal governor was miffed by Dinwiddie's meddling with "their Iroquois." Even influential Virginians who were not part of the Ohio Company did not wish to throw their support behind Dinwiddie's financial venture, especially when there was no apparent gain in it for themselves.

In an effort to secure the support of the Ohio Indians, Dinwiddie called the Indians to a conference at Winchester in September 1753, and Christopher Gist was one of the attendees. All that was accomplished at the conference was Indian approval to build a strong house or storehouse at the Forks of the Ohio to supply the Indians with goods; however, the Indians did not give the Virginians permission to establish settlements in the area.

Most men would have accepted what appeared to be the inevitable, but Dinwiddie pressed on and used the power of his position as royal lieutenant-governor to further his financial interest in the Ohio Company's venture. It was nothing less than brazen patronage. As a start, Dinwiddie conferred military commissions on key members of the Ohio Company and then he began to recruit militia to enforce the company's claim in the Ohio country.

On Wednesday, October 31, 1753, to comply with Darcy's directive on behalf of the king, Dinwiddie drafted a formal message to the French commander demanding that the French explain why their army had occupied land that was "so notoriously known to be the Property of the Crown of Great Britain."[1] The entire message read:

"SIR,

The lands upon the River Ohio, in the Western Parts of the Colony of Virginia, are so notoriously known to be the Property of the Crown of Great-Britain, that it is a Matter of equal Concern and Surprize to me, to hear that a Body of French Forces

With George Washington in the Wilderness

are erecting Fortresses, and making Settlements upon that River, within his Majesty's Dominions.

The Many and repeated Complaints I have received of these Acts of Hostility, lay me under the Necessity, of sending, in the Name of the King my Master, the Bearor hereof, George Washington, Esq; one of the Adjutants General of the Forces of the Dominion, to complain to you of the Encroachments thus made, and of the Injuries done to the Subjects of Great-Britain, in open Violation of the Law of Nations, and the Treaties now subsisting between the two Crowns.

If these facts are true, and you shall think fit to justify your Proceedings, I must desire you to acquaint me, by whose Authority and Instructions you have lately marched from Canada, with an armed Force, and invaded the King of Great-Britain's Territories, in the Manner complained of; that according to the Purport and resolution of your Answer, I may act agreeably to the Commission I am honored with, from the King, my Master.

However Sir, in Obedience to my Instructions, it becomes my Duty to require your peaceable Departure; and that you would forbear prosecuting a Purpose so interruptive of the Harmony and good Understanding, which his Majesty is desirous to continue and cultivate with the most Christian King.

I persuade myself you will receive and entertain Major Washington with the Candour and Politeness natural to your Nation; and it will give me the greatest Satisfaction, if you return him with an Answer suitable to my Wishes for a very long and lasting Peace between us.

I have the Honour to subscribe myself,
SIR,

> Your most obedient,
> Humble Servant,
> Robert Dinwiddie
> Williamsburg, in Virginia
> October 31st, 1753"[2]

George Washington, the younger half-brother of Lawrence Washington, happened to be in Williamsburg at the time. Upon the death of Lawrence the previous year, George had been commissioned by Dinwiddie as adjutant general in charge of militia for one of the four new military districts. It's not known if twenty-one-year-old Washington volunteered to deliver the message to the French commander or whether he was approached by Dinwiddie. Regardless, Dinwiddie's choice of Washington to deliver the message was likely influenced by the fact that Washington's family were stakeholders in the Ohio Company, and Washington could be relied upon to look after Ohio Company interests. Dinwiddie also gave Washington a letter for Christopher Gist, requesting Gist to assist Washington during his travels through Pennsylvania.

Washington departed Williamsburg the same day, Wednesday,

10. Mission to Evict the French

October 31, 1753, for what was more than a one-thousand-mile journey mostly through the rugged, mountainous wilderness of western Pennsylvania during the depth of winter. While making the journey, young Washington's life would be saved on at least on two occasions by Christopher Gist.

After leaving Williamsburg, Washington rode to Fredericksburg, Virginia, where he arrived on Thursday, November 1, 1753. There, he sought out and hired Jacob Van Braam (1727–?), who was his old tutor in sword exercise and military science. Van Braam was a sword master and mercenary who once served in the Royal Navy with Lawrence Washington. Washington hired Van Braam primarily as a translator, because the Dutchman was conversant in both English and French, while Washington's only language was English. In actuality, Van Braam's abilities as a translator were rather tenuous. His native language was Dutch, and any translation from English or French had to first be mentally translated through Dutch, occasionally losing something in the translation.

Christopher Gist was at the Will's Creek storehouse on Wednesday, November 14, 1753, when Washington and Van Braam arrived. Gist wrote, "Then Major Washington Came to my house at Wills Creek and delivered me a letter from the Council in Virginia requesting me to attend him up to the Commandant of the French Fort on the Ohio River."[3]

Gist agreed to accompany Washington and Van Braam, and likely on Gist's recommendation, Washington hired four other men. Barnaby Curran and John McGuire were experienced, savvy woodsmen and Indian traders who were familiar with the upper Allegheny River region, and Henry Stewart and William Jenkins were hired as general assistants.

The group departed Will's Creek the following day, Thursday, November 15, 1753, and stopped to rest after traveling eight miles. While stopped, they were overtaken by a messenger from Gist's son, who was returning from visiting the Cherokees in the south and lay sick at the mouth of the *Conococheague*.[4] Conococheague is a Lenape phrase that means "river of many turns," and its mouth is on the Potomac River at present Williamsport, Maryland. Gist didn't mention which son sent the message, but it likely was Nathaniel, who had been living and trading among the Cherokee.

Washington apparently balked at Gist's going to the aid of his son, and Gist wrote in his journal, "But as I found myself entered again on public business, and Major Washington and all the company unwilling

With George Washington in the Wilderness

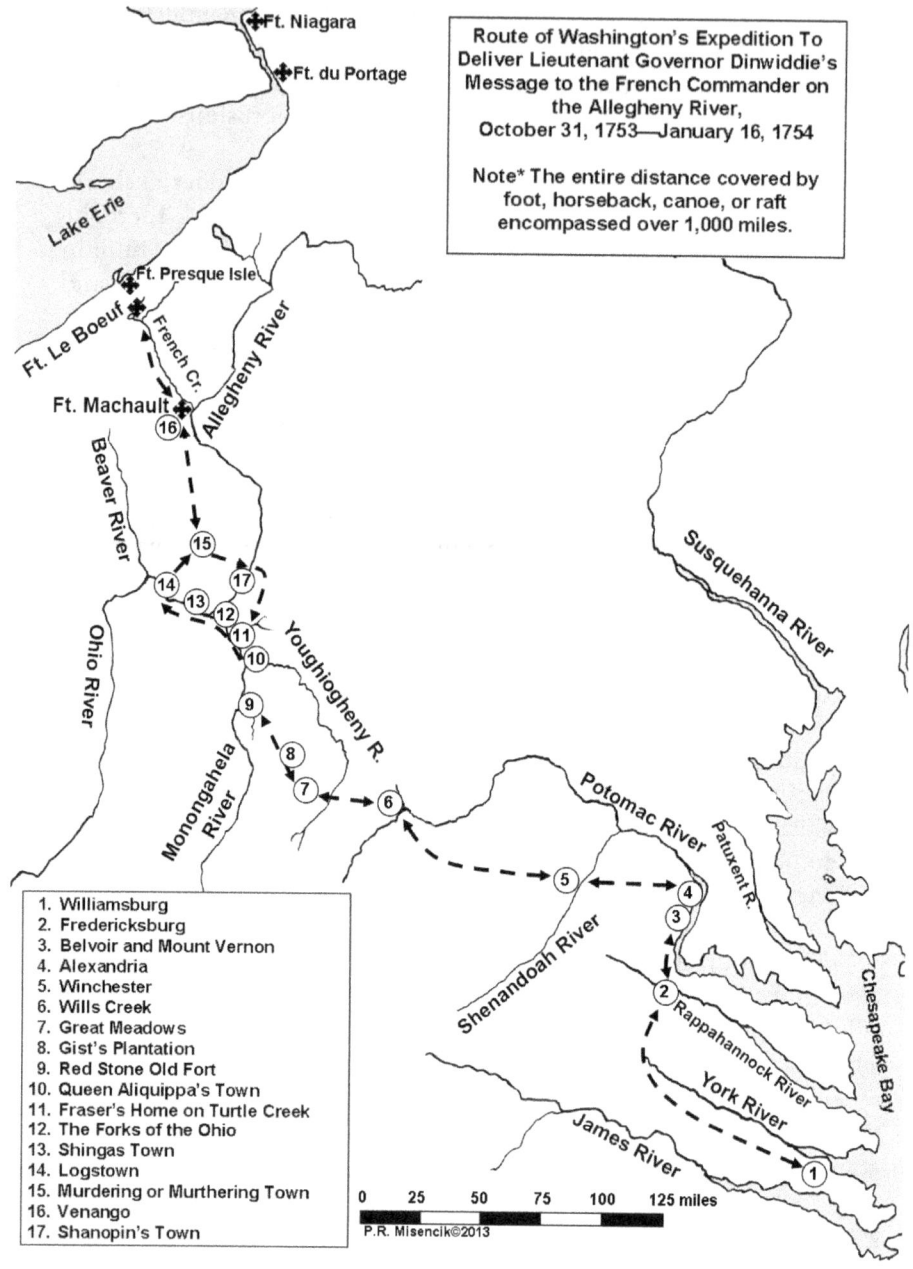

Washington's 1753–1754 expedition to the Ohio Country. Gist joined Washington at Will's Creek.

10. Mission to Evict the French

I should return, I wrote and sent medicines to my son, and so continued my journey."[5]

On Sunday, November 18, 1753, after traveling about twenty-one miles, they reached Gist's home, which he referred to as "the new settlement." Gist added that the snow was about ankle deep. After spending the night, Gist bid farewell to a likely disappointed Sarah, and set off with Washington and his small party to evict the French from western Pennsylvania.

Three days after leaving Gist's settlement, they reached John Fraser's post at the mouth of Turtle Creek on the Monongahela, at present Braddock, Pennsylvania. They spent the night with Fraser, and the next day the trader lent them a canoe to carry their baggage while they rode west about ten miles to the Forks of the Ohio. They camped for the night at the Forks, and Washington, eyeing the junction of the Allegheny and the Monongahela rivers, wrote in his journal, "As I got down before the Canoe, I spent some time in viewing the Rivers, and the Land in the Fork, which I think extremely well situated for a Fort, as it has the absolute Command of both Rivers."[6]

Leaving the Forks, Gist led Washington and his small delegation proceeded about two miles down the Ohio to the town of the Lenape Chief Shingas[7] (c. 1740–1763), which was near the mouth of Chartier's Creek. Shingas agreed to accompany them to Logstown, where they arrived during the evening of Saturday, November 24, 1753. They had hoped to meet with Tanacharison, but instead, the Oneida half-king Scarouady told them that Tanacharison was at his cabin on the Beaver River some fifteen miles away. The following morning, Sunday the 25th, Scarouady sent a messenger to Tanacharison, asking him to come to Logstown. Tanacharison arrived that afternoon and met with Gist and Washington and an interpreter named John Davidson who happened to be at Logstown.

The talks with Tanacharison were somewhat disquieting to Washington, who quickly realized that the half-king was not the backward savage he had expected. In fact, Tanacharison was a very intelligent and savvy diplomat who not only spoke several Indian dialects but also was fluent in French and English. Washington, on the other hand, only spoke and understood English. Tanacharison was not at all impressed with the twenty-one-year-old Washington and his handful of companions, especially since they were the English king's response to a powerful French army advancing down the Allegheny River toward the Forks of the Ohio. The old chief told Washington that he had seen firsthand the might of the French army, and he bluntly asked Washington what he was going to do about it. Tanacharison was undoubtedly even more distressed when the young Virginian told him his mission was to deliver a letter of very great importance to the French commandant and then return to Dinwiddie with the French officer's response.

Nonetheless, Tanacharison told Washington he would accompany him to deliver Dinwiddie's letter to the French but would require a delay of about three days to allow him to return to the Beaver River to retrieve a "French speech belt" from his hunting cabin. The speech belt Tanacharison wanted to retrieve was given to him by the French, and the old chief intended to return it to them. The weaving of wampum belts was a means of record keeping, and the pattern of a belt was associated with an agreement of friendship, a treaty, a transaction, or as mutual acknowledgment of some other event that the parties wished to document. The French had presented speech belts to the Indians, which at the time were accepted in a spirit of friendship and cooperation. They were large white belts, thirteen rows deep with "four Towns and Forts worked in it with black Wampum."[8] This was the belt that Marin referred to during his tirade against Tanacharison. Returning a speech belt was a sign of rejection of friendship and a repudiation of the agreements associated with the belt. The half-king would return the French speech belt to demonstrate that the Iroquois and the Ohio tribes would back the side that was most aligned with their interest. It was a signal to the French that after Marin's unbelievably insensitive outburst that summer, the French had some serious diplomatic ground to make up.

During the discussions at Logstown, Washington became impressed with John Davidson's knowledge of Indian dialects, so he hired the interpreter to accompany him on the mission to the French forts. When they set out from Logstown on Friday, November 30, 1753, Washington's party had grown to twelve with the addition of the half-king Tanacharison, two old chiefs called *Jeskekake* and *Kaghswaghtaniunt* (White Thunder), and a younger warrior called *Guyasuta* (Hunter). Their first stop would be at Fort Machault at Venango, which was the most recently constructed of the French forts, and where they hoped to find the French commander of the Allegheny region.

Gist wrote in his journal for that day, "We set out with the Half-King and two old men and one young warrior, with us. At night we camped at the Muthering town, about fifteen miles, on a branch of Great Beaver Creek. Got some corn and dried meat."[9] The curiously sinister-sounding

10. Mission to Evict the French

town is also referred to as "Murdering Town" on several maps, including maps made by Washington and Gist, but there is no explanation regarding its name. We only know it was a small Lenape village or a close collection of small Lenape communities along the Logstown-Venango Path near present Harmony and Evans City, Pennsylvania. The town would take on even more sinister overtones during Washington and Gist's return from the upper Allegheny River.

Due to the heavy rains, the party was forced to leave the Venango Path and take to the higher ground, which increased the distance to Fort Machault by a third. They arrived at Fort Machault at Venango on Tuesday, December 4, 1753, after traveling over eighty miles by Gist's reckoning to cover the usual sixty miles from Logstown to Fort Machault.

At the fort, they were hospitably received by its commander Captain Phillipe-Thomas Chabert de Joncaire, who in 1749 had marched with Céloron on his expedition around Ohio. Joncaire was a seasoned veteran of frontier diplomacy and, along with being a talented soldier,

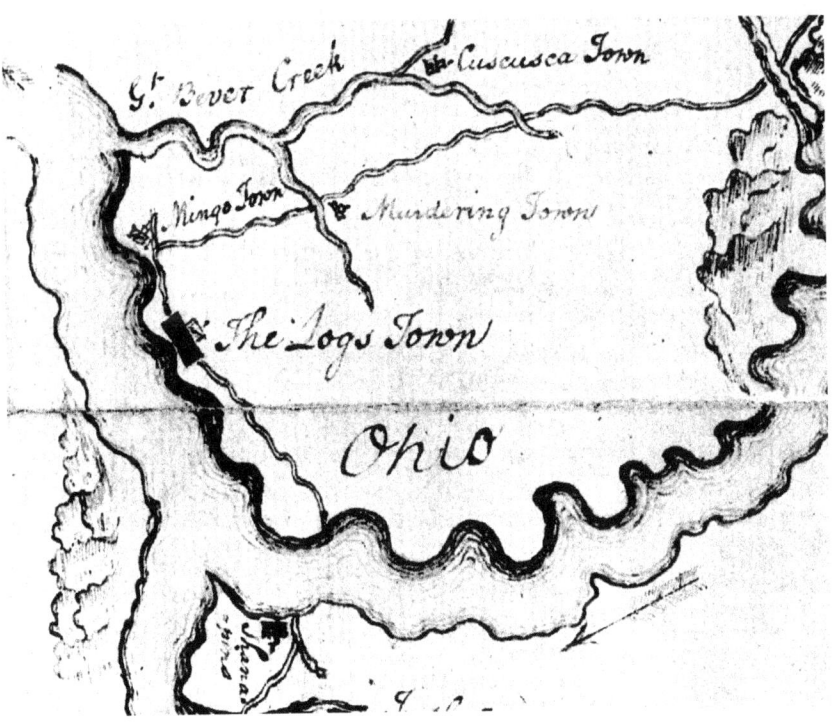

Portion of Washington's 1754 map showing Murdering Town (Library of Congress—G3820 1754.W3 1927 TIL).

was very familiar with Indian tribal cultures. Surprisingly, he had been successful in his dealings with the Iroquois, who traditionally were ill-disposed toward the French. Joncaire was so influential and adept in dealing with the Indians that in 1744 during King George's War, the British offered a reward for him, dead or alive. At that time, New York Royal Governor George Clinton (c. 1686–1761) speculated that Joncaire might be enticed to switch allegiance if he was offered sufficient inducement. In fact, the reason for Joncaire's posting to Fort Machault was to conduct the delicate diplomacy of attempting to secure the support and goodwill of the Lenape, Shawnee, and Wyandot tribes in the Ohio region.

Joncaire treated his visitors in a kindly and hospitable manner, offering them as fine a dinner as could be provided on the frontier, which was accompanied by his best wine. However, the French officer told Washington that he could not accept Dinwiddie's letter. Joncaire admitted that he was in command of the fort, but he was under the command of Marin's successor Jacques Legardeur de Saint-Pierre (1701–1755), who was presently at Fort Le Bœuf, and Dinwiddie's message would have to be taken there. There was no alternative for Washington but to continue on to Fort Le Bœuf to deliver the message to Legardeur and obtain his response.

After spending almost three days at Fort Machault, Washington, Gist, and their party set out for Fort le Bœuf on Saturday, December 7, 1753. On their journey, they were accompanied by one Monsieur René-Hippolyte LaForce (1728–1802) and three other French soldiers. LaForce was ostensibly the Commissary of the French Stores, but as subsequent events would indicate, he may have had a more significant role in the French military command.

The route from Fort Machault to Fort Le Bœuf essentially followed French Creek, with the trail to the east of the waterway. The heavy rains made many of the lower areas impassable, forcing the party to deviate off the trail for considerable distances and abandon the trail altogether for the latter portion of the trip. Many of the smaller streams could not be crossed at their normal fords, which required the party to swim the horses while the men floated their baggage across on hastily constructed log rafts. They passed Custalogas's town at the confluence of Deer Creek and French Creek (near present Carlton, Pennsylvania) and reached *Cussewago* on Sunday the 8th. Cussewago was a Lenape village located at present Meadville, Pennsylvania. At Cussewago, Washington had to leave behind one of the horses that was too worn out to

10. Mission to Evict the French

continue. From Cussewago, the group was forced to make an approximately eight-mile detour to the southeast, looking for a safe crossing over Muddy Creek. From there they were able to proceed directly to the French fort. The trail between the two forts was approximately forty-seven miles in length, but because of the numerous detours, Gist reckoned that they traveled about twenty miles farther. It took the party over five unpleasant and arduous days to reach Fort Le Bœuf, near Rivière au Bœuf, which Washington renamed "French Creek" in his diary.

They arrived at the French Fort on Wednesday, December 12, 1753, and were greeted by the garrison's second in command. Washington was eager to complete his mission and begin the long journey back to Williamsburg, so he hurriedly acquainted the officer who greeted him with his mission and tried to give him the letter from Dinwiddie. However, that officer politely refused to take the letter saying it would have to be given to Captain Legardeur, the fort's commander. Legardeur was absent from the fort but arrived the next day about noon. He was a formidable person coming from a very prominent family. In 1718, his father, who was an officer in the French army, had founded the post at Chagouamigon (present Ashland, Wisconsin). Young Jacques Legardeur, having grown up on the frontier, quickly acquired a comprehensive expertise and knowledge of Indian life, customs, and language. In 1732, Governor-General Charles de la Boische, Marquis de Beauharnois, claimed that Jacques Legardeur "knows the savage language better than the savages, as they themselves admit."[10] Upon Marin's death in October, Legardeur was sent to take over Marin's command and had arrived at Fort Le Bœuf only seven days prior to the arrival of Washington's party.

Legardeur greeted Washington cordially and Washington was impressed with the fifty-two-year-old French commander, writing, "This Commander is a Knight of the military Order of St. Lewis, and named Legardeur de St. Pierre. He is an elderly Gentleman, and has much the Air of a Soldier."[11] The French commander listened politely as the young Virginia major described his mission and handed him the message from Lieutenant-Governor Dinwiddie. The seasoned, military professional Legardeur was undoubtedly more amused than impressed with the twenty-one-year-old major and his motley delegation who had come to evict him from the Ohio territory. Ever the gentleman, Legardeur treated Washington and his party cordially and graciously. To Washington's vexation, the French commander was especially hospitable to the Indians in Washington's delegation. Legardeur accepted the

With George Washington in the Wilderness

letter and said he would adjourn to his private quarters to have the message translated and carefully considered before offering a response. A few hours later, the French commander summoned Washington and Van Braam to examine the translation and make any necessary corrections. Then for the next two days, Washington and his party enjoyed the hospitality of the French at Fort Le Bœuf while Legardeur composed his response to Dinwiddie.

Washington and Gist spent those days carefully studying the French fort, its armament, and the disposition of troops. Washington observed that the garrison consisted of one hundred officers and men, and that the troops were building birch bark canoes and pine batteaux and noted that over fifty canoes and 170 batteaux would be ready in the spring. Each of the fort's four bastions mounted eight six-pounder cannon and a four-pounder was positioned to guard the gate.[12]

On Friday, December 14, 1753, Legardeur met with Washington and explained that he was only a subordinate acting under the direct orders of Governor-General Duquesne in Québec and the governor-general would be the more appropriate recipient of Dinwiddie's letter. The French commander invited Washington to continue on to Québec to deliver the letter personally to Duquesne, but Washington demurred. Nevertheless, Legardeur assured Washington that he would forward the letter to Duquesne, whose answer would govern Legardeur's actions in response to Dinwiddie's demands. Meanwhile, the French commander politely but firmly stated that at present he could not acquiesce to Dinwiddie's order to withdraw from the Ohio. In the meantime, until Duquesne made his response, Legardeur gave Washington a letter for Dinwiddie, which was dated the following day. Legardeur's message strongly reaffirmed his resolve not to leave unless Duquesne ordered him to do so:

"SIR,

As I have the Honour of commanding here in Chief, Mr. Washington delivered me the Letter which you wrote to the Commandant of the French Troops.

I should have been glad that you had given him Orders, or that he had been inclined to proceed to Canada, to see our General; to whom it better belongs than to me to set-forth the Evidence and Reality of the Rights of the King, my Master, upon the Lands situated along the River Ohio, and to contest the Pretensions of the King of Great-Britain thereto.

I shall transmit your Letter to the Marquis Duquesne. His Answer will be a Law to me; and if he shall order me to communicate it to you, Sir, you may be assured I shall not fail to dispatch it to you forthwith.

As to the Summons you send me to retire, I do not think myself obliged to obey

10. Mission to Evict the French

it. Whatever may be your Instructions, I am here by Virtue of the Orders of my General; and I entreat you, Sir, not to doubt one Moment, but that I am determin'd to conform myself to them with all the Exactness and Resolution which can be expected from the best Officer.

I don't know that in the Progress of this Campaign any Thing has passed which can be reputed an act of Hostility, or that is contrary to the Treaties which subsist between the two Crowns; the Continuation whereof as much interests, and is pleasing to us, as the English. Had you been pleased Sir, to have descended to particularize the Facts which occasioned your Complaint, I should have had the Honour of answering you in the fullest, and, I am persuaded, most satisfactory Manner.

I made it my particular Care to receive Mr. Washington, with a Distinction suitable to your Dignity, as well as his own Quality and great merit. I flatter myself that he will do me this Justice before you, Sir; and that he will signify to you in the Manner I do myself, the profound Respect with which I am,

SIR,

>Your most humble, and
>Most obedient Servant,
>Legardeur De St. Pierre.
>From the Fort sur La Riviere au Bœuf
>The 15th of December 1753[13]

With the successful delivery of Dinwiddie's letter, and Legardeur's written refusal to withdraw his troops in hand, Washington was eager to return to Governor Dinwiddie in Williamsburg, and Gist was eager to return home to his wife and family. However, their departure was delayed because they had difficulties extricating the Indians from the French, who were continuously plying them with gifts and liquor. Part of their delay was caused by Legardeur's refusal to accept the speech belt that Tanacharison was determined to return. Finally, the French commander grudgingly accepted the belt, but then began to ply the Indians with liquor and the promise of additional gifts if they would remain at Fort Le Bœuf so they could hold further councils. It was only after Gist and Washington reminded Tanacharison that he gave his word to accompany Washington on the return that he and the other Indians somewhat reluctantly turned their backs on French hospitality and the promise of more liquor and gifts.

11

The Perilous Return

"Not all danger comes with a warning."
—Indian adage

    According to Gist's journal, the party had sent their horses down to Venango earlier to rest and recuperate for the return journey. They were most likely sent with the two handymen, Henry Stewart and William Jenkins and at least one of the frontier traders, Barnaby Curran or John McGuire. Washington, Gist, and the other white men traveled in one canoe, the Indians traveled in another, and LaForce and his party were in a third canoe. The Indians outpaced the white men, but they all joined up during the evening of Monday, December 17, 1753, after the Indians had already made camp.

    The snow and ice made the journey extremely difficult, often forcing the party into the water to pull their canoes over shoals, ice jams, and other debris that made the water route over French Creek almost impassable. In several instances, they were forced to portage their canoes and equipage for considerable distances around obstructions. The canoe carrying LaForce and his companions upset at one point and apparently no one in Gist and Washington's party stopped to render them assistance. Gist wrote in his journal, "The creek began to be very low and we were forced to get out, to keep our canoe from over-setting, several times; the water freezing to our clothes; and we had the pleasure of seeing the French overset, and the brandy and wine floating in the creek, and run by them, and left them to shift for themselves. Came to Venango, and met with our people and horses."[1] They reached Fort Machault at Venango on Saturday, December 22, 1753, and once again availed themselves of Captain Joncaire's hospitality while they rested and prepared for the next leg of their journey.

    Gist reminded Washington that Joncaire had previously attempted to seduce the Indians away from the English and would almost certainly continue that effort. To make matters worse, the old chief

11. The Perilous Return

Kaghswaghtaniunt was unable to walk due to sickness and injuries, and Tanacharison said he would remain at the French fort until the ailing chief was able to travel. And, even then, the Indians would take the longer route by canoe down the Allegheny River. However, Tanacharison offered to send the young warrior Guyasuta with the white men to guide and hunt for them. The half-king said he would meet Washington and Gist at the Forks of the Ohio, because he wanted to dictate a message for Governor Dinwiddie. As it turned out, Tanacharison delayed at Fort Machault longer than anticipated and did not meet Washington and Gist as planned.

Leaving Tanacharison and the two older chiefs at Fort Machault, Washington, Gist, Van Braam, Curran, McGuire, Stewart, Jenkins, Davidson, and the young warrior Guyasuta started off on their return journey. To the dismay of the white men, their horses, which had earlier been sent down from Fort Le Bœuf, had not sufficiently recovered their strength. The group started out on the horses anyway but soon realized that their mounts and packhorses were in such bad shape that their progress was drastically slowed. Washington and Gist dismounted and spread the baggage among all the horses in order to lighten the loads on each, but it didn't help much. The men soon found it impossible to remain mounted and were forced to travel on foot while leading their exhausted animals. Gist wrote, "Monday, [December] 24, [1753]—Here Major Washington set out on foot in Indian dress. Our horses grew weak, that we were mostly obliged to travel on foot, and had snow all day."[2] Washington's "Indian dress" was likely moccasins and a hunting shirt instead of his normal riding boots and regimental coat.

Washington grew frustrated by the slow pace of travel and decided that he and Gist would leave the rest of the group and travel by a more direct route to Will's Creek. He wrote, "The Horses grew less able to travel every Day; the Cold increased very fast; and the Roads were becoming much worse by a deep Snow, continually freezing: Therefore, I was uneasy to get back, to make Report of my Proceedings to his Honour the Governor, I determined to prosecute my Journey the nearest Way through the Woods, on Foot."[3]

Gist had doubts about young Washington's ability to traverse the rugged wilderness on foot in the depths of winter. Indeed, it would be challenging for an experienced frontiersman, but for the inexperienced twenty-one-year-old Washington it would be a grueling winter trek fraught with perils. The young major, though strong, was more used to covering distances on horseback than on foot. Gist wrote his thoughts in his journal on Wednesday, December 26, 1753: "The Major desired me to set out on foot, and leave our company, as the creeks were frozen, and our horses could make but little way. Indeed, I was unwilling he should undertake such a travel, who had never been used to walking before this time. But he insisted on it, I set out with our packs, like Indians, and traveled about eighteen miles."[4]

Washington and Gist left the other members of their party on Wednesday, December 26, 1753, and set off overland, leaving Van Braam in charge of the group along with the horses and baggage. Washington described readying himself for the trek. "I took my necessary Papers; pulled off my Cloaths; and tied myself up in a Match Coat [a heavy overcoat of wool or skins]. Then with Gun in Hand and Pack at my Back, in which were my Papers and Provisions. I set-out with Mr. Gist, fitted in the same manner."[5]

The going was tough, and fortunately they found a cabin in which to spend the night. Gist wrote, "That night we lodged in an Indian cabin, and the Major was much fatigued. It was very cold; all the small runs were frozen, that we could hardly get water to drink."[6]

The following day, Thursday, December 27, 1753, Washington and Gist passed Murthering Town where they encountered an Indian who appeared to be waiting for them. The Indian greeted them and called Gist by name. Gist wrote of the encounter,

> We rose early in the morning, and set out about two o'clock. Got to the Murthering town, on the southeast fork of Beaver creek. Here we met with an Indian, whom I thought I had seen at Joncaire's, at Venango, when on our journey up to the French fort. The fellow called me by my Indian name,[7] and pretended to be glad to see me. He asked us several questions, as to how we came to travel on foot, when we left Venango, where we parted with our horses, and when they would be there, etc. Major Washington insisted on travelling on the nearest way to the forks of the Allegheny. We asked the Indian if he could go with us and show us the nearest way. The Indian seemed very glad and ready to go with us. Upon which we set out, and the Indian took the Major's pack.[8]

Since the Indian appeared friendly and offered to guide them, he did not initially arouse any suspicion. In fact, the Indian was very helpful, and when it was apparent that Washington was fatiguing, he offered to carry Washington's pack. Gist, however, began to get suspicious when he noticed that the Indian was leading them in a more northeasterly direction, but the frontiersman refrained from alerting Washington so as not to unduly concern him. The Indian next offered to carry

11. The Perilous Return

Washington's gun, but for some reason Washington began to mistrust the Indian, and when Washington refused to give up his gun, the Indian's demeanor became brusque and surly. The Indian argued that the white men should change course to avoid the many Ottawa Indians who were around and would kill them if they were discovered. He suggested they go to his cabin, which was located a little farther to the north where they could all wait until the danger had passed.

Washington refused and insisted on proceeding directly to the Forks. Then, Gist noticed the Indian had accelerated his pace and advanced about fifteen yards ahead of the two white men. Gist was about to say something when the Indian abruptly turned and fired his musket in the direction of Washington and Gist. Gist's journal records the event: "We came to a clear meadow; it was very light, and snow on the ground. The Indian made a stop, turned about; the Major saw him point his gun toward us and fire. Said the Major, 'Are you shot?' 'No,' said I. Upon which the Indian ran forward to a big standing white oak, and [began] to loading his gun, but we were soon with him. I would have killed him; but the Major would not suffer me to kill him."[9]

Gist was certainly not happy with Washington's order not to harm the Indian, but he grudgingly obeyed. However, he told Washington, "As you will not have him killed, we must get him away, and then we must travel all night."[10] Not willing to remain constantly on guard against further treachery on the part of the Indian and not wanting to kill him, Gist told the Indian they were too fatigued to continue, but the Indian should go to his cabin, and they would follow his tracks in the morning. Gist built a fire and acted as if they were going to camp for the night, and the Indian disappeared into the darkness. A short time after the Indian departed, Gist and Washington abandoned the campsite and walked until morning to put as much distance as possible between them and any pursuers. Either the Indian was glad to have gotten away with his life or Gist and Washington had given him the slip, because they did not encounter him after that time. But Washington was about to have another close call, from which Gist would rescue him.

Two days later on Saturday, December 29, 1753, Washington and Gist reached the west bank of the Allegheny River about two miles above Shannopin's Town and approximately five miles from the Forks. They had hoped to be able to walk across the frozen river to the east bank, but the solid ice only extended to about fifty yards from either shore with a swift current and treacherous ice floes in the middle of the river. They decided to build a raft to get to the other side. Gist's journal only gives a

With George Washington in the Wilderness

cursory account of the crossing: "We set out early, got to the Allegheny, made a raft, and with much difficulty got over to an island, a little above Shannopin's town. The Major having fallen in from off the raft, and my fingers frost-bitten, and the sun down, and very cold, we contented ourselves to encamp on that island. It was deep water between us and the shore; but the cold did us some service, for in the morning it was frozen hard enough for us to pass over on the ice."[11]

Washington's account captures the perilous endeavor in more detail:

> There was no Way for getting over but on a Raft: Which we-set about, with but one poor Hatchet, and finished just after Sun-setting. This was a whole Day's Work: we next got it launched, and went on Board of it: Then set-off. But before we were Half Way over, we were jammed in the Ice, in such a Manner that we expected our Raft to sink, and ourselves to perish. I put out my setting Pole to try to stop the Raft, that the Ice might pass by; when the Rapidity of the Stream threw it with so much Violence against the Pole, that it jirked me out into ten Feet Water: But I fortunately saved myself by catching hold of one of the Raft Logs. Notwithstanding all our Efforts we could not get the Raft to either Shore; but were obliged, as we were near an island, to quit our Raft and make to it.[12]

Coming ashore on the little island in the Allegheny River,[13] the two soaked and freezing men were saved only by Gist's frontier savvy and his ability to quickly start a fire and construct a crude shelter. The night was bitterly cold, and Gist, who primarily tended the fire and worked to dry their garments, bore the brunt of the elements. Washington wrote that "The Cold was so extremely severe, that Mr. Gist had all his fingers, and some of his Toes frozen."[14]

On Sunday, December 30, 1753, after leaving the little island, Washington and Gist traveled ten miles to John Fraser's cabin at the mouth of Turtle Creek and they rested there until Tuesday January 1, 1754. During their stay with Fraser, they took time to visit the staunchly pro–English Queen Aliquippa,[15] who had recently moved her village to the mouth of the Youghiogheny on the Monongahela at present McKeesport, Pennsylvania. The old queen told the two men the reason she moved from her village at McKee's Rocks was to distance herself from the French and she would never go back to the Ohio River area until the English built a fort there.[16] Leaving Fraser's cabin on January 1, Washington and Gist stopped for two days at Gist's new settlement, where Washington bought a horse and tack before the two men continued on to Will's Creek, arriving there on Sunday, January 6, 1754.

11. The Perilous Return

While Gist and Washington were at Will's Creek, they encountered William Trent, who was most recently employed by the Ohio Company to negotiate with the Indians in the Ohio River area. Trent was now in charge of a party of workmen who were leading seventeen pack horses laden with tools, matériel, and stock to strengthen and improve the Ohio Company storehouse at Redstone Creek. The storehouse at Redstone was often referred to as a "fort"; however, the structure was never intended to be a fort, or ever used as one. The misconception likely resulted from its proximity to the ancient Indian earthworks in the vicinity that were called "Red Stone Old Fort."

Trent's mission was not planned as a military mission, but he was sent to improve the company storehouse to serve as a supply depot for Ohio Company settlers, and also to facilitate Indian trade by shortening the fur traders' supply lines. When they completed their work, some of Trent's workers planned to take up habitation at Gist's settlement. Of course, Gist was well acquainted with Trent, who was a seasoned frontiersman and fur trader. Trent's father, William Trent senior, was a wealthy Philadelphia shipping merchant and founder of Trenton, New Jersey. With the financial backing of his father, young William Trent took on George Croghan as a business partner, and together they developed an effective trading network among the Ohio Indians.

At Will's Creek, Washington and Gist told Trent of the French commander's refusal to withdraw from the Allegheny region and the probability that Trent would encounter hostility from the French or their Indian Allies. Trent took the opportunity to write a letter for Washington to deliver to Dinwiddie, in which Trent said if he was authorized, he could stop the French advance during the winter.[17]

Gist returned to his home and Washington continued on to Williamsburg, arriving there on Wednesday, January 16, 1754. He made his report to the lieutenant-governor and delivered both Legardeur's letter of refusal and the message William Trent had written.

It didn't take Dinwiddie long to take action. On Saturday, January 26, 1754, he commissioned William Trent as commander and captain and sent orders for him to recruit a maximum of one hundred men to work with the friendly Indians to keep possession of the Ohio Valley and repel the French.[18] In addition, no doubt acting on the advice of Washington, Trent was ordered to begin construction of a fort at the Forks of the Ohio. This was a change from the original Ohio Company plan to build the fort at Chartier's Creek.

Trent's commission and orders from Dinwiddie were carried by

With George Washington in the Wilderness

mounted messengers who reached Trent at Redstone Creek around the middle of February 1754. Trent was told to take and use whatever tools, arms, and equipment necessary from the company storehouse to outfit and maintain his troops. At the same time, Dinwiddie ordered Washington to recruit one hundred men from Frederick and Augusta counties and march them to the Forks.

Being ordered to raise a company of one hundred men was one thing and actually raising a company on the frontier was another. Recruiting men to serve in the wilderness was particularly difficult under the best of circumstances, yet Trent tried his best. He sent recruiters and messengers to his friends, acquaintances, and officials throughout the neighboring colonies asking for volunteers, but in addition to the twenty or so he originally brought to Redstone, he could only enlist about fifty-two men in total.[19]

Trent and his small company were armed only with muskets, some rifles, and the necessary tools for fort building, but they marched to the Forks and arrived there on Sunday, February 17, 1754. As soon as they arrived, they immediately set to work felling trees and clearing ground for the construction of the fort Trent would name Fort Prince George, in honor of King George II's son, the future George III. However, the men in Trent's small command insisted on referring to the fortification as "Trent's Fort." Both Gist and Tanacharison were there to meet Trent, and the half-king pledged Indian support and to supply food to Trent's men. Tanacharison also pledged warriors if the French should attempt to interfere with the fort's construction.

While they worked to build a defensible fort, neither Trent nor Gist had any illusion about their chances against Legardeur's artillery-equipped army. In fact, an Indian had reported to Gist that on Tuesday, February 5, 1764, he heard a French officer boast that the English would be expelled from the Forks in less than a month.[20] On Tuesday, February 19, 1754, Trent and Gist hurriedly wrote a message to Washington stating they expected an attack by the French at any time and implored Washington to hurry with reinforcements.

Tanacharison was unimpressed with Trent's tiny command, and for that matter, the English response to the French incursion. On one hand, the English were finally willing to commit troops to challenge the French army that was moving down the Allegheny, but the size of Trent's minuscule force didn't give Tanacharison any measure of confidence when compared to Legardeur's massive artillery-equipped veteran army. However, the half-king was philosophical, believing that

11. The Perilous Return

once the British were in for a penny, they would be in for a pound, and since this small force of Virginians was all he had, that would have to suffice, at least for the present. As the first logs of the fort were laid, Trent's men and Tanacharison's Indians drank toasts in celebration of winning the race to the Forks, but no one really believed that the contest was over. They knew the French would arrive in the spring.

The implications of Dinwiddie's commission and orders to Trent are interesting, to say the least. In actuality, Trent and his men were no more than employees of the Ohio Company of Virginia. Now, Dinwiddie used the authority of his office as lieutenant-governor to transform his employees into military troops of the colony of Virginia, and by extension, troops of the British Empire. Even worse, Dinwiddie had empowered them to act for the benefit of a private land speculation venture in which he was a major shareholder.

At the Forks, Trent and his men were making a great effort to complete the fort in anticipation of the imminent arrival of the French army. Rumors were rife that the French were preparing to move down the Allegheny. George Croghan reported, after a visit to Trent's construction site, that the men at the Forks were working very hard, which "seemed to give the Indians great pleasure and put them in high spirits."[21] Observing the fort's construction, Tanacharison urged that a palisaded stockade be built first to facilitate defense, but Trent's initial effort was to construct a stoutly built stronghouse of squared logs, pierced with loopholes for muskets. Both Trent and Tanacharison were correct to hurry the preparation of defenses at the Forks, because the French were in fact on the move.

Reports of English activities reached Governor-General Duquesne in Québec, and Duquesne had taken the extraordinary measure of launching a mid-winter expedition to secure the Forks before the English could effectively fortify it. But first, he had to appoint a new commander. The previous fall, shortly after arriving as Marin's replacement, Legardeur requested to be relieved, citing ill health as the reason.[22] On Christmas Day in 1753, Captain Claude-Pierre Pećaudy de Contrecœur (1705–1755) replaced Legardeur as commander of French troops along the Ohio. Contrecœur was a colonial officer of regular troops who had been in the king's service since age sixteen. He had been second-in-command during Céloron's 1749 expedition and commanded at Fort Niagara during Marin's march down the Allegheny in 1753. Contrecœur's journal and family letters indicate that neither he nor his wife were enthusiastic about the new assignment as Marin's

103

replacement. After years of hard existence apart on the far frontiers, Contrecœur and his family were finally living together and enjoying comfortable quarters. However, orders were orders, especially when issued by the governor-general, and Contrecœur duly reported to Québec and took command of the expedition. Duquesne's orders were "to take possession of the Belle Rivière, where you will have Fort de Chiningué built."[23] Logstown was sometimes referred to by the names Chiningué or Chenango. That implied that in addition to building a fort at the Forks, Contrecœur was ordered to extend the chain of French strongpoints at least as far as Logstown. Duquesne realized that the English might arrive at the Forks first, so the governor-general added that Contrecœur should "hasten to interrupt and even destroy their work from the start."[24] In a subsequent message dated Sunday, January 27, 1754, the governor-general specified that he expected the fort at the Forks of the Ohio to be named Fort Duquesne.

Contrecœur's force of five hundred French regulars and militia left Québec on Tuesday, January 15, 1754, and were joined by three hundred troops in Montréal. They marched out of Montréal on Saturday, February 2, 1754, dragging sledges laden with ammunition, food, and equipment sufficient for two months. The first stages of the more than six-hundred-mile winter journey were extremely arduous, requiring exhausting snowshoe travel most of the way while pulling their heavily laden provision sleds. Often their daily progress was so trifling that they scarcely moved beyond sight of their previous night's bivouac. After they crossed the Niagara portage, the ice on Lake Erie had thawed sufficiently to allow the troops to travel via batteaux as far as Fort Presque Isle, which they reached on Friday, March 8, 1754. The trek south over the Presque Isle portage and down French Creek continued to be exhausting. Although the air temperature was rising with approaching spring, the road that had been so laboriously constructed the previous year was now in terrible condition and needed considerable repair. Water travel was restricted by tangles of fallen trees and other debris that choked French Creek after an earlier severe winter storm had battered the area. The French force stopped at Fort Le Bœuf where Contrecœur formally relieved Legardeur of command; then Contrecœur continued on to Fort Machault, where he and his men arrived toward the end of March 1754.

Shortly after Contrecœur marched into Fort Machault, the military engineer and artillerist Captain François-Marc-Antoine Le Mercier and an additional 350 reinforcements arrived. They had been recuperating in Québec from the previous summer's grueling expedition

11. The Perilous Return

to the Allegheny with Marin. Le Mercier brought further orders from Duquesne specifying that Contrecœur leave only a handful of troops at Forts Presque Isle, Le Bœuf, and Machault, and take the rest of the army to the Forks with all possible speed. Apparently, Duquesne had received an intelligence report from Michel Maray de La Chauvignerie's (c. 1710–?), a tough and experienced frontier officer, who erroneously inflated Trent's command at the Forks as numbering about one thousand.

Duquesne had been correct in assuming that the English had begun construction of a fort at the Forks. Concerned that an alarming number of English troops had arrived at the strategic location ahead of the French, the governor-general believed that it would require a maximum effort to dislodge them. Duquesne was so disquieted by Chauvignerie's reports of a potent English army at the Forks that he considered it necessary to further reinforce Contrecœur. In May 1754, the governor-general dispatched additional troops under Captain Michel-Jean-Hughes Péan (1723–1782) to support Contrecœur's operation. Péan's orders specified that if in Contrecœur's opinion, Péan's services were not needed or if the increased French troop strength was insufficient to dislodge the British, Péan should abort the rendezvous with Contrecœur and resume his journey to Fort Detroit. Péan dawdled, and by the time he reached the Fort Presque Isle portage in June 1754, he learned that Contrecœur no longer needed his assistance. So, he tarried at Fort Presque Isle for about a month until the end of July, then continued on to Fort Detroit.

With Trent at work on Fort Prince George, Lieutenant-Governor Dinwiddie needed to find troops to garrison and defend the fort. Since Washington had recently returned from his mission to the Ohio and had some knowledge of the area and experience dealing with the French and Indians, Dinwiddie tasked Washington with raising the initial contingent of troops and ordered him to march to defend the Forks. Once again, Dinwiddie more than likely selected Washington because of his family's ties to the Ohio Company of Virginia rather than for Washington's frontier experience, which in reality was very minimal. The lieutenant-governor undoubtedly considered that the young Virginian's financial interest in the Ohio Company would enhance his diligence regarding the success of the enterprise.

But first Dinwiddie had to make it possible for Washington to raise troops for the venture. The daily pay for Virginia militia volunteers was fifteen pounds of tobacco, and if that didn't entice sufficient volunteers, the lieutenant-governor was prepared to conscript the rest. Dinwiddie also turned to his neighboring colonial governors for troops, but they were not eager to send their citizens to support Dinwiddie's Ohio Company business venture. Even the Virginia colonial legislators in Williamsburg balked at Dinwiddie's request for funds for additional troops. Some members argued that reports of the French advance were blatant attempts to sway the burgesses to support the interests of the Ohio Company, and at least one member even expressed the opinion that the Forks of the Ohio in actuality belonged to France. To Dinwiddie's dismay, the burgesses also stated that the Virginia militia could not be used outside the colony, and the Forks of the Ohio likely fell into that category. The best concession Dinwiddie was able to wrest from the burgesses was an appropriation of £10,000 for protection of the frontier.[25]

Thwarted by his own colony's legislature, Dinwiddie looked at other means of raising troops. There were several units of British regulars in the colonies, including independent companies that were not attached to any regiment. After sending requests to their respective governors, one company based in New York and one in South Carolina were placed at Dinwiddie's disposal. The more immediate problem was getting a sufficient number of troops mustered and marched to the Forks. Even if the independent companies of regulars from New York and South Carolina could reach the Forks in time, their combined numbers were only about two hundred, which was still too small a force to defend against a sizable French army. It would require an additional several hundred militia troops to augment the regular companies in order to stand any chance against the veteran French army that was presently poised to move down the Allegheny River.

Dinwiddie had originally planned for a force of six hundred to seven hundred militia but recruiting became unexpectedly difficult. Volunteers were few and far between, and the quality of those enlisted was generally disappointing. Washington complained to Dinwiddie that "You may, with almost equal success, attempt to raise the dead to life again as to raise the force of this country."[26] To spur enlistments, Dinwiddie offered an inducement bonus of 200,000 acres of land to divide among those who enlisted, but even so, volunteers only trickled in, and those were usually of very poor quality.

Unwittingly, Dinwiddie's proclamation, offering the two hundred thousand acres of land, served to undermine many of the Ohio Company claims in the Ohio region. He likely figured there was enough land to satisfy both ventures, but that was not the case. For one thing, Governor Hamilton of Pennsylvania argued that the land that Dinwiddie was promising was within the Province of Pennsylvania. Also, those bounty

11. The Perilous Return

lands overlapped a good portion of the Ohio Company lands, and later those claimants prevailed at the expense of the Ohio Company.

Washington gamely continued to try to recruit militia, but on Saturday, March 9, 1754, he frustratingly wrote that those who enlisted were generally "loose, Idle persons, that are quite destitute of House, and Home; and I may truely say many of them of Cloaths; which last render's them very incapable of the necessary Service as they must unavoidably be expos'd to inclement weather in Marches etc.; and can expect no other, than to encounter almost every difficulty that's incident to a Soldiers Life. There is many of them without Shoes, other's want Stockings, some are without Shirts, and not a few that have Scarce a Coat, or Waistcoat, to their Backs; in short, they are as illy provided as can well be conceived."[27]

Frustrated by the slow pace of recruitments, Dinwiddie decided he would send a smaller force because he believed it was imperative to have troops on the Ohio as soon as possible. He opted to make do with a regiment of three hundred men instead of waiting until he recruited the full six hundred, which was his original plan. A full-strength eighteenth-century regiment numbered between six hundred and one thousand men. Dinwiddie's smaller Virginia regiment would be less than half the size of a full-strength regiment and would comprise six companies of fifty men each. To augment his abbreviated regiment, Dinwiddie hoped to entice Indian warriors from the Carolinas, but Royal Governor James Glen (1701–1777) of South Carolina believed Dinwiddie was trying to take over the lucrative southern Indian trade, so he successfully campaigned to convince the Indians to stay at home.

During March of 1754, messages arrived continually at Williamsburg from Trent and Gist warning that the French were on the move and that reinforcements were urgently needed at the Forks. Trent reported that Monsieur René-Hippolyte LaForce had told the Indians that if they sided with the English, "neither they nor the English there would see the Sun above 20 Days longer; 13 of the Days being then to come."[28] Dinwiddie felt he couldn't wait any longer. On Sunday, March 31, 1754, he ordered Washington to march at once for the Forks with whatever men he had, and Dinwiddie's choice for overall commander, Colonel Joshua Fry, would follow as soon as possible with whatever men he could raise.

While Washington was attempting to raise troops, Dinwiddie appointed Colonel Joshua Fry (1700–1754) to command the force that would defend the Forks, and Washington would be Fry's second-in-command with the rank of lieutenant-colonel. Gist was

With George Washington in the Wilderness

acquainted with Fry from the Logstown Conference of 1752, in which Fry was one of the three commissioners representing Virginia. Prior to that, he had been a professor of mathematics at the College of William and Mary, and around 1744 he and his family moved to Goochland County between present Charlottesville and Scottsville, Virginia. In 1749, he and Peter Jefferson (1708–1757), the father of Thomas Jefferson, were commissioned to determine a section of the Virginia-North Carolina boundary, and in 1751, he collaborated with Peter Jefferson in compiling the "Map of the Inhabited Parts of Virginia."

12

Fleur-de-Lis at the Forks

"It is easy to be brave from a distance."
—Indian adage

At the Forks, Trent and Gist were doing the best they could with their small band of laborers, but the work wasn't progressing nearly fast enough for the half-king Tanacharison. In truth, even Trent and Gist were concerned about the slow progress. If Tanacharison's Indians would have helped with the work, it might have progressed faster, but for the most part they were unwilling to take part in the strenuous construction. The Indians did, however, consume a fairly significant portion of Trent's meager food supply and soon there was nothing to eat other than some Indian corn and whatever scant game the Indians brought in.

Christopher Gist planned to return home to his settlement, but the increasingly anxious and impatient Tanacharison prevailed on Gist to travel all the way to Williamsburg, if necessary, to speed the arrival of supplies, reinforcements, and artillery.

At the same time, Trent was also very concerned that his minuscule force and partially finished fort would not have any chance against the French. His repeated requests for reinforcements, provisions, and equipment only resulted in vague assurances that help would be dispatched. In desperation, Trent decided to travel to Will's Creek to get what he could from the Ohio Company storehouse, and from there send messengers to plead for whatever assistance he could get. John Fraser, who was at his post at Turtle Creek, had been commissioned a lieutenant in Trent's small force, and until the arrival of Colonel Joshua Fry and George Washington, he was second-in-command to Trent and should have taken charge when Trent departed.

However, the threat of the French army coming down the Allegheny and the likelihood that they would pillage and destroy English trading posts made Fraser desperate to save his furs, equipment, and trade goods. As a result, he was adamant that rather than supervise the

With George Washington in the Wilderness

construction of Fort Prince George, he needed to take care of his personal business, which meant packing up and transporting everything east. So, Trent had no choice but to leave his brother-in-law, Ensign Edward Ward,[1] in command of the small force at the Forks.

Before he left, Trent directed Ward to first complete the outer walls of the fort, which the ensign concentrated on. They were nearing completion on Saturday, April 13, 1754, when Tanacharison's scouts brought word that a large French force equipped with artillery was descending the Allegheny nearby. Ward rushed the eight miles to Fraser's house on Turtle Creek and asked the trader to return with him to the Forks to assume command of the garrison and direct the defense of the fort. Even though Fraser was technically in command, he unabashedly refused. He asked the astonished Ward, "What can we do?"[2] He added that "he had a shilling to loose for a penny he should gain by his Commission at that time. And that he had Business which he could not settle in under Six Days."[3] Ward was disgusted with Fraser's attitude and returned to the Forks alone, declaring that he would not only complete the fort but would defend it against the entire French army and that he would "hold out to the last extremity before it should be said that the English retreated like cowards before the French forces appeared."[4] When Lieutenant-Governor Dinwiddie learned of John Fraser's unwillingness to take command at the Forks, he suggested that Fraser should be court-martialed and punished, but the court-martial exonerated both Fraser and Trent.

In the meantime, Washington with his two rather small companies was struggling to reach the Forks in time to help defend Fort Prince George, but it was rough going. Washington, dressed in a fine regimental uniform, rode at the head of the column, but his men for the most part were dressed in homespun linen, linsey-woolsey,[5] or buckskin, and while some had shoes, most wore moccasins. Their baggage train consisted of a line of lumbering wagons that carried food, supplies, and ammunition. They had no artillery except for a few small-caliber swivel guns, which were very small cannon, which depending on their size could fire up to a one-pound ball or one pound of shot. They were short-range antipersonnel weapons generally mounted on a swiveling fork or rotating stand that provided them with a very wide range of movement.

After departing Alexandria on Tuesday, April 2, 1754, Washington and his men traveled a mere six miles before they were forced to camp for the night. The following days, they were able to increase their rate of march to about eleven miles a day, but even at that rate it would take them several weeks to cover the roughly 220 miles to the Forks.

12. Fleur-de-Lis at the Forks

Swivel gun at Fort Ligonier (authors' photo).

At Winchester, Washington was met by Captain Adam Stephen (1718–1791)[6] and the militia company that Stephen had recruited from the area. These reinforcements brought Washington's regiment up to approximately 160 men, but it was still only about half the force

With George Washington in the Wilderness

Washington and Fry hoped to have at the Forks. Even the youthfully optimistic Washington realized they would need a considerably larger number of troops to stand a chance against the French army. Two of the officers, Captains Andrew Lewis and Robert Stobo, remained in Alexandria where they attempted to recruit additional men, and Colonel Fry was working his way through Virginia to join Washington while also trying to attract volunteers to augment his force.

On Wednesday, April 17, 1754, Washington met Christopher Gist who at the urging of Tanacharison was on his way to hasten the arrival of reinforcements. Gist reported that work on the fort had begun, but construction was progressing slowly. He also related that the half-king was so concerned by the French advance and angry at the English delay that he and his Indians threatened to abandon the area around the Forks rather than face the French juggernaut with only Trent's minuscule force. Gist having encountered Washington and his troops, and learning that Colonel Fry was on the way, decided to travel back toward the Forks with Washington's column.

On Friday, April 19, 1754, still some thirty miles from Will's Creek, they met a messenger from Trent who brought the alarming news that a French army numbering more than eight hundred and supported by artillery was coming down the Allegheny in a flotilla of canoes and batteaux. Washington relayed the message on to Williamsburg adding his own urgent request for immediate reinforcements. They were too late. Two days previous, on Wednesday, April 17, 1754, the French army had arrived at the Forks.

On Saturday, April 13, 1754, Ensign Ward at the Forks received word that a massive French force of more than one thousand men would arrive on or about April 17. The small detachment worked at a frenzied pace to complete the defenses before the French arrived, and somehow, they were just able to get it done. The gates to the palisaded stockade were hung on Tuesday, April 16, 1754, the day before the French arrived.

From his spies who had constantly observed the construction of Fort Prince George, Contrecœur had a good grasp of what to expect as far as the fortification was concerned. However, he was not as confident of the intelligence he received regarding the size of the English garrison that would defend it. Most recently, his spies reported that the English personnel at the Forks numbered only about fifty men, but that number drastically conflicted with the earlier reports of upwards of one thousand English troops in the area of the Forks. Unwilling to meet a potentially large, hostile force before his men were in battle formation,

12. Fleur-de-Lis at the Forks

Contrecœur landed his troops at Shannopin's town on the Allegheny, about three miles above the Forks. He bivouacked there for the night of Tuesday, April 16, 1754. The next day, Wednesday, April 17, with updated intelligence, Contrecœur and his army proceeded the remaining three miles downriver and disembarked a short distance from Fort Prince George. Ward and his small garrison were huddled in the fort as Contrecœur's professional soldiers quickly swarmed ashore and established a perimeter while four of the French cannon were disembarked and assembled on carriages.

Ensign Ward and his small command watched with increasing trepidation from behind their palisaded walls as the French troops smartly formed up on shore while their artillery deployed to cover them. Then with flags flying and drums beating, the French ceremoniously marched to about 150 yards from the fort, which was just beyond musket range, and Captain François-Marc-Antoine Le Mercier continued forward with a small guard and called for a parley.[7] Ward was unsure of what to do, and as far as he was concerned there did not seem to be any good options. Undoubtedly cursing both Trent and Fraser for being absent, Ward quickly assembled a small guard and nervously marched out of the fort to meet with the French representatives. Tanacharison accompanied Ward to the meeting with Le Mercier. Thankfully, Ward found Le Mercier gracious to a fault and though he treated Ward with sympathetic kindness, he left no doubt whatsoever that he was there to evict the English from the Forks. He handed Ward a letter that Contrecœur had written the previous day that was filled with polite Gallic prose but minced no words in demanding the immediate surrender of the fort and English withdrawal from New France.

"A Summon by order of Contrecœur, Captain of one of the Companies of the Detachment of the French marine, Commander-in-Chief of his Most Christian Majestie's Troops now on the beautiful River, to the Commander of Those of the King of Great Britain at the Mouth of the River Mohongialo.

> Sir:
>
> Nothing can surprise me more than to see you attempt a Settlement upon the Lands of the King my Master, which obliges me, now, Sir, to send You this Gentleman, Chevalier Le Mercier, Captain of the Bombardiers, Commander of the Artillery of Canada, to know of you, Sir, by Vertue of what Authority You are come to fortify Yourself within the Dominions of the King my Master. This action seems so contrary to the last Treaty of Peace concluded at Aix-la-Chapelle between his Most Christian Majesty and the King of Great Britain, that I do not know to whom to

With George Washington in the Wilderness

impute such an Usurpation, as it is incontestable that the lands situated along the beautiful River belong to his Most Christian Majesty.

I am informed, Sir, that your Undertaking has been concerted by none else than by a Company who have more in View the advantage of a Trade than to endeavor to keep the Union of Harmony which subsists between the Crowns of France and Great Britain, altho' it is as much the Interest, Sir, of your Nation as Our's to preserve it.

Let it be as will, Sir, if you come into this Place charged with Orders, I summon you in the Name of the King my Master, by Vertue of Orders which I got from my General, to retreat peaceably with your Troops from off the Lands of the King (and not to return, or else I find myself obliged to fulfill my Duty and compel You to it. I hope, Sir, You will not defer an Instant, and that You will not force me to the last Extremity); in that case, Sir, You may be persuaded that I will give Orders that there shall be no Damage done by my Detachment.

I prevent You, Sir, from the trouble of asking me one Hour of Delay, nor to wait for my consent to receive Orders from your Governor; He can give you none within the Dominions of the King my Master. Those I have received of my General are my laws, so that I cannot depart from them.

If, on the contrary, Sir, You have not got Orders, and only come to trade, I am sorry to tell you that I cannot avoid seizing You and to confiscate your Effects to the Use of the Indians our Children, Allies, and Friends, as You are not allowed to carry on a contraband Trade. It is for this Reason, Sir, that we stopped two Englishmen last year who were trading upon our Lands; moreover, the King my Master asks nothing but his Right, he has not the least Intention to trouble the good Harmony and Friendship which reigns between his Majesty and the King of Great Britain.

The Governor of Canada can give Proof of having done his utmost Endeavors to maintain the perfect Union which reigns between Two Friendly Princes, as he has learned that the Iroquois and the Nepissingues of the Lake of the Two Mountains had struck and destroyed an English Family towards Carolina, he has barred up the Road and forced them to give him a little Boy belonging to that family, which was the only one alive, and which Mr. Wlerich, a Merchant of Montréal, has carried to Boston; and what is more, he has forbid the Savages from exercising their accustomed Cruelty upon the English our Friends.

I could complain bitterly, Sir, of the Means taken all last Winter to instigate the Indians to accept the hatchet and to strike Us while We were striving to maintain the Peace.

I am well persuaded, Sir, of the polite Manner in which You will receive Monsieur Le Mercier, as well out of Regard to his business as his Distinction and personal Merit. I expect You will send him back with one of your Officers, who will bring me a precise answer. As You have got some Indians with You, Sir, I join with Monsieur Le Mercier an Interpreter, that he may inform them of my Intentions upon the subject.

> I am, with great Regard, Sir,
> Your most humble and most obedient Servant,
> Contrecœur
> Done at our Camp, April 16th, 1754"[8]

12. Fleur-de-Lis at the Forks

Ward was in a quandary. The young ensign was charged with defending the Forks and did not want to surrender his post without a fight, but being outnumbered twenty to one by a veteran army supported with artillery could only end in the slaughter of his small command. Tanacharison advised Ward to try to delay by stating that he was not authorized to make such a decision. Ward explained to Mercier that as a mere ensign, he did not have sufficient authority to surrender the fort. That could only be done by Captain Trent, who had gone to Will's Creek, or Lieutenant Fraser at Turtle Creek. Ward asked for time to at least summon Lieutenant Fraser from his home eight miles away as Fraser was technically in command during Trent's absence and was the more appropriate person to carry on negotiations with the French commander. Le Mercier politely but firmly refused Ward's request and told Ward that he had exactly one hour to accept the terms and "retreat peaceably with your troops"[9] or the French army would remove them by force. Ward realized that resistance would be futile and agreed to abandon the Forks much to the frustration of the enraged Tanacharison who angrily watched as the English surrendered their fort to the French without so much as a shot being fired.

Contrecœur's terms allowed the English to spend the night camped near the fort but specified they must leave the Forks by noon the following day. They were allowed to take their weapons and all of their possessions with them. In an outward gesture of politeness, but more likely to obtain intelligence, the English and their Indian allies were invited to dinner in the French camp. The French commander asked many questions concerning the British government, to which Ward professed ignorance. Wine flowed freely and one of the topics discussed was the disposition of the Virginians' construction tools: axes, saws, mattocks, et cetera. Contrecœur knew that Ward's garrison was desperately short of provisions, and he offered rations and money in exchange for the tools.[10] Some sources indicate that Ward took advantage of Contrecœur's offer and sold him the construction equipment,[11] but Ward steadfastly claimed that he refused Contrecœur's offer. Ward's deposition letter of Tuesday, July 2, 1754, to Dinwiddie states, "That the French Commander desired some of the Carpenter's Tools, offering money for them, to which he [Ward] answer'd he loved his King and Country too well to part with any of them."[12]

On the morning of Tuesday, April 18, 1754, Ward and his small command began their march east as the French raised the fleur-de-lis flag over the fort. One of the French soldiers wrote, "We took possession of the fort in which there were only fifty men and four cannons, but no provisions at all."[13] The "four cannons" mentioned were most likely swivel guns. Other than swivel guns, the Virginians did not have any proper, large-caliber artillery at the Forks at that time.

Contrecœur graciously provided three days rations to help sustain Ward's troops during their march east. Tanacharison watched as the English and the French waged their strangely genteel form of warfare, and the half-king was beside himself with anger and frustration.

13

The World on Fire

> "The volley fired by a young Virginian in the backwoods of America set the world on fire."
> —Horace Walpole

Meanwhile, Christopher Gist, in the company with Washington's troops, was on the way to the Forks. However, when they reached Cresap's post at Old Town, they learned that the French had indeed evicted Ward's small force and had begun construction of Fort Duquesne, using much of the matériel salvaged from Fort Prince George.

Washington and Gist arrived at Will's Creek about the same time that Ensign Ward and his small detachment straggled in from the west. Ward described how he was obliged to surrender to more than a thousand French regulars under the command of Captain Contrecœur, who arrived in sixty bateaux and three hundred canoes, and equipped with eighteen pieces of artillery. Along with Ward's retreating contingent, Tanacharison had sent two young warriors to see for themselves if and how the English were responding.

Of course, with the news that a formidable and well-equipped French army was in control of the Forks, Washington's original orders to garrison and defend Fort Prince George were no longer applicable. Washington's force of about 160 men, even with the addition of the thirty or so who were with Ensign Ward, would be no match for Contrecœur's artillery-equipped force. However, if Colonel Fry and Robert Stobo were successful in recruiting a large number of volunteers, they might be able to challenge the French for control of the Forks. In the meantime, Washington decided to march his men to Red Stone to await reinforcements and for Colonel Fry to take over command.

Washington's decision to lead his troops into disputed territory was risky; his small force would be exposed to a possible attack by a veteran French army that was at least six times larger than his and was supported by field artillery. The likely reason for placing his abbreviated

With George Washington in the Wilderness

regiment in harm's way was that Washington wanted to demonstrate to Tanacharison and the Ohio Indians that British support was on the way. To further demonstrate that fact, on Wednesday, April 24, 1754, Washington sent one of the Indians with a message to Tanacharison, which read,

> To the Half-King, and the Chiefs and Warriors of the Shawanese and Loups our Friends and Bretheren. I received your speech by brother Bucks who came to us with the two young men six days after their departure from you. We return you our greatest thanks and our hearts burn with love and affection towards you, in gratitude for your constant attachment to us, as also your gracious speech, and your wise counsels.
>
> This young man will inform you, where he found a small part of our army, making towards you, clearing the roads for a great number of our warriors, who are ready to follow us, with our great guns our ammunition and provisions. I cannot delay letting you know the thoughts of our hearts, I send you back this young man, with this speech, to acquaint you therewith, and the other young man I have sent to the Governor of Virginia, to deliver him your speech and your wampum, and to be an eye-witness of the preparations we are making, to come in all haste to the assistance of those whose interest is as dear to us as our lives. We know the character of the treacherous French, and our conduct shall plainly show you how much we have it at heart. I shall not be satisfied if I do not see you before all our forces are met together at the Fort which is in the way, wherefore, I desire with the greatest earnestness, that you, or at least one of you, Scruneyattha [Scarouady] and send a necklace of wampum, should come as soon as possible and meet us on the road, and to assist us in council. I present you with these bunches of wampum, to assure you of the sincerity of my speech, and that you may remember how much I am your Friend and Brother.
>
> Signed
G° Washington or
Conotocarious[1]

The name *Conotocarious* (Taker of Towns) had been given to Washington by Tanacharison the previous winter during their trek to deliver Dinwiddie's message to Legardeur.

Christopher Gist continued along with Washington, but the progress was slow due to the amount of labor expended in improving the trail in anticipation of Colonel Fry's artillery and supply wagons. At one point, they were barely able to progress twenty miles in fifteen days.[2]

Rather than continue at the present snail's pace, Gist moved on ahead and reached his home while Washington's troops were still miles away on the east side of the Alleghenies. On Friday, May 17, 1754, Washington had reached the Great Crossing of the Youghiogheny River, between present Addison and Markleysburg, Pennsylvania,

13. The World on Fire

and was joined by Ensign Ward who was returning from reporting to Lieutenant-Governor Dinwiddie. Ward told Washington that Dinwiddie approved of Washington's intent to take his small force to Red Stone. He also told Washington that two companies of regulars were on the way. One was the Independent Company of Regulars from South Carolina, and the other was the Independent Company of Regulars from New York, and each of the companies was composed of about one hundred men.

That same evening, two Indians came into Washington's camp claiming they had been at the Forks of the Ohio five days previous. They told Washington that the construction of Fort Duquesne was progressing rapidly and most of the troops were employed in construction duties. They said when they left, the fort was "already breast-high, and of the thickness of twelve feet, and filled up with Earth. Stone, &c."[3] The Indians estimated the number of French troops to be about six hundred, but they said the French claimed they had eight hundred and expected their numbers to double to about sixteen hundred within the next few days.

At the same time, Contrecœur at Fort Duquesne sent Lieutenant LaForce[4] in command of about fifty French troops and Indians to scout the area to the east. During the early part of May 1754, under the pretense of searching for French deserters, LaForce arrived at Gist's Plantation. It's not known whether Gist had returned home by that time or if he was hiding to avoid the French party. Reportedly, the French were inclined to destroy Gist's home and trading post but were dissuaded by Indians there who were friendly with Gist.

LaForce returned to Fort Duquesne and reported to Contrecœur who in addition to LaForce, had been keeping track of Washington's advance by several scouting parties. The French commander had an accurate estimation of the size and strength of Washington's troops but was in a quandary regarding their intentions. Surely, they did not mean to try reclaiming the Forks with such a small number of men. On Thursday, May 23, 1754, the French commander sent Ensign Joseph Coulon de Villiers de Jumonville (1718–1754) and a small detachment of some thirty troops to discover the whereabouts of the English force and to find out if they had in fact entered French territory. Jumonville was ordered to first report the location of the English troops to Contrecœur and then present the intruders with a peaceful summons that demanded their immediate withdrawal from French territory. Ensign Jumonville was thirty-five years old and had an undistinguished military

With George Washington in the Wilderness

career. His military service was unlike those of his three brothers, who had all distinguished themselves in the regular army. It is supposed that Jumonville was given the mission by Contrecœur to help him with his advancement. However, while Jumonville was technically in command, the party included two officers, Lieutenant LaForce, who likely was there to mentor the untested Jumonville, and Ensign Pierre Jacques Drouillon de Macé (1727–1780), who was sent along as an interpreter.

On Friday, May 24, 1754, Washington's force had reached Great Meadows. During the trek from Will's Creek, about a dozen men had deserted and the rest were exhausted to the point of collapse. The young commander received rumors almost daily of advancing French troops, and frustratingly, there was still no sign of the promised reinforcements. In the valley where they stopped lay an open alpine grassland called Great Meadows (present Farmington Township, Pennsylvania) that was watered by a stream called Great Meadow Run and intersected by a tributary brook called Indian Run. The grassy field was a few hundred yards wide and stretched about two miles long.

Washington realized that his men desperately needed a period of rest and recuperation, so he decided to establish a camp at Great Meadows before tackling the 2,500-foot-high Chestnut Ridge, which loomed above them to the west. Great Meadows was not a bad choice because it was level with adequate pasturage and a plentiful supply of water. In addition, the location of Great Meadows was strategic. It lay fifty-one miles from Will's Creek and eighteen miles from the Great Crossing of the Youghiogheny, twelve miles from Christopher Gist's plantation, twenty-six miles from Red Stone Creek, and about fifty-five miles from the French garrison at the Forks of the Ohio. It was a good place to set up a camp, rest the men, and plan how best to proceed.

No sooner had they made camp, when Indian runners brought a message from Tanacharison that had been written for him by John Davidson. While Davidson was a good translator, he was a barely literate writer. The message read:

"To the forist his Magesties Commander Offeverses to hom this meay concern.

An acct. Of a French armey to meat Miger Georg Wassiontton therfor my Brotheres I deisir you to be awar of them for deisind to strike the forist English they see tow deays since they marchd I cannot tell what number the hif King and the rest of the Chiefes will be with you in five dayes to Consel—no more at present but give my serves to my Brother's the English.

The Half King
John Davidson"[5]

13. The World on Fire

The poorly written message undoubtedly perplexed Washington. It mentioned a French army on the march, but it gave no hint of its size or location. Washington had been hearing from other sources about French parties scouting the area. However, this was the first warning he received of an army of French regulars heading in his direction.

Around that time, the French troops led by Jumonville and LaForce were in the vicinity of Gist's Plantation. They knew that the half-king Tanacharison was to a certain extent in league with Washington, and by finding the half-king it would lead them to the Virginians. At mid-day Sunday, May 26, 1754, Lieutenant LaForce and most likely the interpreter Drouillon de Macé visited Christopher Gist's homestead, this time finding the frontiersman at home. LaForce enquired if Gist knew where Tanacharison was at the time, but Gist said he had no idea, and the two Frenchmen left. Gist followed the two men to Jumonville's detachment, and then trailed the French troops to within five miles of Washington's encampment at Great Meadows.

Early the next day, Monday, May 27, 1754, Gist visited Washington and told him about the French party that was in the area, and also about the earlier visit when friendly Indians saved his house from being vandalized by the French. To Washington's mind, this was confirmation of Tanacharison's warning about hostile French troops. He immediately put his weary men to work clearing brush and positioning his wagons to serve as makeshift defensive fortifications.

If Christopher Gist's original intention was to keep a low profile in hopes of coexisting with the French, he certainly was going about it in an unusual manner.

Washington wrote in his journal, apparently combining the two visits to Gist's home by LaForce, "May 27th. Mr. Gist arrived early in the morning, who told us that Mr. la Force, with fifty men whose tracks he had seen five miles from here, had been at his plantation the day before, towards noon, and would have killed a cow, and broken every thing in the house, if two Indians, whom he had left in charge of the house, had not prevented them from carrying out their design."[6] To this point, Washington had heard rumors from several people about French units of various sizes, but it was more concerning to Washington when someone as precise as Gist warned of a sizable contingent of French troops.

Washington dashed off a message to Dinwiddie, adding, "We have with Natures assistance made a good Intrenchment, and by clearing ye[7] Bushes out of these Meadows, prepar'd a charming field for an

With George Washington in the Wilderness

encounter."[8] When he was finished, Washington gave the message to Gist to deliver to Dinwiddie who was due to arrive in Winchester.

At Great Meadows, after ensuring that all the weapons were serviceable and ammunition was adequate, the Virginians spent an uneasy night. Sentries were on the alert for any sign of the French, and the remainder of the troops nervously tried to sleep fully dressed and with their weapons handy. To make matters worse, a steady rain began to fall. Washington was desperate for the arrival of Colonel Joshua Fry and his long-awaited reinforcements because he was convinced that an attack by the French army was imminent.

About eight o'clock in the evening of Monday, May 27, 1754, an Indian named "Silverheels"[9] came into Washington's camp with a message from Tanacharison informing the Virginians that the half-king who had been on his way to Great Meadows came across the tracks of two men, which he followed. The tracks led to a very secluded area where Tanacharison believed a large force of French soldiers were hidden. Silverheels said that the half-king and his Indians were camped near the French bivouac, which was about six miles from Great Meadows. This information was consistent with Gist's earlier report about a French war party in the vicinity. It also reinforced the thought that the French were planning to attack the Virginians.

Night had fallen and the steady rain turned the darkness into an inky blackness, but rather than wait for the enemy's attack, Washington decided to reconnoiter the French force to obtain a better idea of what he was up against. He left his camp at Big Meadows on high alert with sentries and pickets posted, and with Silverheels guiding, he set off with about forty men to find Tanacharison's camp. Washington wrote in his journal: "I sent out forty men and ordered my ammunition to be put in a place of safety, fearing it to be a stratagem of the French to attack our camp; I left a guard to defend it, and with the rest of my men, set out in a heavy rain, and in a night as dark as pitch, along a path scarce broad enough for one man; we were sometimes fifteen or twenty minutes out of the path before we could come on it again, and we would often strike against each other in the darkness: All night long we continued our route, and on the 28th about sun-rise we arrived at the Indian camp."[10]

Washington and his men were stressed by fatigue, and their anxiety was exacerbated by the proximity of what they believed was a potent enemy force. Tanacharison and Washington held a hurried council, and the half-king told Washington that since the French were obviously planning to attack, it would be more prudent to attack them first. Both

13. The World on Fire

Washington and Tanacharison concluded that an early morning surprise attack would give them a better chance against the veteran French regulars.

Jumonville's detachment of about thirty men was camped in a hollow at the foot of a stone cliff that rose sharply from the floor of the glen. The bivouac was fairly well hidden and protected. The location was most likely selected in an attempt to find protection from the incessant rain rather than as a place of stealth and concealment. There were no sentries posted, and the French soldiers had stacked their arms off to one side in a protected area under an overhang where they would be less susceptible to the constant rainfall.

It's difficult to explain why Jumonville did not exercise basic military discipline and post armed sentries, or why the more experienced Monsieur LaForce did not intervene in that matter. One likely explanation is that they believed their role was diplomatic rather than military and did not require a defensive perimeter. Jumonville's orders were to discover the English party and after reporting its location to Contrecœur

Jumonville Glen, from Washington's position, looking toward the French bivouac near the cliff wall.

With George Washington in the Wilderness

at Fort Duquesne, he was ordered to merely deliver a peaceful summons from the French commander to "the first English officer that he could find,"[11] which was a message that invited the English to withdraw from French territory. Contrecœur's summons read:

> Word has reached me by way of the savages, that you have come with an armed force upon the lands of the King, my master; but I am hardly able to believe it. Since I ought to neglect nothing to be informed correctly about it, I am sending Sieur Dejumonville to find out, and in case he finds you there, he is to summon you in the name of the king, in virtue of the orders I have received from my general, to retire peaceably with your troops. Otherwise, Monsieur, I shall be obliged to compel you in all the ways that I believe most efficacious for the honor of the arms of France. The sale of the Belle River territory by the savages gives you such poor title that I could not be prevented from meeting force with force.
>
> I warn you that if any act of hostility occurs after this summons, which is the last I shall send you, you will have to answer for it, since our intention is to maintain the concord which now reigns between the two friendly princes. Whatever your intention may be, I am convinced you will show M. Dejumonville all the consideration that he deserves and send him back at once to inform me of your intentions.[12]

The French may have considered themselves to be on a diplomatic mission, but Washington with Tanacharison's prompting came to a different conclusion. To the young Virginian, the French had bivouacked in such a hidden and secretive location for a more sinister reason than merely to shelter from the rain. He concluded they had been skulking around, because they had nefarious intentions regarding Washington and his command.

Washington deployed his troops on two sides of the French party and sent Tanacharison and his Indians to seal off the far end of the little glade. Once that was accomplished, Washington signaled a stealthy advance on the French encampment.

When the advancing Virginians stepped into the open, French soldiers who were preparing for breakfast spotted them almost immediately. The sight of an armed force marching toward them in line of battle startled them, and they quickly raised the alarm and rushed for their stacked muskets to defend themselves. Now that he was discovered, Washington swiftly advanced his line to less than fifty yards, well within killing range of his muskets, when a shot rang out. Nobody recalled who fired first, but within seconds a full-scale engagement erupted. Captain Adam Stephen's troops poured fire from the tops of the rock face down into the milling French troops, and Washington's men fired

13. The World on Fire

volley after volley from the floor of the glen. In the first exchanges, several French and a few Virginians were bowled over by the heavy musket balls, but it was obvious to both sides that the French were getting the worst of it. The French troops began a fighting withdrawal to the

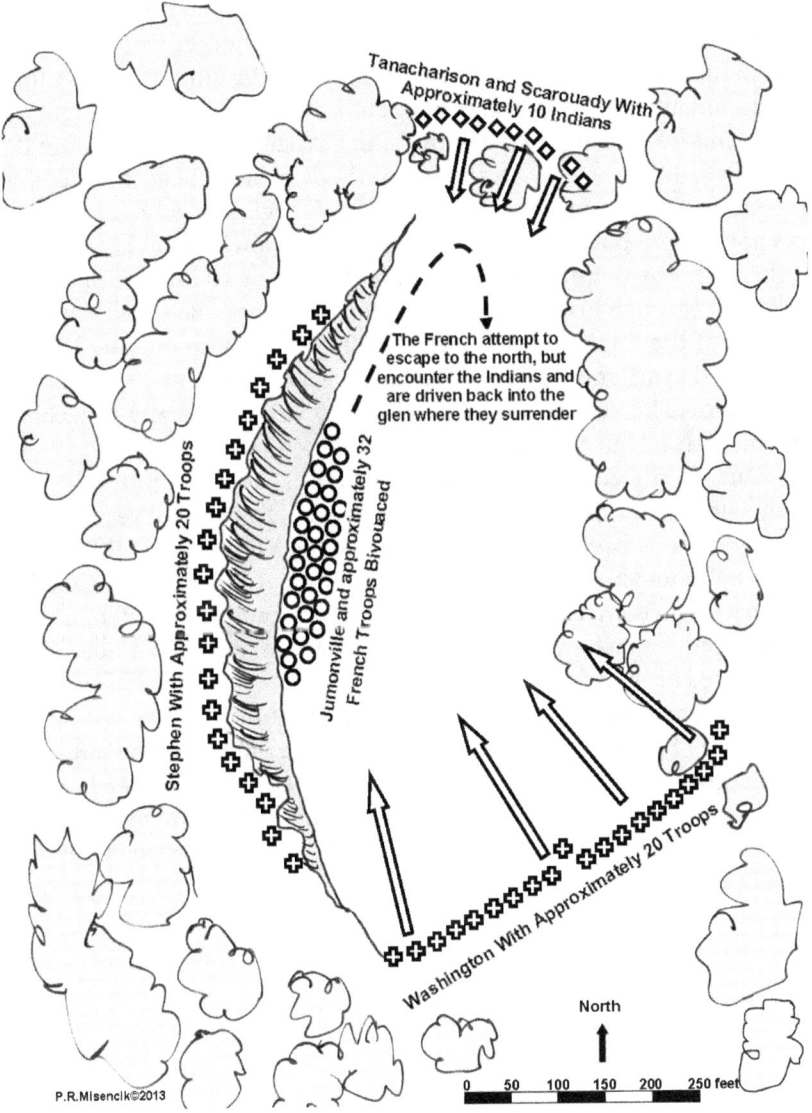

Skirmish at Jumonville Glen.

With George Washington in the Wilderness

north, but soon ran into Tanacharison and his Indians who forced them back into the ravine. The fight lasted no more than fifteen minutes and it ended when Jumonville cried out for a cease-fire. The firing slackened off and eventually stopped, but before the shocked Washington could intervene, the Indians rushed forward and tomahawked all but one of the wounded Frenchmen, and then they began to scalp the dead. It was when Tanacharison demanded that the unwounded French be turned over to the Indians to be killed and scalped that Washington firmly took charge and denied the half-king's demand.

Sometime during or after the short skirmish, Ensign Jumonville was killed. The most persistent and perhaps believable account comes from John Shaw, a private in Washington's regiment who admittedly was not present but related in a sworn statement what others who were in the ravine at the time had told him. According to Shaw, Jumonville called out through his interpreter that he had something to tell the commander of the English force, after which Washington and his Virginians closed in around Jumonville to hear what he had to say.[13] Jumonville began to read his summons aloud in French, which ironically Tanacharison understood but Washington did not.

During the reading, Tanacharison approached Jumonville and softly said, *"Tu n'es pas encore mort, mon père"* [You are not yet dead, my father],[14] and before Washington or any of the Virginians could act, the half-king swung his tomahawk and split Jumonville's skull, which killed him instantly. Then as the horrified Virginians and their French prisoners watched, Tanacharison scooped out a handful of Jumonville's brains and washed his hands with them.

After the short but bloody fight, Washington was torn with emotion. It was the first time he led men in battle, but after the euphoria of emerging unscathed and victorious, he began to wonder how his actions would be judged by his superiors, and indeed by the king himself. There was no doubt that he had just started a war between England and France.

14

Surrender on the Fourth of July

"Wars spring from unseen and generally insignificant causes, the first outbreak being often but an explosion of anger."
—Thucydides

Washington sent his French prisoners under guard to Williamsburg and began construction of a more substantial fortification at Great Meadows. His letter to Dinwiddie included the sentence, "Began to erect a small fort with small palisades, fearing that when the French should hear the news of that defeat we may be attacked by considerable forces."[1]

By Sunday, June 2, 1754, a rough palisade had been constructed of split logs about fifty feet in diameter with the walls twelve feet high, and a small building of squared timbers was erected in the center of the stockade. Tanacharison, who had arrived at Great Meadows with Queen Aliquippa and about eighty-five Indian men, women, and children, was unimpressed with the defensive structure. Washington had grandly christened it "Fort Necessity," but the half-king disdainfully referred to it as "that little thing upon the meadow."

On Thursday, June 6, 1754, Christopher Gist returned from Winchester with the grave announcement that Colonel Joshua Fry had been severely injured by a fall from his horse. Fry lingered for a few days and then died at Will's Creek on Friday, May 31, 1754. Gist's message added that because of the death of Fry, Dinwiddie had elevated the twenty-two-year-old Washington to the rank of colonel. Washington was to remain in command of the English troops until such time as Colonel James Innes arrived with his contingent of reinforcements. Innes would then take over as commander-in-chief of the expedition and Washington would be his second-in-command. In the meantime, Innes

With George Washington in the Wilderness

Reconstructed Fort Necessity at Fort Necessity National Battlefield.

and his troops were dawdling ineffectually across Virginia and would not reach Winchester for more than another month, much too late to be of any use to Washington at Great Meadows.

When Innes and his men finally reached Winchester, they received word of Washington's defeat at Great Meadows, and most of Innes's force simply dispersed and returned home to North Carolina. Gist also told Washington that Lieutenant Colonel George Muse and Captain Robert Stobo were bringing the three companies that had been with Fry, and Muse would act as Washington's second-in-command. Muse and Stobo arrived on Sunday, June 9, 1754, but they only had about 140 men, which was about the normal strength of one full company. Word also reached Great Meadows that the South Carolina Independent Company of Regulars would soon arrive at Great Meadows.

Gist, along with George Croghan, had been appointed deputy commissary under Major John Carlyle, who was the commissary of the Virginia Regiment. As such, Gist reportedly used most of his family's personal supply of provisions to feed Washington's troops, and the frontiersman often paid for additional supplies out of his own purse. Gist also had detractors, among whom were Governor Horatio Sharpe of Maryland. Sharpe complained that Gist was in over his head as commissary, blatantly dishonest, or at best a naïve victim of unscrupulous contractors.

14. Surrender on the Fourth of July

When Governor Sharpe toured the camps, he complained that there was no salt, which was a necessity for curing meat, therefore the cattle could not be butchered. Sharpe laid blame directly on Gist. Also, Sharpe received complaints that Gist and Carlyle were not paying their bills, even though the money had been advanced them. Dinwiddie attempted to defend Gist by directing the blame solely at Carlyle. Sharpe answered Dinwiddie in a letter, which read in part,

> I was importuned a good deal by Mr. Gists Creditors with some of whom I am indeed somewhat suspicious that he had hardly acted the honest part....I was told that he did receive several Sums of Money of you to discharge a good many Debts but instead of appropriating it in that manner He paid off with part thereof some old Debts that he had contracted on his own private Account & with the Remainder purchased a Quantity of Goods to trade with also on his own Account. Gist acknowledged to me that He had received £45. for Andrew Montour but Montour did not receive a Farthing thereof.[2]

Sharpe later admitted that Gist said he used the money he was supposed to pay Andrew Montour to instead purchase provisions for the troops.

Even so, Sharpe did not trust and apparently did not like Christopher Gist. Even Dinwiddie, who staunchly defended Gist, wrote to William Fairfax, another Gist supporter, "I always had and have a good Opinion of Mr. Gist's Capacity and Integrity, yet I did not think him a proper Person to act as Commissary with the forces."[3]

In the late fall of 1754, Gist was in a quandary. He realized that Washington's attack on the French troops signaled war between France and England, and his settlement was in the middle of the battlefield. It didn't help any that on Sunday, June 16, 1754, Washington took most of his men over the ridge to Gist's Plantation where they began to construct fortifications, with an eye to fighting the French there. The Virginians appropriated Gist's horses, tore down his fences and smaller buildings, and used the timbers for construction of a small palisade. In addition, they worked on fortifying Gist's house.

Several Ohio Indians had been at Gist's Plantation when Washington arrived, and additional Lenape, Shawnee, Wyandot, and Mingo were streaming into the plantation. Washington held a council with the Indians in an attempt to gain their loyalty and assurance they would support the British in a war against the French. In that respect, the council was a failure; the majority of the Ohio Indians wanted nothing to do with Washington's plan to battle the French. In fact, a number of Indians at the council had been sent by the French to act as spies. When the council ended, the Indians melted away. Even Tanacharison, who had

With George Washington in the Wilderness

arrived for the council, departed with his Mingos. Washington was left with only a few Lenape Indians who agreed to stay and act as scouts.

Work progressed at Gist's until the evening of Friday, June 28, 1754, when Washington received reports that as many as sixteen hundred French and Indians were on the march and heading for Gist's Plantation. Washington called the officers together for a series of councils of war to consider the most prudent strategy, and it was unanimously decided that fortifying and making a stand at Gist's was impractical. It would take too much time and effort to construct strong defenses, and another disadvantage was that Gist's was accessible to the French via the Monongahela, which was only five miles away. They decided to return to Great Meadows where better defenses had already been prepared and where supplies and reinforcements would more quickly be received. Some officers even recommended withdrawing all the way to Will's Creek to await adequate reinforcements and artillery, but Washington decided they would continue strengthening the defenses at Great Meadows.

To add a measure of urgency, French deserters informed Washington that the French were expecting additional reinforcements, and worse, two English deserters informed the French of the strength and deployment of Washington's troops. There was no time to tarry, and everything useful that could be carried was taken from Gist's, as Washington led his men back over Chestnut ridge to Great Meadows and Fort Necessity.

With the departure of Washington's troops, Gist prepared to move his family east to relative safety, and those other homesteaders in Gist's community who had not already left the area departed with Gist and his family. Gist temporarily settled his family at Will's creek, before returning to Great Meadows.

During the last week of June 1754, a French army under the command of Captain Sieur Louis Coulon de Villiers (1710–1757) traveled by water up the Monongahela to Red Stone, where they disembarked on Sunday, June 30, 1754. Villers was the half-brother of Ensign Joseph Coulon de Jumonville, who was killed by Washington's force after the fight in the glen on Tuesday, May 28, 1754. It was unfortunate for young George Washington that it was Villiers who was leading the French troops. He was perhaps the most distinguished warrior in a family of talented military men, and the French referred to him as "Le Grand Villiers."[4] When Villiers learned of the death of his half-brother, he immediately requested and was granted command of the force that would

14. Surrender on the Fourth of July

avenge Jumonville's death and also drive the English out of French territory.

Villiers's force consisted of six hundred French and Canadian troops and about 150 Indians,[5] and on Tuesday, July 2, 1754, they reached Gist's Plantation. The French commander described it in his journal as "consisting of three houses surrounded by some pieces standing on end, and by some enclosures the interiors of which was found to be commanded by the neighboring heights."[6]

Gist's buildings appeared to be fortified, with a stockade of sorts surrounding them, and thinking the Virginia troops were barricaded within, Villiers ordered several volleys of musketry fired at the buildings. When there was no response, he advanced his troops and found the settlement deserted. As Villiers surveyed the abandoned and unfinished defenses at Gist's Plantation, Indian scouts brought in a Virginian who had deserted from Washington's force. The man told Villiers that Washington's troops had left Gist's settlement only two days previous. He said that when Washington learned of the French advance, he led his troops back to Great Meadows where they had previously begun building fortifications.

With a better knowledge of Washington's location, Villiers marched his men along the trail that Washington's troops had so laboriously hacked out over Chestnut ridge. It began to rain, and around noon of Tuesday, July 2, 1754, they arrived at the site of the skirmish where Jumonville had been killed the previous May. Villiers ordered his troops to bury the remains of the scalped and mutilated men, including his half-brother, and then they descended the mountain and camped a few miles from Great Meadows.

Early in the morning of Wednesday, July 3, 1754, the rain was falling steadily as Villiers cautiously led his troops forward. Almost immediately they encountered Washington's pickets who were screening Great Meadows. The veteran French and their Indian allies drove the pickets back, and about eleven o'clock in the morning, Villiers caught sight of Washington's tiny fort through the rain and mist. After forming up his men at the edge of the forest, Villiers, for some reason, ordered a volley fired in the direction of the English troops at the impossible range of about six hundred yards. Washington's troops responded with a fusillade from their swivel guns, but at that range, neither side scored any hits on their enemy.

The exchange of shots signaled the opening of hostilities. Anticipating a set-piece battle as fought in Europe, Washington formed his

With George Washington in the Wilderness

men up in straight lines and ordered them to stand firm and wait until they were ordered to fire when the enemy ranks closed within musket range. Villiers, however, was not a product of European battles but rather was a canny commander, schooled in forest warfare as fought on the frontier. As Washington's troops stood and waited for the French to advance and trade musket volleys across the meadow, Villiers ordered his men to swiftly deploy into the forest along the sides of the meadow. Within minutes, they enveloped Washington's compactly dressed ranks, and from the cover of the trees, began to pour a devastating flanking fire into the densely aligned English troop formations.

Stunned by the ferocious fire from the forest edge, Lieutenant Colonel George Muse, Washington's second-in-command, pulled his 2nd Division from the line without orders and took refuge in the trenches. The withdrawal of Muse's division exposed the South Carolina Independent Company to the galling French fire, and Washington had no choice but to order all of the troops to fall back to the protection of the fort and the trenches.

The rain was falling in torrents and the ground was a quagmire. Worse yet, the trenches were completely filled with water, making it

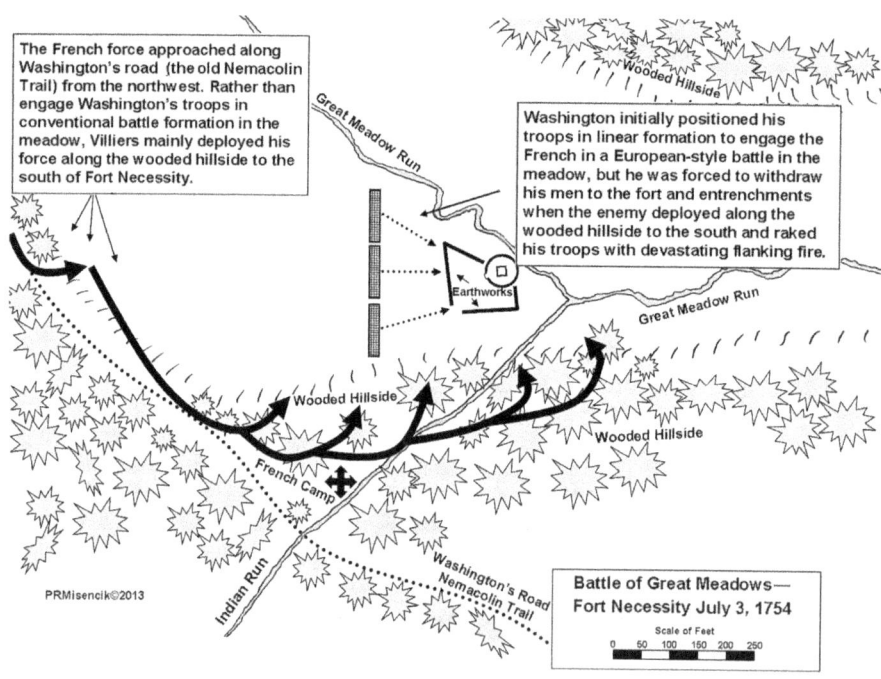

Battle of Great Meadows, July 3, 1754.

14. Surrender on the Fourth of July

almost impossible to keep cartridges dry or prevent muskets from fouling. Fortunately for Washington's troops, Villiers had no intention of launching an assault against the Fort Necessity positions. Instead, the French and Indians sniped at anything that moved, killing horses, cattle, and dogs along with the troops huddled in and around the tiny fort. Within a short time, every cow, horse, and dog had been killed.

The pouring rain began to render the muskets of Washington's troops unserviceable until only a desultory and sporadic English gunfire answered the steady French and Indian musketry from the woods. Being sheltered under the canopy of trees, the French and Indians found it somewhat easier to keeps their weapons serviceable. Reportedly, Christopher Gist also took part in the battle, but he did not record it in his journal or other writings.

As the afternoon wore on, it became ever more desperate for the English troops. The numbers of Washington's men killed and wounded were steadily rising, while the French did not appear to have suffered many losses at all. The uneven contest continued for over nine hours, and as dusk approached, Washington surveyed his troops and found that about a third of his men were casualties, either dead or wounded. He was concerned that with nightfall, the Indians would swarm over the defenses and massacre his surviving troops.

About eight o'clock in the evening, the French fire ceased, and a voice called out from the tree line that the French were willing to parley. Villiers had decided to give Washington a chance to surrender with a semblance of honor. Le Mercier, who was Villiers's spokesperson, offered Washington the opportunity to send two officers into the French camp to discuss the terms of surrender. Washington had only two officers who could read, write, and converse in French; they were Jacob Van Braam and the seriously wounded Ensign William La Peyronie.

In the French camp, the two were surprised when Villiers said that since France and England were not officially at war, he was willing to offer very generous terms. Washington and his troops would surrender their positions with full honors of war, and with flags flying and drums beating, they would be allowed to return home with all their personal effects. They would also be permitted to take their weapons and one swivel gun with them. Taking the swivel gun was in accordance with "the honors of war," where a defeated force was generally allowed to haul away at least one piece of artillery. Villiers added that Washington must accept the terms quickly, because five hundred more Indians were expected, and the French commander was concerned that once they arrived, he would not be able to control them and prevent a massacre if Washington delayed in accepting the terms of capitulation.

Van Braam presented two copies of the capitulation agreement to Washington, which they read in the pouring rain with the aid of flickering lanterns. Since La Peyronie was wounded, Van Braam did all of translating, and he relied mostly on his conversation with Villiers rather than on laboriously translating the written document. Washington signed the capitulation agreement, and a copy was returned to the French camp. However, there were a few sentences which Washington would later take great exception to. The translated capitulation agreement is as follows:

> Capitulation granted by Mons. De Villiers, Captain of infantry and commander of troops of his most Christian majesty, to those English troops actually in the fort of Necessity which was built on the lands of the King's dominions July the 3rd, at eight o'clock at night, 1754.
>
> As our intention had never been to trouble the peace and good harmony which reigns between the two friendly princes, but only to revenge the assassination which has been done on one of our officers, bearer of a summons, upon his party, as also to hinder any establishment on the lands of the dominions of the King, my master. Upon these considerations, we are willing to grant protection of favor, to all the English that are in the said fort, upon conditions hereafter mentioned
>
> Article 1
>
> We grant the English commander to retire with all garrisons, to return peaceably into his own country, and we promise to hinder his receiving any insult from us French, and to restrain as much as shall be in our power the Savages that are with us
>
> Article 2
>
> He shall be permitted to withdraw and to take with him whatever belongs to them except the artillery, which we reserve for ourselves
>
> Article 3
>
> We grant them the honors of war; they shall come out with drums beating, and with a small piece of cannon, wishing to show by this means that we treat them as friends
>
> Article 4
>
> As soon as these Articles are signed by both parties they shall take down the English flag
>
> Article 5
>
> Tomorrow at daybreak a detachment of French shall receive the surrender of the garrison and take possession of the aforesaid fort

14. Surrender on the Fourth of July

Article 6

Since the English have scarcely any horses or oxen left, they shall be allowed to hide their property, in order that they may return to seek for it after they shall have recovered their horses; for this purpose they shall be permitted to leave such number of troops as guards as they may think proper, under this condition that they give their word of honor that they will work on no establishment either in the surrounding country or beyond the Highlands during one year beginning from this day

Article 7

Since the English have in their power an officer and two cadets, and, in general all the prisoners whom they took when assassinated Sieur de Jumonville they now promise to send them with an escort to Fort Duquesne, situated on Belle River, and to secure the safe performance of this treaty article, as was as of the treaty, Messrs. Jacob Van Braam and Robert Stobo, both Captains shall be delivered to us as hostages until the arrival of our French and Canadians herein before mentioned. We on our part declare that we shall give them an escort to send back in safety the two officers who promise us our French in two months and a half at the latest.

Made out in duplicate on one of the posts of our blockhouse the same day and year as before.[7]

In effect, it stipulated that the French would hold Van Braam and Robert Stobo as hostages until all of the Frenchmen who were taken prisoner in the Jumonville skirmish were returned. That was a fairly customary provision, and the terms in themselves were as negotiated, and generous indeed for the circumstances; however, what they missed, which would later become an issue, were the phrases that read "only to revenge the assassination which has been done on one of our officers, bearer of a summons, upon his party" and "the prisoners whom they took when assassinated Sieur de Jumonville." In essence, by signing the document, Washington had admitted to the assassination of a diplomatic emissary. Notwithstanding the fact that the French words *L'assisin* and *l'assasinat* should have caught the attention of Washington at the time, Van Braam bore the brunt of the blame for not bringing it to the attention of Washington or his officers, and for sullying the honor of the future "father of his country."

The following day, ironically the fourth of July, Washington's troops buried their dead, and since they did not have a single horse remaining, they marched out of Great Meadows on the road back to Will's Creek. Many of the wounded could not make the long walk back, so with Villiers's approval, an ensign, a sergeant, and eleven soldiers remained with the wounded and any personal effects that could not be carried until wagons could be sent to recover them.

With George Washington in the Wilderness

Captain Robert Stobo and Captain Jacob Van Braam, in accordance with the terms of the capitulation, were to be held hostage until such time as the English released the twenty-one French prisoners who were captured in the fight with Jumonville and who were now in Williamsburg. It's not certain how Stobo and Van Braam were selected or whether they volunteered. Some credit the fact that they were not married and had no other families in Virginia as the reason they were chosen. Some anecdotal evidence suggests that Stobo volunteered, but Van Braam was assigned, perhaps because of his role in labeling Washington as an assassin.

Christopher Gist likely marched out with the retreating troops, although there is no documentary account of his participation in the battle or of his retreat to Will's Creek.

15

Fort Cumberland at Will's Creek

"An army is like a serpent, it moves on its belly."
—Frederick the Great

After defeating Washington at Great Meadows, Captain de Villiers burned Fort Necessity to the ground and then started back toward Fort Duquesne. On Friday, July 5, 1754, he stopped at Gist's settlement and ordered his troops to destroy all the entrenchments and other defensive works, and then they burned every one of the houses and outbuildings in the area. On Saturday, July 6, 1754, they burned the Ohio Company storehouse at Red Stone before returning to report to Contrecœur at Fort Duquesne.

The loss of Gist's settlement in addition to the crushing debts he already carried were catastrophes from which he never recovered. He hoped that the Ohio Company of Virginia would provide some recompense for his losses, but the Ohio Company had troubles of its own. The opening of hostilities essentially marked the end of the Ohio Company's tenuous hold on the land west of the mountains, and the commissioners were not inclined to throw good money after bad by paying for Gist's losses. Gist also petitioned the Virginia House of Burgesses for reparation, but in spite of his many meritorious accomplishments on behalf of Virginia, Gist's pleas for compensation was rejected. The burgesses apparently considered Gist's claim for recompense to be a private matter between him and the Ohio Company of Virginia.

After the destruction of Christopher Gist's settlement by de Villiers, the frontiersman moved to Will's Creek for a short time, and then relocated farther east to Opequon Creek somewhere between its confluence with the Potomac River and present Kernstown, Virginia, near Winchester. Historian Kenneth P. Bailey (1912–2000) wrote of the destruction of Gist's Plantation and his move to Opequon: "The razing

With George Washington in the Wilderness

of these structures and equipment left Gist in a desperate financial status from which he never fully recovered. His home had been broken up, never again completely to reunite. By this time his five children were adults. His wife had probably died at the Plantation although possibly not until after their new home was built at Opekon [sic] off the Potomac, in 1755."[1] As Bailey indicated, Sarah Howard Gist, Christopher's wife, died at some unknown time between late 1754 and 1757. A search of family ancestry records seems to indicate the later year, but nothing definitive has been found. However, a letter from William Fairfax to George Washington dated Saturday, July 17, 1757, states, "I am glad that Capt. Gist is likely to be employed in Indian Affairs to his advantage. His Daughter lives with Us and is kindly treated by M^{rs}. Fx and Miss Hannah—."[2] Although Fairfax does not mention the daughter by name, he was referring to Anne, or Nancy as she was commonly called, and she lived with the Fairfax family for at least two years. According to Gist family members, Anne was very attractive, and indeed was courted for a time by young George Washington who wrote her one or two love letters.[3]

Fairfax's letter is also a good indication that Gist's wife Sarah had by that time passed away, otherwise Anne would have likely continued to reside at home with her mother. Other than the reference mentioned above, there is no specific evidence regarding the location of Gist's home on Opequon Creek. Bailey only states in a footnote that "the Opekon [Opequon] Creek empties into the Potomac slightly west of the famous Philadelphia Wagon Road. Gist's home was not far from that of the Fairfaxes."[4] Opequon Creek extends about sixty-five miles from present Winchester north to the Potomac River, and though there is no documentary evidence regarding the exact location of Gist's home, local historical lore indicates it was closer to Winchester, Virginia.

After the battle of Great Meadows, George Washington rode back to Williamsburg to report to Lieutenant-Governor Dinwiddie. Since there were no defensive strongpoints standing in the path of a French invasion of the Middle Atlantic colonies, Washington recommended that a magazine and fortification be erected at Will's Creek. When Colonel James Innes of North Carolina finally arrived at Will's Creek, he assumed command and stripped the Ohio Company storehouse that was located there of supplies and matériel to construct a fort.

At the urging of his old friend Robert Dinwiddie, Colonel Innes raised a regiment of volunteers in North Carolina, and with the unexpected death of Colonel Joshua Fry, Innes was appointed by Dinwiddie

15. Fort Cumberland at Will's Creek

to take over command of the troops at Great Meadows with Washington as his second-in-command. However, Innes's march from North Carolina was so inept and mismanaged, that it took him took over a month to reach Winchester, Virginia, which was still about 115 miles short of Great Meadows. Innes had started with 350 troops, but desertions reduced his command to about 150 by the time he reached Winchester on Tuesday, July 9, 1754, five days after Washington had capitulated to de Villiers at Great Meadows. When Innes's men learned of Washington's defeat, most simply walked off without orders and returned home to North Carolina. Innes continued on to Will's Creek where he assumed command and began construction of the fort, which he initially named Fort Mount Pleasant. Maryland Governor Horatio Sharpe learned of Innes's ineptitude and summarily relieved him of his position, but Innes stayed on, giving himself the grandiose title of campmaster general.

During the remainder of 1754 and into 1755, Gist maintained his position as commissary for the Virginia Regiment, while at the same time, Dinwiddie appointed him as Indian agent. However, there was some ambiguity as to who he was actually working for. The Ohio Company of Virginia still existed as an entity, but in effect it existed in name only. Dinwiddie and the other company stakeholders tried to keep it viable, but the land they needed to keep the company afloat was firmly under control of the formidable French army.

In October 1754, George Washington resigned his military commission and returned to civilian life. He didn't resign as a result of his defeat at Big Meadows but rather because of a reorganization plan for the colonial forces that was implemented by Lieutenant-Governor Dinwiddie. To Washington, the most onerous aspect of Dinwiddie's plan was to reorganize the Virginia regiment into independent companies commanded by captains, and Washington would command one company. That meant Washington's rank would be reduced from colonel to captain, and even though it might be considered a regular army commission or "King's commission," it was too much for twenty-three-year-old George Washington's pride to accept. He replied to Dinwiddie, "I think, the disparity between the present offer of a Company, and my former rank, too great to expect any real satisfaction or enjoyment in a Corps, where I once did, not thought I had a right to, command."[5]

Washington was drawn to and indeed enamored by the military, so it's somewhat of a surprise that he tendered his resignation. To be honest, his military career had not gotten off to an auspicious start. By the

With George Washington in the Wilderness

time he was twenty-two years old, he had created an international incident by killing a French emissary, started a major war between France and England, and been mentioned with some derision by the king of England. When King George II learned that Washington wrote "I have heard the bullets whistle; and believe me there is something charming in the sound," the king, who actually commanded troops[6] at the Battle of Dettington in 1743, muttered, "He would not say so if he had been used to hear many."[7]

For an ordinary person, that would have been the end of their military career, but young Washington was no ordinary person, and not only would he return to military life, but he would do so on his own terms.

In February 1755, Washington learned that Major General Edward Braddock had arrived in Hampton, Virginia, with two line regiments, the 44th and the 48th. Braddock was the new commander-in-chief for the Thirteen Colonies, and the man who would lead the expedition against the French at Fort Duquesne.

In March 1755, Washington received a letter written by General Braddock's aide-de-camp Robert Orme (c. 1725–c. 1781–90). The letter mentioned Washington as "universally esteemed" and alluded to Washington's desire to accompany Braddock's expedition. Most likely, it was Dinwiddie who initiated the correspondence, because it would have been very much in character for Dinwiddie to attempt to place someone in a position close to Braddock who would reliably act in the interests of the lieutenant-governor. The letter read:

> Williamsburg, 2 March, 1755
>
> Sir: George Washington
>
> The General having been informed that you expressed some desire to make the campaign, but that you declined it upon some disagreeableness that you thought might arise from the regulations of command, has ordered me to acquaint you that he will be very glad of your company in his family, by which all inconveniences of that kind will be obviated.
>
> I shall think myself very happy to form an acquaintance with a person so universally esteemed, and shall use every opportunity of assuring you how much I am Sir, your most obedient servant.
>
> Robert Orme, aid de camp[8]

On Saturday, March 15, 1755, Washington replied to Orme, stating that he was honored to have been offered a place in Braddock's official family or headquarters staff. He admitted that he had declined Dinwiddie's offer of a captaincy but was willing to serve with Braddock as a volunteer in order to learn more of the military art under Braddock.

15. Fort Cumberland at Will's Creek

Washington, however, asked that he be allowed to join the expedition at Will's Creek rather than at Alexandria, and that he be released from duty as soon as the "grand affair is over," and also if there were any space of inaction long enough to permit Washington to periodically return to Virginia. Washington claimed his justification was the recent inheritance of his brother's Mount Vernon estate. "I hope it will not be taken amiss when it is considered how unprepared I am at present to quit a family, an estate scarcely settled, and in the utmost confusion."

Orme responded to Washington on Saturday, March 22, 1755:

"Sir: George Washington

The General orders me to give you his compliments, and to assure you his wishes are to make it agreeable to yourself and consistent with your affairs, and, therefore, he desires you will settle your business at home, and to join him at Wills Creek if more convenient to you; and whenever you find it necessary to return, he begs you will look upon yourself as entirely master, and judge what is proper to be done."[9]

Incredibly, twenty-three-year-old Washington had inveigled his way into General Braddock's official family on his own terms. As the historian Thomas Crocker wrote, "It was a remarkable achievement by a twenty-three-year-old colonial in dealing with a sixty-year-old major general with the disposition of an Iroquois."[10]

Christopher Gist, on the other hand, was unhappy about his uncertain financial future. For the past five years, he had been gainfully employed by the Ohio Company, and at that time he believed that he had achieved a secure future for himself and his family. But now, with the destruction of his settlement in the Monongahela Valley, he was in more perilous financial straits than ever before. Whatever he earned as the Ohio Company's agent to the Indians, and by delivering messages for Lieutenant-Governor Dinwiddie, the Ohio Company, and George Washington, it was barely enough for his family to survive on. Fortunately, Lieutenant-Governor Dinwiddie or possibly Washington recommended Gist to General Braddock, and Gist was offered the position as the general's guide[11] and chief of scouts,[12] which he eagerly accepted as a chance to earn extra money.

Gist hoped that Braddock's expedition against Fort Duquesne would reclaim the trans-Allegheny region and revive the Ohio Company land grant. More importantly, it would allow the resettlement Gist's Monongahela community, which he hoped would prove to be a lucrative venture. It certainly started out with much promise.

Dinwiddie told Braddock that four hundred southern Indian

With George Washington in the Wilderness

warriors would join the army at Will's Creek, and the Irish trader George Croghan signed on to lead them. Two other future notables signed on to join the expedition. They were the young wagon masters twenty-year-old Daniel Boone and nineteen-year-old Daniel Morgan. Daniel Boone would later become a heroic Kentucky frontiersman, and Daniel Morgan would gain fame during the Revolutionary War as the leader of Morgan's Riflemen, whose deadly accuracy with their long rifles cut the British to pieces at the Battle of Saratoga in 1777. Reportedly, Gist's two sons Nathaniel and Thomas also signed on as scouts, but Nathaniel was sent back down south to recruit Cherokee warriors for Braddock's expedition.

Apparently, Nathaniel recruited a sizable number of four hundred or five hundred Indian warriors, but on the return to join Braddock, Richard Pearis, who still bore animosity toward Nathaniel from their previous argument over land, dissuaded the Indians from continuing with Nathaniel. Pearis was respected by the southern Indians, and the warriors listened as the trader told them that Gist did not have a commission from Braddock to recruit warriors, and that Braddock would never send someone so young and unimportant on such a mission. The fact that Nathaniel had no written commission or even presents to give the Indians caused the warriors to believe Pearis, and they decided not to continue with Nathaniel. When Nathaniel returned without any Indians, Lieutenant-Governor Dinwiddie of Virginia was so angry that he offered a reward for Pearis's apprehension.[13]

Braddock's army marched out of Alexandria in segments between Friday, April 11, 1755, and Sunday, April 20, 1755, and General Braddock arrived at Frederick, Maryland, on Monday, April 21, 1755. There Braddock was joined by George Washington and met with Maryland Governor Sharpe and deputy Postmaster-General of the American colonies, Benjamin Franklin. Franklin was instrumental in securing wagons to transport Braddock's ammunition, equipage, and supplies, and he also offered Braddock some military advice:

> To be sure, sir, if you arrive well before Duquesne, with those fine troops, as well provided with artillery, that place not yet completely fortified, and as we hear with no strong garrison, can probably make but a short resistance. The only danger I apprehend of obstruction to your march is from ambuscades of Indians, who by constant practice are dexterous in laying and executing them; and the slender line, near four miles long, which your army must make may expose it to be attacked by surprise in its flanks and be cut like a thread into several pieces which from their distance cannot come up in time to support each other.[14]

15. Fort Cumberland at Will's Creek

Braddock took exception to Franklin's advice and commented condescendingly on the postmaster-general's obvious ignorance of military matters: "These savages may indeed, be a formidable enemy to your raw American militia, but upon the King's regular and disciplined troops, sir, it is impossible they should make any impression."[15] Less than two and one-half months later, Braddock would be made tragically aware of the prescience of Franklin's comments.

Braddock learned there was no road from Frederick, Maryland, to Will's Creek, so he was forced to turn back to the southwest toward Winchester, Virginia, and join the road being graded by Sir John St. Clair's (fl. 1755–1767) work parties.

Somewhere along the route of march, Christopher Gist joined up with Braddock's expedition. Most likely it was at Will's Creek, where Braddock's force prepared for the remaining 105 or so mile march against Fort Duquesne.

Braddock reached Will's Creek on Saturday, May 10, 1755, and after surveying what Colonel Innes called Fort Mount Pleasant, which was still under construction, the general renamed it Fort Cumberland. That was to honor Prince William Augustus, Duke of Cumberland (1721–1765), the third and youngest son of King George II. General Braddock must have been somewhat impressed by Innes's fort, because he named Innes "Governor of Fort Cumberland" and tasked Innes with commanding the reserve force at the fort during Braddock's expedition.

By Thursday, May 15, 1755, Braddock had expended so much money on hiring men, renting wagons, and purchasing supplies that he had seriously depleted his war chest. Realizing he would need to replenish his purse, he ordered young George Washington to ride as speedily as possible to Hampton, Virginia, to obtain £4,000 from the army's agent there. Washington made the four-hundred-mile round trip in twelve days.

A good portion of Braddock's war chest had been given to Thomas Cresap who was contracted to supply the commissary with food for the expedition. The barrels of meat and other foodstuffs were obtained from the Cresap storehouse on Conococheague Creek, which was being administered by Cresap's son Daniel. However, later during the expedition, it was discovered that Cresap had not provided anywhere near the contracted amount of provisions, and worse yet, the meat barrels contained spoiled meat that had to be destroyed. That caused a serious food shortage, and Braddock was forced to send precious horse-drawn wagons back to Winchester and Conococheague to obtain beef and flour.

With George Washington in the Wilderness

Because of the Cresaps' dereliction, Braddock sent troops to arrest them, but the rascally frontier trader and his son had already fled from the general's reach.

The lack of provisions weighed heavily on Braddock, who realized that it would be impossible to live off the land as would be the case of an army marching through an area populated with farms and cities. In an attempt to procure provisions, he encouraged farmers from miles around to bring their produce to Will's Creek and sell them to the army. Unfortunately, it was too early in the season for harvested crops, and even more of a problem was the fact that Fort Cumberland was a remote wilderness outpost with few farms in the area. Some of Braddock's picket patrols began to forage on their own and either bought or otherwise confiscated produce from the scattered homesteads. Some enterprising troopers began to intercept the few farmers who were bringing food to the fort, which they purchased cheaply or simply confiscated, and then resold to Braddock's commissary for their own profit. When Braddock learned of this practice, he issued an order that made it a crime punishable by death.[16]

Lieutenant-Governor Dinwiddie had promised Braddock that four hundred southern Indian warriors would be waiting to join the expedition at Will's Creek, but when the general arrived, the Indians were nowhere to be seen. Instead, there were about a hundred Indian men, women, and children who had come to trade at the Ohio Company storehouse but had no intention of accompanying the expedition. A day or so later, George Croghan arrived with about fifty Pennsylvania warriors, and when Braddock asked Croghan where the rest of Dinwiddie's promised Indians were, Croghan simply answered that he didn't know anything about Dinwiddie's Indians.

In addition to promising Braddock four hundred Cherokee warriors, Lieutenant-Governor Dinwiddie also promised that five hundred head of cattle and other supplies would be delivered to the fort. Like the four hundred Indians, the promised beef did not materialize. Those unfulfilled promises on the part of the Virginia lieutenant-governor caused Braddock to consider cancelling the entire expedition.

Fortunately, on Tuesday, May 20, 1755, a group of Quakers arrived at Will's Creek with several wagons loaded with flour, food, cheese, meat, and other provisions. No sooner had the Quakers brought in their supplies, than another eighty wagons full of provisions arrived. The much-needed supplies were all due to Benjamin Franklin's lobbying of the Pennsylvania Assembly. That wasn't all; in the ensuing days, other

15. Fort Cumberland at Will's Creek

wagon loads of food and supplies arrived in camp, mostly due to Franklin's tireless efforts.

For the troops at Will's Creek, the Indian families who were there to trade became a source of great interest to Braddock's soldiers. At first, the soldiers were instructed not to have any communication with the Indians, lest they cause some affront to the natives. The men generally followed those orders, until one of the troops learned that during Indian dances, it was the custom of the Indian women to dance with any man she fancied and then sleep with him. After that, she would return to her husband, who apparently was unfazed by his wife's actions.

Many of the soldiers offered extra rations to entice the women to their tents, and even Braddock's officers took part in the curious custom. When the general learned what was occurring, he attempted to put a stop to it by prohibiting Indian women from entering the army's campsite. That merely caused the soldiers to become more resourceful in meeting and enjoying the company of the Indian women.

Braddock held two councils with the Indians, during which he presented gifts and fed the Indians one of the oxen. He harangued them about the perfidy of the French and told them that it was in the Indians' best interests to support the English against the French. Braddock told the Indians to send their families back to Pennsylvania so that the warriors would be unencumbered in taking up the hatchet against the French. As was the custom of the Indians, they nodded in agreement, and proclaimed their eternal friendship and allegiance to the English, not wanting to insult or anger Braddock who was hosting the councils, feeding them and presenting them with gifts.

Unfortunately, the following day, all but eight of the Indians had vanished into the forest, and none of them returned. The half-king Scarouady (fl. 1750–1757) was one of those who remained. Scarouady[17] was an Oneida of the Iroquois Confederacy, and like Tanacharison who died the previous October, he represented the Iroquois Council in providing oversight of the Ohio Indians. Scarouady was sympathetic to the English but considered Braddock a "bad man." He complained that Braddock was full of pride and arrogance, did not listen to the Indians, and looked upon the Indians as little more than dogs. According to Scarouady, Braddock told the Indians that when the French were defeated, no savage should inherit the land, and only the English would inhabit it. Furthermore, Braddock said that any Indians who did not come into camp and declare themselves allies of the English would be considered enemies. With that sort of message, it's surprising that even the eight warriors remained with Braddock's expedition.

One of the first things Braddock did after arriving at Will's Creek was to appoint George Washington as his aide-de-camp. Washington wrote his brother John Washington (1736–1787) regarding his new duties: "The Gen'l had appointed me one of his Aide de Camps, in which Character I shall serve this Campaigne, agreeably enough, as I am thereby freed from all commands but his, and give Orders to all, which must be implicitly obeyed."[18]

While the army was preparing to move out of their encampment at Will's Creek, the soldiers were becoming increasingly nervous. Indian scouts spying for the French were seen in the vicinity, and the outlying pickets were fearful of an attack at any minute. Relations between Braddock's troops and the small party of Indians under Scarouady suffered a setback on Friday, May 23, 1755, when a party of Indians were returning to Will's Creek after a scouting mission and were fired on by English troops who thought they were the enemy. Fortunately, at that time, there were no casualties.

16

March to the Monongahela

"If my soldiers were to begin to think, not one of them would remain in the army."
—Frederick the Great

The first contingent of Braddock's army marched from Fort Cumberland on Thursday, May 29, 1755, and the going was incredibly arduous. They were the engineers and laborers under Sir John St. Clair whose job it was to make the road passable for the wagons and artillery. Almost from the very beginning, wagons careened off the rocky hillsides and were smashed to pieces, while others were damaged and had to be repaired. St. Clair's engineers worked tirelessly on the road construction while the rest of the troops pushed and pulled the heavy equipment over the road that was barely wide enough for the wagons. In that fashion they inched along, seldom progressing as much as six miles in eight hours, but often considerably less.

By Friday, June 6, 1755, nine days after starting out, St. Clair's advance work parties were a mere twenty-four miles from Fort Cumberland, and the next day, Saturday, June 7, 1755, the main body of Braddock's army set out to begin the 116-mile trek from Will's Creek to Fort Duquesne. They marched out in the midst of a fierce storm with lightning and thunder echoing through the mountains, and the road so laboriously graded by St. Clair's work parties became a quagmire. Braddock had arranged for Royal Navy officer Lieutenant Charles Spendlow[1] and six sailors to accompany his expedition. It was thought that the sailors' expertise with rigging block and tackle would facilitate hoisting the wagons and artillery over the steepest hills. It was a good idea, because without them, more wagons and artillery would likely have been lost on the treacherous mountain road. Braddock himself marched out from Fort Cumberland with the rest of his troops on Tuesday, June 10, 1755.

With George Washington in the Wilderness

On Tuesday, June 17, 1755, frustrated by the slow pace of his army and concerned that the army's provisions would be exhausted before reaching Fort Duquesne, Braddock halted his army at Little Meadows, twenty miles from Will's Creek. There he told his officers that he decided to split his force and create a flying column of the best troops who would move rapidly ahead unencumbered by the heaviest wagons and siege artillery. Colonel Sir Peter Halkett's 44th Regiment would be in the advance column, while Colonel Thomas Dunbar would command the reserves following behind.

As the army marched from Will's Creek, there was frequent evidence of hostile French Indians, but once across the Great Crossing the encounters increased and turned more deadly. Any individual who strayed a short distance from the main group or even small groups of men or work parties were especially vulnerable and frequently attacked. During one stop by the flying column about seven miles past the Great Crossing, four men were killed and scalped in the vicinity of the camp. Because of that, the soldiers named the campsite "Scalping Camp." After passing the scene of Washington's defeat at Great Meadows the previous July, encounters with enemy Indians and French troops and militia increased, and in a brief skirmish one French-allied Indian was killed.

On Friday, June 27, 1755, the flying column crossed the crest of Chestnut Ridge and descended toward the Monongahela valley, making camp at the burnt-out ruins of Christopher Gist's plantation. It was nine days less than a full year since Washington had signed the capitulation document on July 3, 1754, which surrendered Fort Necessity to Captain Sieur Louis Coulon de Villiers. What is noteworthy of the date is that once Washington, and indeed Christopher Gist, as well as any other troops that may have participated in the Battle of Great Meadows crossed Chestnut Ridge, they were in violation of the surrender terms to which they pledged their word of honor. One clause of those terms specified that "under this condition that they give their word of honor that they will work on no establishment either in the surrounding country or beyond the Highlands during one year beginning from this day." Interestingly, this historical fact seems to be studiously ignored by Washington historians.

On Thursday, July 3, 1755, Braddock ordered George Croghan to send out some of his Indians to reconnoiter Fort Duquesne, but despite threats and bribes, the Indians flatly refused. The next day, on Friday, July 4, 1755, Croghan was able to convince two Indians to scout the French fort, but after their earlier reticence to take on the mission,

16. March to the Monongahela

the general was concerned they might be less than diligent. As a backup, Christopher Gist was engaged to also conduct a reconnaissance of Fort Duquesne and to bring back his independent assessment.

Braddock and the advance army were now less that twenty miles from Fort Duquesne, and the number of attacks on the army increased the closer they got. On Sunday, July 6, 1755, Indians attacked the rear of the column and killed and scalped a man and a camp follower. They wounded two men and were in the process of scalping one of them when the men were rescued by the rear guard. Stragglers were not the only ones who were in danger. Indians would rush out of the thick forest on either side of the column and fire point blank or even tomahawk men who were marching with the main group.

Understandably, all of the troops were on edge as they peered into the depths of the forbidding forest. A couple hours after the previous Indian attack, the soldiers spotted some French Indians lurking in the woods and immediately opened fire on them. A few of the remaining Indians who still accompanied Braddock rushed up to help and were met with a volley from the English troops. One of Indians who was killed by the "friendly fire" was *Monacatuca*, the son of the Oneida half-king Scarouady. Braddock offered Scarouady condolences as well as presents and ordered a full military funeral for Monacatuca. Scarouady was heart-broken and said that if his son had been killed in battle, it would have been one thing, but to lose him to his own allies was most regrettable.

On Saturday, July 6, 1755, the Indian scouts who had been sent out a couple days earlier returned saying they had seen a few soldiers around the fort, and a few soldiers and Indians between the fort and Braddock's column. They also brought in the scalp of a young French militia man who was hunting about a mile from the fort.

A few hours later, Christopher Gist returned from his scouting mission to Fort Duquesne, and his report was similar to that of the Indian scouts. The only difference was that Gist observed some smoke between Braddock's column and the French fort, but when he tried to get nearer to the fort, he was discovered by some Indians who chased and very nearly captured him. For his efforts, Braddock ordered that Gist be formally recognized for his scouting trip and he awarded Gist 50 thirty-six shilling pieces. The entry in the notes of the expedition read: "This is to certify that Mr. Christopher Gist executed the office of head Guide with great Sobriety Prudence & Fidelity to which Office he was appointed by Genl Braddock the 27th of May 1755. And I do farther certify that he was sent to bring intelligence from the French Fort which service he performed with great Risk being for a long time pursued. Upon his return the Genl being well satisfied with his behavior ordered Mr. Shirley the Secretary to pay him his 50 thirty-six Shilling Pieces."[2]

The very next day, Monday, July 7, 1755, Gist was taken to task for a route he recommended. They were eight miles from Fort Duquesne, and Gist and the other guides were summoned to advise on the best places to ford Turtle Creek. Apparently, Gist recommended a route that proved impossible for the wagons and artillery, so the army was forced to camp before retracing its course and following a more suitable route. As a result, that night's camp was designated "Blunder Camp."

On Tuesday, July 8, 1755, the army camped at present East McKeesport, Pennsylvania, which was less than two miles from the Monongahela River. At two o'clock in the morning of Wednesday, July 9, 1755, the first units of the army marched east to ford the Monongahela River. The plan was to march about two miles up the west side of the Monongahela past the mouth of Turtle Creek to another ford where they would cross back to the east side of the river. The reason for the double crossing was to avoid the bluffs and narrow path along the forest on the east side of the river, which were more conducive for an ambush. When Braddock's army recrossed the Monongahela, they were about ten miles from Fort Duquesne.

The lead elements of the army arrived at the second crossing about eight o'clock in the morning, and scouts reported seeing some Indians on the other side of the river, which was about three hundred yards across. To cover the crossing, two field cannon were unlimbered and positioned to rake the far bank, then the lead companies began crossing the knee-deep ford.

17

Death in the Forest

"Who would have thought?"
—General Edward Braddock

Once across the Monongahela, the army formed up and began to advance toward Fort Duquesne. Two hundred yards from the river, they passed the abandoned home and shop of John Fraser where Washington and Gist stopped during their trek to and from Fort Le Bœuf a year and a half prior.

By early afternoon of Wednesday, July 9, 1755, Braddock's entire flying column was safely across the river. Suspecting that the enemy was observing from the depths of the forest, Braddock had marched his army across the shallow ford with regimental flags flying, fifes playing, and drums beating. It was meant to awe the French and particularly the Indians with the might of the British empire, and in truth, nothing like it had ever been seen before in the American wilderness.

To the officers, the crossing was perhaps the most likely place for a French and Indian ambush, and when that did not materialize, there was a collective sigh of relief. Safely across the ford, the British were confident of a quick and easy victory. In fact, now that they were a mere seven miles from Fort Duquesne, Braddock and his officers expected to hear the sound of the French blowing up their fort before retreating up the Allegheny River toward Canada.

To be sure, the French commander, Sieur de Contrecœur, was considering that very option. His scouts had been observing Braddock's army almost from the time they left Will's Creek, and he was well aware of the lopsided odds he faced. The French commander knew that Braddock's lead force outnumbered the French and Indians at Fort Duquesne by almost two and one-half to one, and the English general's ten pieces of artillery were far superior to the few four- and six-pounder cannon at Fort Duquesne. Contrecœur's garrison consisted of about three hundred French regulars and militia and perhaps six hundred Indian allies who were camped outside the fort. The French commander was well aware that Indians depended on stealth and fighting from cover and had little temperament to fight a pitched battle against massed ranks supported by artillery. He knew that when Braddock arrived to invest the fort, the Indians would likely melt away into the forest.

Rather than wait for the inevitable, two officers, Captain Daniel Liénard de Beaujeu (1711–1755), who was sent to replace Contrecœur but had not yet taken command of the fort, along with Captain Jean Dumas (1721–1794), decided to gather a force of volunteers and launch a preemptive strike against the English while they were still somewhat vulnerable in their line of march. At first, the French Indians were reluctant to attack the large and powerful British army, but Beaujeu, who dressed in Indian garb and painted his face in the Indian fashion, was able to convince them to follow him. In addition to the four to six hundred Indians who would accompany Beaujeu and Dumas, around one hundred French regulars and about 150 French militia joined in. That was a large war party by frontier standards, but still nowhere near equal to the formidable 2,100 troops in Braddock's force.

A short distance beyond the river crossing, the lead elements of Braddock's column spotted what appeared to be a large body of men running toward them. The opposing sides spotted each other at about the same instant, and Beaujeu swiftly signaled his men to rush forward along the forest edge on both sides of the red-coated column. Gage's light infantry were in the forefront, and when they spotted the approaching enemy, Gage calmly formed his infantry in line of battle and fired several volleys at the attackers. In one of the initial volleys, the French leader Beaujeu was killed by a musket ball to the head, but Dumas immediately took charge and pressed forward with the attack.

Braddock's two six-pounder cannon, loaded with case shot,[1] were unlimbered and fired at the enemy who continued to shift farther along the flanks of Braddock's column and kept up a sustained fusillade of musketry into the massed flanks of the British troops. The lead elements of the army began to fall back but collided with the main body who were attempting to move forward, and within minutes the entire column was in chaos.

The battle raged for several hours during which time twenty-six of the eighty-six officers in Braddock's force were killed, and another thirty-seven officers were wounded, many of whom would not survive. Christopher Gist was near when Colonel Peter Halkett and his son James were shot down. An eyewitness wrote,

17. Death in the Forest

This savage levelled his piece at Sir Peter as he rode about, which one Capt. Ghist [sic], a captain of Militia and huntsman perceiving who had just discharged his musket, he made haste to reload, in order to prevent the danger with which Sir Peter was threatened, but could not make much dispatch but that the Indian had shot Sir Peter down, before he was in readiness to oppose him. Ghist however immediately after step'd up and blew out the miscreant's brains; Sir Peter's servant [actually, it was his son James, who was a subaltern in the regiment] went up to his master's body to see if he was not mortally wounded, or if dead, to take care that the body was decently disposed of, but the poor fellow in that Instant was shot and fell upon his master.[2]

Braddock had several horses shot out from under him until finally he was shot from the saddle. With Braddock down, George Washington rallied the troops, organized a fighting withdrawal, and took charge of the rear guard covering the army's retreat. That earned him recognition as "Hero of the Monongahela" and contributed to his fame as an American warrior.

The French and Indians did not pursue the fleeing troops en masse, but small parties of Indians followed the retreating army and picked off stragglers and the burial parties who stopped to bury those who died along the way.

Braddock died from his wounds on Sunday, July 13, 1755, and his last words were, "Who would have thought?" He was buried at midnight in the middle of the trail, and the entire army marched over his grave so that the footprints of men, horses, and wagon wheels would obliterate every trace. That was done so the Indians could not find the grave and take the general's scalp or otherwise desecrate his body.

There does not appear to be any other information regarding Gist's activities immediately before or during the battle. As Braddock's guide, one might wonder what his duties might have been, particularly with regard to scouting ahead and providing some warning of the French and Indian attack. In Gist's favor is the fact that of all the recriminations that came to light as a result of the crushing defeat, no one blamed Gist personally. Thomas Gage, who along with his light infantry were in the lead of the column, commented that there had been a lack of guide or scouts to provide an adequate warning. Colonel Thomas Dunbar made a similar comment, without mentioning any names specifically, but it must be remembered that he was with the rear column a day or so behind Braddock's force.

Remarkably, Gist, who was in the thick of the fighting during the battle and as part of Washington's rear guard, survived unscathed. That was not the case with the large percentage of Braddock's force. As

With George Washington in the Wilderness

previously mentioned, almost three-quarters of Braddock's eighty-six officers were casualties, and of the approximately 2,100 English troops in the battle, 456 were killed outright and 422 were wounded, many of whom later died. Fifty women camp-followers were with Braddock's column and only four survived. By comparison, eight French troops were killed and four were wounded, while the Indians lost fifteen killed and twelve wounded. It was a lopsided victory for the French and Indians, who had no field artillery, and numbered less than half of Braddock's force.

The battered survivors finally reached Fort Cumberland at Will's Creek on Wednesday, July 16, 1755, one week after the battle. The fort for the most part became a field hospital where the surgeons tried to save those who were still alive. Tragically, it was found that many of the musket balls removed from wounded soldiers were the larger caliber type commonly used in British Brown Bess muskets. Those wounds were almost certainly caused by wild friendly fire volleys from panicked English troops. Washington sent a dispatch to Dinwiddie, dated Friday, July 18, 1755, and in it the young Virginian was brutal in his assessment of Braddock's regulars. He wrote,

> Our numbers consisted of abt. 1300 well arm'd Men, chiefly Regular's, who were immediately struck with such a deadly Panick, that nothing but confusion and disobedience of order's prevail'd amongst them: The Officer's in gen'l behav'd with incomparable bravery, for which they greatly suffer'd, there being near 60 kill'd and wound'd. A large proportion, out of the number we had! The Virginian Companies behav'd like Men and died like Soldiers; for I believe out of the 3 Companys that were there that day, scarce 30 were left alive.... In short the dastardly behaviour of the English Soldier's expos'd all those who were inclin'd to do their duty to almost certain Death; and at length, in despight of every effort to the contrary, broke and run as Sheep before the Hounds, leav'g the Artillery, Ammunition, Provisions, and, every individual thing we had with us a prey to the Enemy; and when we endeavour'd to rally them in hopes of regaining our invaluable loss, it was with as much success as if we had attempted to have stop'd the wild Bears of the Mountains.[3]

18

Captain of Scouts and Indian Agent

"A man's dignity can never be taken away, unless it is surrendered."

—Anonymous

After Braddock's disastrous defeat at the Monongahela, it was apparent to Gist that the Ohio Company venture in the trans-Allegheny region was in serious jeopardy, and with it Gist's very livelihood. To Gist, it was likely the British government would sign another treaty with France recognizing their right to the land west of the Alleghenies as they did in three previous treaties. If that were the case, the Ohio Company venture was dead and buried.

Gist was still burdened by his crushing £10,000 debt to the British Fur Company as a result of the loss of his warehouse in 1732, and now the destruction of his home and equipment in the Monongahela valley added to his financial woes. As a result, Gist was eager to take on any job that would provide an income. Fortunately, his friendship with George Washington resulted in his obtaining a commission from Lieutenant-Governor Dinwiddie as Captain of the Company of Scouts.

Dinwiddie commissioned Washington as colonel and appointed him commander of the Virginia Regiment. The majority of militia companies were infantrymen, but the regiment also contained one company of mounted troops and the company of scouts, which was commanded by Gist. In addition, Washington was able to obtain a lieutenant's commission for Nathaniel Gist, who would serve as a scout in his father's company.

In the Virginia regiment, a colonel's pay was ten shillings (10s) or one-half pound per day, and a private received one shilling (1s) per day. As officers, Christopher and Nathaniel were at the higher end of the scale, which was a livable wage. In addition, Gist was given the task of recruiting men for his company, but Washington specified which men were suitable. Washington told Gist that the men must be frontiersmen between the ages of sixteen and fifty-four, over five feet four inches tall, in good health, and capable of strenuous and difficult work. Gist was promised two *pistoles* for every new recruit he obtained. A pistole was a Spanish coin in common usage that was valued at approximately sixteen shillings, or a little more than three-quarters of a British pound sterling (£).[1] Gist was also allowed a fund to support the recruits until they were incorporated into the regiment.

In spite of Washington's instructions regarding the minimum qualifications for new recruits, Gist wasn't particularly scrupulous about following Washington's guidelines, and the majority of recruits appear to be anyone who could be persuaded to join.[2] Indeed, Gist recruited a substantial number, and asked for more money to continue his recruiting. On Monday, November 24, 1755, Gist wrote to Washington from Pennsylvania: "I have Sent twenty of My Soldiers to York Town [present York, Pennsylvania,] who are all in good Sperritts there and Two I now send to them. to Morrow I Shall follow them. I have been forced to Borrow Money; and if Could have had Money enough I believe I should have had 50 Men by this Time, I hope I Shall be properly Supply'd with Cash to Answer what I have done and if We want Men I think I Can Soon get them."[3]

The reason Gist was short of money was because he was paying the men their recruitment bonus out of his own pocket until he was later reimbursed by the regiment. The recruitment bonus was usually one shilling for each man who joined the military. When he received Gist's message, Washington was concerned that Gist was falling further behind in his finances. In a letter to Adam Stephen, dated Tuesday, May 18, 1756, Washington wrote: "Your ordering Captain Gist an hundred pounds: he will fall greatly short when his accompts [accounts] are settled; and I believe is very unable to pay the Balances."[4]

Apparently, Washington was correct. In a letter to Dinwiddie, Washington wrote: "Captain Gist has some Accompts [accounts] against the Country for necessary services. I doubt not your Honor will consider the justice of them and assist the poor man in the affair, as he is put to great inconvenience for want of money, has been obliged to advance his own, as far as it would go, and people to whom he owes balances upon that account are daily threatening him with suits."[5]

Recruiting soldiers was one thing but keeping them in the military was quite another. Some signed on only for the bonus while

18. Captain of Scouts and Indian Agent

others found army life not to their liking, and in both cases, they simply deserted. Since most of the deserters were shielded by friends and relatives, the army resorted to offering rewards for their recapture, and even took to having announcements and descriptions of deserters read during church services. Interestingly, several recaptured Maryland men who deserted from Gist's company told Governor Sharpe that they were detained beyond the end of their enlistment. Washington queried Gist, who said he told the men they would be "discharged at the end of the war or expedition, which might possibly be ended in 6 or 8 months."[6] Washington told Sharpe to return the men, and if it appeared they were telling the truth, Gist's conduct would be investigated. However, there are no indications that an investigation was ever initiated.

Through the end of 1757, the Virginia Regiment was involved in numerous skirmishes with Indians along the frontier. One such fight about eighteen miles from Winchester resulted in a detachment under George Mercer (1733–1784) losing nearly a third of its men.[7] Though Gist appears to have been involved in some of the skirmishes, his primary duties involved recruiting and carrying messages for Washington. In fact, Gist made three trips delivering messages between Winchester and Williamsburg between Wednesday, April 20 and Monday, June 6, 1757.

Through 1757, Gist was stationed variously at Fort Loudoun at Winchester, Fort Maidstone,[8] across the Potomac River from present Williamsport, Maryland, and occasionally at Fort Cumberland. Fort Maidstone was associated with the Conococheague storehouse across the river.

In May of 1757, Gist voluntarily took a reduction in rank from captain to lieutenant. The reason was that the regiment was becoming top-heavy, from attrition, desertions, and lack of recruits. As a result, the companies were much smaller than usual, so a decision was made to reduce the number of companies from sixteen to ten, which would bring those ten companies up to normal strength. The six extra captains were asked to accept demotion to lieutenant or resign. Only Christopher Gist agreed to accept demotion with the stipulation that his seniority was second only to Captain John McNeil (fl. 1737–c. 1765), who was first commissioned in 1754.

If his terms were not accepted, it's difficult to imagine that Gist would have resigned. His income as an army officer was all he had, and if he left the military, he would have also jeopardized his personal relationships with Washington, Dinwiddie, and William Fairfax.

With George Washington in the Wilderness

He needn't have worried, because on July 25, 1757, Gist was appointed to the position of Deputy Superintendent of Indian Affairs in the Southern Department. Prior to that time, Indian affairs were conducted by the governors of the individual colonies. That was until Edmund Atkin (1707–1761), a Charleston, South Carolina, merchant and planter, who also had been a member of the provincial council. In 1755, he traveled to England, and at the request of the Board of Trade, wrote a treatise outlining his plan to reorganize colonial Indian affairs.

Rather than leaving it up to the individual colonial governors, Atkin recommended a coordinated system of managing Indian affairs by dividing the colonies into the northern department and the southern department. The two departments would conform to the newly created military districts. The respective military commanders would have overall control of Indian affairs within their districts, but they would depend on the superintendents for the actual administration.

Atkin's plan included giving the superintendents the authority to negotiate treaties and to cultivate friendships with the Indians, and work to prevent them from forming an allegiance with the French, and also to induce the Indians to trade only with English traders. To prevent friction between the Indians and colonists, the Indians would be encouraged to refrain from entering British towns without consent of the superintendent, and in return the Superintendent would agree to build fortified trading posts that were convenient to the Indians. The posts would have blacksmiths and gunsmiths to repair the Indians' weapons and hunting equipment, and more importantly, would contain a plentiful supply of moderately priced trade goods.

Atkin apparently impressed the right people, particularly those in the Board of Trade, and in 1756, he was appointed Superintendent of Indian Affairs in the Southern Department. Sir William Johnson was appointed Superintendent in the Northern Department.

Atkin returned first to New York in October 1756, and after a lengthy stay, traveled to Williamsburg where he arrived and presented his credentials to Lieutenant-Governor Dinwiddie. Dinwiddie accepted Adkin's appointment but argued that Virginia was a long way from South Carolina and it was Virginia's frontier that was presently being fought over. He said that Colonel Washington had recommended that a deputy superintendent remain in the Virginia Colony to deal with the Indians there. Washington's message to Dinwiddie, dated Monday, May 30, 1757, read in part, "I therefore beg leave to recommend (not from an inclination to *dictate;* much less from a disposition to intermeddle,

18. Captain of Scouts and Indian Agent

but with due submission) that some person of good Sense and probity, with a tolerable share of the knowledge of their customs, be appointed to transact, under your Honors direction, or *that* of the Southern agent, the Indian Affairs of this Colony, of every kind whatever."[9]

The idea appealed to Atkin who in turn asked if Dinwiddie had a recommendation, and the Virginia lieutenant-governor referenced another paragraph from Washington's letter: "I wou'd beg leave to recommend Mr. Gist as the most proper person I am acquainted with to conduct the Business. He knows but little of their language it is true, but is well acquainted with their manners and customs; especially of the Southern Indians. And for his honesty and zeal I think I dare vouch."[10]

To bolster his recommendation, Washington also wrote to John Robinson, Speaker of the Virginia House of Burgesses, who also was in communication with Atkin. Washington wrote, "I know of no person so well qualified for an undertaking of this sort as the bearer, Captain Gist. He has had extensive dealings with the Indians, is in great esteem among them, well acquainted with their manners and customs, is indefatigable and patient, most excellent qualities indeed where Indians are concerned. And for his capacity, honesty, and zeal, I dare not venture to engage."[11]

Gist also had other supporters, among whom was William Fairfax, and other influential Virginians, most of whom had been shareholders in the Ohio Company. Indeed, with Dinwiddie's personal experience with Gist, and Washington's recommendation, Dinwiddie was confident that Gist could be relied on to look out for Virginia interests should Atkin tend to promote those of South Carolina. In essence, Virginia could handle its Indian affairs as it saw fit regardless of Atkin's position and authority. In actuality, Gist really was the best choice, since he was very knowledgeable about the southern Indians and the Indians of the Ohio territory, having traveled, lived, and worked among them. Atkin was certainly pleased with the choice of Gist as his deputy, no doubt believing that Atkin would formulate the strategic plans, make the decisions, and take the credit, while Gist did the work. Virginia would also be responsible for Gist's salary.

That June, Atkin decided to offer the job to Gist, but Dinwiddie was concerned about the impact of Gist's salary to the colony. Since Gist received a captain's pay of ten shillings a day (10s), Dinwiddie thought he should be paid no more than the same amount. Gist accepted the position on Wednesday, July 25, 1757, and his per diem salary was set at ten shillings Sterling, or in Virginia currency, twelve shillings six pence.

With George Washington in the Wilderness

When news of Gist's appointment was made public, Richard Pearis, whose animosity for Nathaniel now carried over to the entire Gist family, objected. He claimed that the Cherokee regarded him as the legitimate manager of Indian affairs for England and claimed as proof that he had led Indian raiding parties against the French and had received a captain's commission from Maryland Governor Sharpe. Dinwiddie considered Pearis a scoundrel because of his interference in recruiting Indians for Braddock in 1755, and both he and Atkin criticized Maryland Governor Sharpe for validating Pearis. Sharpe did not hold Gist in high regard, and the rebukes from Dinwiddie and Atkin created additional friction between Governor Sharpe and Christopher Gist.

Gist resigned from the Virginia Regiment on the day he took office as deputy superintendent. His position as deputy superintendent would not be confirmed by the Virginia Council until October, but he immediately immersed himself in the job. His first duty was to settle the accounts for Indian gifts that were purchased by Washington, Adam Stephen, and other officers in the Virginia Regiment. In September 1757, Atkin and Gist, along with an interpreter, left Winchester to visit the southern Indians in order to recruit warriors for the Virginia Regiment.

Since Winchester was the major rendezvous point for the recruited Indians, Dinwiddie ordered more goods to be purchased and sent there for the Indian service. In addition, he hired an interpreter to remain in Winchester permanently to facilitate communications with the Indians. To avoid friction with the white inhabitants of Winchester, Dinwiddie strongly advised Gist to keep the Indians out of town and to ensure that they were not given whiskey or other intoxicating spirits. Gist had been given 240 pounds to purchase goods and supplies for the Indians, and Dinwiddie ordered Gist to regularly furnish an exact accounting of how the money was spent.

Gist took exception to Dinwiddie's demands for precise accounting, and he complained to Washington about Dinwiddie's apparent lack of confidence in him. While there was an interpreter stationed in Winchester, Gist didn't have the benefit of an interpreter when he was in the field. He complained to Dinwiddie that "the country is troubled with an Agent they cannot confide in"[12] and that he was not receiving appropriate support. He said that he did not have sufficient goods for the Indians, and with no interpreter, he could not communicate with them.

Dinwiddie listened to Gist's complaints and argued that the Virginia colony purchased goods for the Indians, and Gist's job did not include purchasing the gifts, but only to deliver them. The lieutenant-governor

18. Captain of Scouts and Indian Agent

pointed out that an interpreter was supplied to the Indian agents, and that he and Atkin should determine how best to utilize him. Regarding the matter of insufficient funds, Dinwiddie said that Atkin mentioned he had given Gist £240 in cash and £800 worth of Indian goods. In addition, Dinwiddie had given Gist £100 for rum and other necessities for the Indians. Apparently, the matter was resolved to their satisfaction since there did not seem to be any further discussion between the two regarding the matter.

Atkin, on the other hand, was the recipient of considerable criticism for mismanagement of Indian affairs and the delivery of gifts to the natives. To be sure, Atkin had a very large area to manage, and was encountering jurisdictional disputes with George Croghan and Sir William Johnson, whose northern department abutted that of Akins and Gist.

In November 1757, Atkin moved south to the Carolinas to administer the southern portion of the department, and he left Gist solely in charge of Indian affairs in Virginia. Before he left, he gave Gist detailed instructions particularly with regard to the Indians who were traveling across Virginia from the south to join Washington's Virginia Regiment. Atkin wanted a regular report, no later than every three months, regarding the number of Indians and what was provided to them in the way of clothing, gifts, supplies, and weapons. He also pointed out that the routes the Indians traveled between the Carolinas and Winchester were through the more settled areas of Virginia, and difficulties regularly occurred between the whites and the Indians. Atkins recommended that Gist should encourage the Indians to use a more western route through the unsettled areas of Virginia by establishing stations farther west, either at the head of the Roanoke River or the James River and on the South Branch of the Potomac. To encourage the Indians to use the western trails, they were told that gifts would be waiting at those western posts. That in itself posed a logistical problem since someone would have to be at the western posts to distribute the gifts. To assist Gist, three assistants were hired to interpret and guide the Indians along the western route. Richard Smith and John Watts would guide the Cherokee, and Thomas Rutherford would do the same with the Catawba. Atkin also instructed Gist to build accommodations for the Indians at each of the stations, and he specified the buildings should be ninety feet by twenty-six feet and cost about £35.

Gist utilized the Indians as scouts and raiders, and they were encouraged to bring back French prisoners. A live prisoner earned an Indian a

With George Washington in the Wilderness

bounty of £45, while he received only £40 for an enemy scalp. Even so, most Indians presented scalps for their bounty instead of live prisoners, since the Indians quickly learned how to make four scalps out of one.

Gist organized the Indians' work details so that on alternate days one-half were scouting or carrying out raids, while the other half were at the stations to defend them from attack. The Indians were hired for three-month tours and were armed and equipped by Gist.

Interestingly, The Indians complained that white troops from the Virginia Regiment wanted to accompany the Indians on their scouting missions. The Indians said that the whites were not fit enough or accustomed to the way the Indians operated and couldn't keep up with the Indians' rapid movement. They were also too noisy in the woods and built big fires. As a result, Gist told Washington and his officers that white soldiers could not accompany the Indians unless the Indians specifically requested them. At Winchester as with other posts where there were both whites and Indians, Gist kept the Indian camps outside the forts and away from the white settlements.

Things ran fairly smoothly, mostly because Gist was the buffer between the white troops and the Indians, and all dealings with the Indians had to go through Gist. To be sure, Gist was fortunate that George Washington, the commander of the Virginia Regiment, was his good friend, and also because Gist's sons Nathaniel and Thomas were officers in the regiment. Even so, money and the scarcity of gifts for the Indians was a chronic problem. We generally think of gifts and presents as something given gratuitously, or complimentary, but in reality, they were the Indians' wages or pay for their service. Unfortunately, Dinwiddie and indeed the Virginia Council retained the mentality that the Indians were ignorant savages that could be exploited by being late in fulfilling promises, or not fulfilling them at all.

Because of Gist, Washington was aware of the negative impact on Indian recruiting if Indians returned to their homes without the promised gifts. As a result, Gist and Washington both appealed to Dinwiddie for more money for gifts for the Indians. Dinwiddie, who was soon to be replaced as lieutenant-governor, said that Atkin had given Gist over £1,000 worth of merchandise for Indian gifts. Gist argued that he did not know how much Atkin had actually paid for the merchandise, but Gist could have bought it locally for £300. Rather than not equipping the Indians as promised, or sending them home empty handed, Washington gave the Indians weapons and necessary articles from the military stores, and Gist purchased goods with his own money.

18. Captain of Scouts and Indian Agent

On Thursday, January 26, 1758, Robert Dinwiddie was replaced as lieutenant-governor by Francis Fauquier (1703–1768). Understandably, Gist did not have the time to develop any sort of rapport with the new lieutenant-governor. However, even as Gist worked on securing Indians for the defense of the frontier, he was forced to deal with other concerns.

In February 1758, Richard Pearis once again surfaced and began to cause trouble for Gist. Pearis disparaged the gifts from Gist as worthless trifles and said that Gist's interpreter had been given instructions to lie to the Indians. He insisted that he was rightfully the person who should deal with the Indians, and he told the Indians to go to Annapolis to meet with Governor Sharpe, saying they would not receive gifts if they didn't. The Indians instead decided to meet with Gist, who was at the post on the South Branch of the Potomac, and the issue was settled to the satisfaction of the Indians. Gist then sent the Maryland governor a letter requesting that he rectify the situation since Sharpe had commissioned Pearis in the first place.

During the spring of 1758, Gist was involved in equipping a large influx of Indians who were coming to Winchester. By April 1758, over 250 Cherokee and fifty Catawba had arrived, mostly in groups of less than thirty, and it fell mostly upon Gist to organize and equip them.

19

The Forbes Campaign against Fort Duquesne

"The supreme art of war is to subdue the enemy without fighting."

—Sun Tsu

During the spring of 1758, plans began to take effect for a British two-pronged offensive against the French. The Earl of Loudoun had been replaced by General James Abercrombie[1] (1706–1781) as the commander-in-chief of British forces in North America, and a second attack against Fort Duquesne was being planned. General John Forbes (1707–1759) was chosen to lead the attack against Fort Duquesne while Abercrombie planned to attack French Fort Carillon (later known as Fort Ticonderoga).

Forbes's choice of a route caused a degree of consternation among the Virginians, since he would avoid the old Braddock Road on the Nemacolin Trail and open a new, more direct road from Carlisle, Pennsylvania. Forbes's new road would for the most part follow the course of present US 30, the Lincoln Highway. The road was more direct and closer to the Pennsylvania grain supplies, and strategically, it would be a surprise to the French, who were anticipating an assault over Braddock's old road.

The Virginians would have preferred that Forbes used Braddock's road since it conveyed more of an impression that the entire route, and indeed the Forks of the Ohio, were part of the Virginia Colony. They were angered by the belief that Forbes chose the northern route across Pennsylvania because of pressure, influence, and lobbying by Pennsylvanians.

Since Gist was the deputy agent for Virginia, his importance and responsibilities increased greatly with the preparations for Forbes's expedition. Gist was now at the peak of his career, and it didn't come as

19. The Forbes Campaign against Fort Duquesne

a surprise that he would attract a rival. That person was a South Carolinian by the name of Captain Abraham Bosomworth (c. 1700–?).

Bosomworth was competent and experienced in dealing with the Indians, but his overriding trait was his aggressive ambition. Now that the Southern Department of Indian Affairs was running smoothly and important to the war effort, Bosomworth wanted to be in charge of all Indian affairs that were connected with the military command. He first traveled to Williamsburg to state his case to John Blair (c. 1687–1771), the president of the council, and then Bosomworth went to Winchester where he brazenly attempted to organize the Indian scouting missions. Gist intervened and gave Bosomworth the more menial task of dispersing gifts to the Indians.

Bosomworth's next ploy was to write a letter on his own authority directly to General Abercrombie, bypassing all intermediate authorities like Washington, Colonel Henry Bouquet, who was General Forbes's second-in-command, and indeed even General Forbes. His letter to Abercrombie was in the form of a demand: "That you will grant me full Powers & Authority to demand and require the aid and assistance of Mr. Atkin's Deputy [Gist] and all Interpreters and Conductors whatever who are all Subordinate to your Excellys Command & they must follow & obey such Orders & Directions as I shall think Proper to give for the Good of the Service & the better Regulation & Management of Indians going to War particularly when accompanying the Army."[2]

Abercrombie assumed that General Forbes was aware that Bosomworth's demand likely ran counter to Atkin and Gist's commission, so, rather than making a decision, he simply acknowledged receipt and forwarded the message to Forbes, who likely interpreted it as Abercrombie's endorsement of Bosomworth's request. It was in that unusual set of circumstances that Bosomworth was able to insinuate himself as liaison between the Indians and the army.

Bosomworth immediately began to inflate his authority and importance while at the same time denigrating Gist's policies, performance, and even Gist's integrity. Apparently, Bosomworth's comments found some willing recipients, but it's difficult to determine from the perspective of over 260 years whether those slurs were deserved or not. It's a fact that Christopher Gist suffered chronic financial difficulties, but for the previous three years he had a steady, better than average income, which would likely continue to improve. His reports of his explorations for the Ohio Company were honest and thorough, as were his expense accounts.

With George Washington in the Wilderness

However, after Abraham Bosomworth ingratiated himself into the confidence of General Forbes and his official family, some of those officers began to write snide and unflattering comments regarding Gist. For example, Sir John St. Clair commented about goods and cash stored at Winchester, writing, "I shall not say but some of the money may remain with Gist but in the Employment he is, there is no avoiding trusting him."[3] To put St. Clair's comments in some perspective, he had a reputation of being somewhat unusual. General Forbes had little regard for his qualities and commented about St. Clair in a message to Bouquet: "He is a very odd man, and I am sorry it has been my fate to have any concern for him.... He was extremely inefficient, and his only talent was for throwing every thing into confusion. Yet he found fault with everyone else, and would discharge volleys of oaths at all who met his disapproval. From this cause or some other Lieutenant Colonel [Adam] Stephen, of the Virginians, told him that he would break his sword rather than be longer under his orders."[4]

Even Colonel Henry Bouquet made several disparaging comments regarding Gist while at the same time endorsing and promoting Bosomworth in messages to General Forbes. It's difficult to ascertain who influenced the other regarding Gist, or whether Bouquet and St. Clair were swayed by Bosomworth or came to their conclusions independently.

Bouquet wrote,

> I do not know anything about the way Indians are managed, but I believe that everything concerning them should be turned over to a single person who would account to you for everything. The variety of measures which have been taken has done much harm, as well as the presents given by different hands and in different places. I think we should have only one storehouse, in which should be deposited the presents from the Provinces (if they give any) and from the King; and by transporting this general storehouse to the place where it is necessary to have Indians, it seems obvious—judging by their greediness—that they would be led there more easily. I should not dare recommend anyone in such a delicate matter, but since the agents or superintendents are leaving you, it seems to me that you will be obliged to take care of their duties. If Bosomworth succeeds in retaining the Cherokees, and can lead them to Fort Loudoun or Reas Town [Ray's Town], wouldn't he be more suitable than Gist to manage them during the campaign?[5]

Bouquet also wrote,

> Bosomworth will go to Cumberland tomorrow to supply them, and will try to bring them here. He continues to manage his Indians very well.[6] ... Mr. Gist being too premature (as he generally is) in his intelligence.[7] ... There are no Indians except a few Tuscaroras at Winchester, 'tis above a fortnight ago

19. The Forbes Campaign against Fort Duquesne

since I had the Account of the Catawbas & Cherokees both which I judged to be without foundation then, Capt Gist should not upon such slight surmises write to the General, and indeed I think at all times his Correspondence ought to be conducted through some other Channel excuse haste.[8] ... Gist's Catawbas and Cherokees exist only in his imagination, and are reduced to 28 Tuscaroras and Nantaways [Nottoways], better fitted to carry off our presents than to fight. We must no longer count on any but ourselves.[9] ... Some blankets are needed to outfit them [the Indians], and especially some vermillion. Gist pretends that he has procured them. This is not very important, but he had no part in it.[10]

Some historians attribute the difficulties that Gist encountered, and to a lesser extent Washington and the Virginians in general, to the jealousy of Maryland Governor Horatio Sharpe and the South Carolinians for Virginia's predominance not only in the war effort but in colonial political affairs. That jealousy found a ready ally in the British officer corps, which had a natural lack of respect and indeed disdain for colonial Americans.

Bosomworth may have endeared himself to Colonels Bouquet and St. Clair, but Washington was definitely not impressed with the pretentious South Carolinian. When meeting Washington, Bosomworth haughtily referred to himself as the Superintendent of Indian Affairs, and Washington wrote contemptuously of the meeting to Colonel St. Clair: "Capt. Bosomworth was here, a Superintendant [*sic*] (as he said) of Indian Affairs."[11] Unfortunately, Bosomworth's attempted erosion of Gist's efforts along with Pearis's attempts to demean Gist with Maryland Governor Sharpe likely had a negative impact on Indian affairs.

In the meantime, Gist's efforts resulted in an anticipated thousand or so Indians on their way to rendezvous at Winchester. In preparation, Gist sent Forbes a listing of goods to be used as gifts and articles necessary to equip the Indians for war, which amounted to a projected expense of about £8,000. Forbes was ordered by Abercrombie to keep the Indians contented, so St. Clair, who was Forbes's quartermaster, followed Gist's recommendations by supplying the Indians with equipment and provisions from military stores.

Forbes apparently was in no hurry to begin his advance toward Fort Duquesne. He would not begin his march until he was completely satisfied that every contingency was considered and taken into account. However, the southern Indians were unfamiliar with the curious way the British waged war and were growing increasingly impatient. Both Washington and Gist knew that if Forbes delayed his march much longer, the exasperated Indians would simply leave and return home.

With George Washington in the Wilderness

Even so, their impatience caused the Indians to wander about and enter the settled towns and villages, which alarmed the citizenry and caused them to complain. Forbes in turn drafted a letter to Washington telling him to keep the Indians away from the settled areas, and Washington relayed the message to Gist. He was largely unsuccessful, because some of the townspeople had invited the Indians into their towns to trade, but never in the numbers they were now encountering. Both Gist and Washington laid much of the blame on the settlers for inviting the Indians in the first place, but that did little to alleviate the situation.

It was even worse along the western route between the Carolinas and Winchester where in one case, Indians stole horses belonging to frontier settlers. The frontiersmen went after the Indians to recover their property, and skirmishing broke out in which men were killed on both sides. In another instance, a group of frontiersmen attacked a party of Cherokee who were returning home and killed about thirty Indians. The Indians were likely more to blame for the fighting, but it caused many of the Indians to refuse to travel north to join the British expedition, and worse yet, many began to go over to the French.

Gist soon found that the number of Indians actually coming to Winchester was considerably less than promised, and even those Indians who arrived at Winchester began to slip back into the woods after receiving arms, equipment, and gifts. That situation was likely the reason Bouquet wrote his disparaging comment that "Gist's Catawbas and Cherokees are better fitted to carry off our presents than to fight."

By Tuesday, July 4, 1758, Forbes had finally moved his army to Carlisle, which would be the main supply depot for his expedition. Forbes's plan was to advance with a two-week supply of provisions and build a fort about every forty miles. There, he would restock with another two-week supply of provisions from Carlisle and advance about another forty miles where he would build another fort. In this way, Forbes's entire army would continue their march intact and well-supplied, thereby eliminating the chronic supply problems that forced Braddock to split his force and race ahead with only a portion of his army.

Gist joined Forbes at Carlisle, and along the way he found fifty Indians at Fort Cumberland and another eighty at Rays Town, which he took with him to Carlisle. At Carlisle, the British troops were eager to continue the march toward Fort Duquesne, but Forbes delayed there six weeks while he built up his main supply depot.

During the next month, and when Forbes finally started his march in August 1758, Gist traveled regularly between Winchester and wherever

19. The Forbes Campaign against Fort Duquesne

Forbes's headquarters happened to be at the time. On Thursday, August 3, 1758, while in Winchester, he encountered an employee of Colonel William Byrd (1728–1777), a member of the Virginia Council, who told him that he had come from *Attakullakulla*, Little Carpenter (1708–1777), a Cherokee chief, who said his warriors would stay at home until the autumn unless General Forbes or Colonel Byrd specifically asked for them. Gist immediately wrote a letter to Colonel Byrd asking him to urge the Cherokee to move north expeditiously to join Forbes.

In early September 1758, Gist was at Rays Town when he received a message from Virginia Lieutenant-Governor Fauquier asking Gist to furnish him with a detailed report of the status of Indian affairs. Fauquier had also written to Washington asking for a detailed status report regarding the Virginia Regiment. Fauquier had not had the opportunity to establish rapport with either Gist or Washington, and he apparently wanted to acquaint himself with those details since he was relatively new in his position, but the order to Gist and Washington added to the two men's already heavy workload.

By September 1758, the lead regiments of Forbes's army had advanced to Loyalhanna and immediately began construction of Fort Ligonier. Loyalhanna was the site of a large Lenape Indian village previously visited by Christopher Gist in November 1750 and was about forty-seven miles from Fort Duquesne. Fort Ligonier would be the last fortification in Forbes's chain of forts stretching back to Carlisle, and from there the final assault on Fort Duquesne would be launched.

However, trustworthy intelligence had been a problem from the start of the expedition. Indians often brought back conflicting reports regarding the strength and preparedness of the French at Fort Duquesne. Scouts came back with varying estimates of the strength of the French garrison and reported the number of French troops and Indian allies to be anything from a smaller number to a body of troops that greatly outnumbered Forbes's army. In addition, some reports claimed that French reinforcements were arriving regularly.

Unwilling to commit without a sound assessment of the enemy's strength and capabilities, Forbes ordered Major James Grant (1720–1806) of the 77th Regiment to reconnoiter the French defenses with a force of about 850 men. Thinking the enemy were few in numbers, Grant on his own initiative divided his force into several components. Then he attempted to trap the enemy by enticing the French to attack one, while the others lie in wait. On Thursday, September 14, 1758, the decoy force marched out with pipes and drums playing. A French force of five hundred French militia and Indians smashed into Grant's troops, quickly overrunning the decoy force and routing the bulk of Grant's troops before they could spring the trap. Of the 850 men in Grant's command, 104 were killed, 220 were wounded, and 18 were captured, including Major James Grant and twenty-three-year-old Thomas Gist, Christopher's youngest child.[12] The French force suffered eight killed and eight wounded in the fight.

By Thursday, October 12, 1758, over two thousand British regulars and militia were at Fort Ligonier under command of Colonel James Byrd. Forbes with the greater part of his army were a few days behind. Outside the fort, Colonel Byrd had stationed a chain of pickets to protect the army's grazing animals when a force of about 440 French regulars and militia and 150 Indians attacked. They drove in the pickets, but the sound of gunfire alerted the troops in the fort, and within minutes the entire garrison was under arms. The British artillery along with their superior numbers successfully repulsed the French attack, and the French withdrew at nightfall, taking about two hundred of the British horses back to Fort Duquesne. The British casualties were twelve killed, eighteen wounded, and thirty-one missing, while the French casualties were estimated to be light.

At that time, Gist was back at Winchester, where he met *Attakullakulla* (Little Carpenter) and about thirty Cherokee warriors, whom he equipped and outfitted and then sent north to join Forbes's army. Little Carpenter led his Indians to Fort Bedford at Rays Town and then to Fort Ligonier, as he and his Indians collected presents along the way, including gifts, supplies, and equipment from General Forbes. Then in the middle of November, after growing impatient while waiting for the British to launch their attack, Little Carpenter and his Cherokees deserted, taking everything they could carry back to their homes in the south.

By Thursday, November 2, 1758, Forbes had over five thousand troops assembled at Fort Ligonier. On Sunday, November 12, 1758, troops under Washington were involved in a brief skirmish and captured a French prisoner who told them that a large number of Canadian militia and most of the Indians had left, and that only a small garrison was defending Fort Duquesne. That spurred Forbes and Bouquet into action, and they immediately moved the army toward the Forks. Nearing the Forks of the Ohio, Forbes's army heard the sounds of explosions and saw smoke from large fires, and when they arrived at the Forks, they found that the French had destroyed Fort Duquesne before retreating in the direction of Canada.

20

The Last Trail

"We will be known forever by the tracks we leave."
—Native American proverb

When the British army marched into the ruins of Fort Duquesne, Christopher Gist was at Fort Loudoun near Winchester, Virginia. As Deputy Superintendent of Indian Affairs for Virginia, he continued to recruit Indians to serve as scouts and carry out raids against the French-allied Indians in the Ohio territory. Men like Bosomworth and Pearis, as well as British officers who were for the most part ignorant of how to equitably deal with Indians, simply assigned the blame for any shortcomings to Gist. For example, Gist was blamed for the desertion of the Cherokees under Little Carpenter at Fort Ligonier, when in actuality, it was Forbes's lengthy delay in initiating an attack against Fort Duquesne that caused the Indians to lose patience and return home.

Another of Gist's difficulties, which he was criticized for, was keeping the Indians away from white settlements on the way to and from Winchester. The Indians were told to follow the westernmost trails to keep them away from white settlements, but they were often invited into communities where they were given liquor and taken advantage of by unscrupulous whites. In retaliation, the Indians stole horses and other plunder, causing a number of serious incidents in which people were killed on both sides, and Gist received much of the blame. After his first few months as Indian Superintendent, Edmund Atkin admitted that the position required "one man to do the job fifty could not handle."[1]

While Gist had his detractors, he also had a following who respected his accomplishments. He developed a good rapport with the Indians, who for the most part appreciated Gist as someone they could trust. The Catawbas in particular referred to him as "Father Gist." Washington was another who continued to support Gist and was very familiar with the difficulties and challenges Gist faced as well as his accomplishments. Washington knew Gist probably better than anyone else and

With George Washington in the Wilderness

solidly supported the frontiersman, as did George Mercer and the former lieutenant-governor Robert Dinwiddie.

Robert Dinwiddie had been succeeded as lieutenant-governor by Francis Fauquier in 1758, but Dinwiddie's 1754 Proclamation promising land-bounties to spur recruitment in the Virginia Regiment now came into effect and caused Christopher Gist to take on additional duties. With the expulsion of the French from the Forks of the Ohio, Gist was given the task of surveying those bounty lands for settlement. That assignment required a considerable amount of travel from Gist's headquarters near Winchester to Williamsburg and also to the bounty lands in the Monongahela valley.

In the spring of 1759, Gist was still tasked with managing the Indians along the Virginia frontier. French rangers along with Indian raiding parties struck isolated homesteads or tiny frontier communities, killing the inhabitants as well as taking many prisoners. A letter written to Gist by Robert Leake (fl. 1756–1784), Commissary General of North America, dated Sunday, August 5, 1759,[2] read in part, "Do Dear Gist Incite the Indians by all the influence you have over them to exert themselves to drive the Barbourous Inhumane Enemy out of their Lurking Places Tell them that they lately took one Capt Jacobs an Indian who had His Majestys Commission and whipt him for three Days & at last tore out his Bowells. He was a Worthy Sober Brave & gallant Soldier."[3]

Among Gist's duties was the ransoming of prisoners who were taken by the Indians, a task that often required as much diplomacy as ransom payment. Many of the hostages had been adopted into Indian communities, and the Indians were reluctant to give them up. Also, many of the hostages had assimilated into the native communities and did not want to be repatriated. While Gist worked to ransom white captives, he certainly was hoping to find his youngest son, Thomas, who had been taken hostage during Major Grant's reconnaissance the previous October. Thomas had been taken to a Wyandot village near Fort Detroit and had been adopted into the native community there. After living among the Indians for about a year, he escaped and made his way back to Virginia.

In the spring of 1759, a smallpox epidemic ravaged the southern Indians. Most of the southern nations suffered heavy losses, but the Catawbas were particularly hard hit and lost an estimated 50 percent of their population to the disease. In July 1759, Christopher Gist was escorting about sixty-two Catawba warriors north toward Winchester when he became infected with smallpox, and on Wednesday, July 25,

20. The Last Trail

1759, Christopher Gist, frontiersman and explorer of Ohio, Kentucky, and West Virginia, died along the trail between Williamsburg and Winchester.

His death went unremarked except by those closest to him, and there are few surviving accounts that mention his passing. Five days after Gist's death, on Monday, July 30, 1759, Captain James Gunn (?–1775) of the Virginia Regiment at Winchester sent a message to Major John Tulleken of the Royal American Regiment, which read, "I thought it proper to advise you that Capt: Gist Duputy [sic] Agent for Indian Affairs here, died on the Road from Williamsburg 25th Instant with the Small Pox. This I mention, that if the General expects any Indians, Some Person be ordered by him to take the Direction of them, Otherwise they Cant be Supplied with Necessaries."[4]

On Sunday, August 12, 1759, Gist's friend George Mercer at Winchester wrote to General John Stanwix (c. 1690–1766) regarding the impact of Gist's death on the Indians.

> Sir, The Detachment of Virginia Troops marched from hence on Thursday last, and I should have joined Them e'er this, but was detained by a Message from the Catawbas with whom I was personally acquainted who desired to speak to Me. I met Them early this Morning near the Town which I would not allow Them to enter upon Account of the Small Pox, and have been very much perplexed, til now tis 8 o'Clock P.M. with their trifling Arguments and Excuses, insisting as they did not know you & their Father Capt Gist as they called him was dead, it was better to return Home, as the Presents they were promised were not ready for them here. After all these Shifts I have at Length engaged Them to go to See you, but have been first obliged to supply them with some Necessaries they were absolutely in want of.[5]

Those are essentially the surviving documents that mention Christopher Gist's passing, and it's sad to note that they are only in the context of work with the Indians, which someone would have to continue. Gist was either fifty-three or fifty-four years old when he died, and though a good deal of his life is undocumented, it's still difficult to comprehend the incredible events, accomplishments, and sheer distances that Gist experienced and traveled in his relatively short life. His life is even more impressive when one considers the people he interacted with as well as the notable historic events he experienced and was part of. In addition to his close relationship with George Washington, whose life he saved on at least two occasions, Gist interacted with icons of history like Robert Dinwiddie, George Mason, Benjamin Franklin, the Lee and Fairfax families, George Mercer, the Cresaps, George Croghan, the

With George Washington in the Wilderness

half-king chiefs Tanacharison and Scarouady, General Braddock, General Forbes, and Colonel Henry Bouquet, to name a few. As remarkable as Gist's life and accomplishments were, it's even more extraordinary that most students of history are unaware of them except perhaps for a few anecdotal facts concerning his wintertime trek with George Washington during the winter of 1753–1754. We believe that he deserves recognition alongside the other famous people of American history, but it probably wouldn't bother Christopher Gist that fame and notoriety had escaped him. He certainly would have been aware of the old Indian adage that says, "A man will be known forever by the tracks he leaves," and Christopher Gist left tracks that were straight, strong, and true.

Epilogue

"When you carry your own water, you will value every drop." —Anonymous

Researching the life of Christopher Gist was a challenge. His journals for the Ohio Company of Virginia were complete and detailed, yet he wrote very little about his personal life or his family. Most of what we know of Gist's personal life, we ascertained from journals and accounts of people he interacted with, men like George Washington, Robert Dinwiddie, Colonel Henry Bouquet, and Thomas and William Fairfax. As it was, Gist was educated and quite literate, but other than accounts of his exploration in his journals for the Ohio Company of Virginia, he did not keep a personal journal. Apparently, his wife Sarah and their children didn't keep diaries or other accounts either. Living on the frontier presumably left little time for writing about one's daily activities, or most likely, Gist and his immediate family never saw a reason to document their lives. In that, the Gists were not unique.

As we were neared completion of our manuscript about Christopher Gist, we wondered about many of the people with whom he interacted and what became of them after Gist's death. Some like George Washington and George Mason became very prominent in American history, while others seem to have faded away with little or no trace.

Some of the characters who interacted with Gist have well documented biographies, while others exited the stage of American history leaving little or no trace.

Aliquippa (c. 1670s–1754)

Queen Aliquippa and her band left Great Meadows with Tanacharison and the other Indians prior to the arrival of the French troops.

Epilogue

She along with the half-king sought refuge at Aughwick, Pennsylvania, near Croghan's trading post. By this time, she was around eighty years old and rather frail from her constant moves. Her poor health was likely exacerbated by the continued stress of worrying for her people. She lived about six months at Aughwick, dying there on Monday, December 23, 1754. John Croghan noted her passing in his journal, "Alequeapy, ye old quine is dead."[1]

Boone, Daniel (1734–1820)

In the mid–1760s Daniel Boone was taken to court in North Carolina for nonpayment of debts, so after his father's death in 1765, he sold the family homestead along the Yadkin River to pay off his debts and looked for a new place to settle. After a short foray to Spanish Florida in search of a suitable place to settle, Boone returned, and in 1769 turned his attention toward the present state of Kentucky, which Gist had explored some eighteen years prior in 1751. It was largely settlers like Boone who fought the Indians in Kentucky, precipitating Lord Dunmore's War of 1770, which forced most of the Shawnee to relinquish their claim to the Kentucky territory.

In Kentucky, Boone blazed "Boone's Trace," which became known as the Wilderness Road through the Cumberland Gap, and he also helped establish the short-lived Transylvania Colony in 1775 and founded the town of Boonesborough.

During the Revolutionary War, the Kentucky territory was considered part of Virginia, and Boone was appointed lieutenant-colonel of the Fayette County Militia. He joined George Rogers Clark's invasion of the Ohio country in 1780, and in 1781 he was elected as a representative to the Virginia General Assembly. In 1782, he was elected sheriff of Fayette County, and also fought the British and their Indian allies in the disastrous Battle of Blue Licks, in which his son Israel was killed.

In 1799, Boone moved his family to present Missouri, and when Missouri became a state in 1804, he was appointed captain of militia. He died on Tuesday, September 26, 1820, at the age of eighty-five, and he was buried near his daughter Jemima's home near present Marthasville, Missouri. In 1845, Boone and his wife's remains were disinterred and reburied in Frankfort, Kentucky, but it's questionable whether it was actually the Boones' remains that were moved. Both graveyards claim that the correct remains are interred in their respective cemeteries.

Epilogue

Bosomworth, Adam (c. 1700–?)

No relevant biographical data regarding Adam Bosworth could be found.

Bouquet, Henry (1719–1765)

Bouquet was a Swiss mercenary who rose to prominence in the British army. In 1763, at the end of the French and Indian War, the Ottawa war chief Pontiac formed an alliance of Indians who sought to remove the British from the former French territory west of the Appalachian Mountains. During that war, known as Pontiac's Conspiracy, Bouquet became infamous for his use of smallpox as a weapon against the Indians. During the Indian siege of Fort Pitt, Bouquet at the urging of William Trent parlayed with the Indians and ordered Captain Simeon Eucyer to give the Indians blankets and hand cloths that had been exposed to the smallpox virus. The smallpox epidemic that decimated the besieging Indians contributed to the lifting of the siege of Fort Pitt.

In August of 1763, Bouquet defeated the Indians at the Battle of Bushy Run, which was the turning point in Pontiac's War. Later that year and in 1764, Bouquet led an expedition into the Ohio Country to quell the remaining rebellious Indians and also repatriate white people who had been previously captured by the Indians. Many of those captives resisted because they had assimilated into Indian society and had Indian spouses and children. Many of those former white captives had to be forcibly repatriated.

In 1765, Bouquet was promoted to brigadier general in command of the army in the southern colonies, but he died in September 1765, in Pensacola, Florida, at the age of forty-eight, likely from yellow fever.

Céloron de Blainville, Pierre Joseph (1693–1759)

After his lead plate burying expedition of 1749, Céloron was posted to command Fort Detroit. There Céloron's half-hearted planning and subsequent failure to follow Governor-General Jonquièr's orders to destroy the recalcitrant Miamis at Pickawillany earned him the governor-general's enmity. Céloron's rationale for noncompliance was his claim that the mission would likely be disastrous to the French in the long run. Although

Epilogue

Céloron was unquestionably brave and loyal, there were other complaints regarding his conduct. He was accused of being haughty and injudicious and not a very good administrator. Apparently, he was better suited for military operations than for administrative duties. When Duquesne became governor-general, he recalled Céloron and made him the town-major of Montréal. Later however, Duquesne wrote that although Céloron was a very good officer, he was not suited for routine administrative work. Little else is known of Céloron's subsequent activities. He died in Montréal on April 12, 1759. He was sixty-six years old. Interestingly, his widow joined the Grey Nuns after his death and remained in Canada, thereby forfeiting the annual pension of 300 livres that the king had awarded her.

Contrecœur, Claude-Pierre Pécaudy de (1705–1775)

Contrecœur remained as commander of Fort Duquesne until 1756, but after Braddock's defeat, he realized that it was only a matter of time before another expedition would be launched against the fort. He made repeated requests for significant numbers of troops and matériel with which to strengthen the post and to consolidate the French gains in the Ohio territory. However, those requests were mostly futile. Citing poor health and fatigue, Contrecœur finally asked to be relieved of command of Fort Duquesne rather than be responsible for the fort's eventual loss. He also petitioned the ministers that he be awarded the cross of the Order of St. Louis, which he received in March 1756. At the same time, he asked for promotions for his two sons who were in the military, one an ensign and the other a cadet. Captain François-Marie de Marchand de Lignery (c. 1703–c. 1760) took over as commander of the Ohio territory, with his headquarters at Fort Duquesne.

Contrecœur's military career was essentially finished, although he did not officially retire until January 1759. After the war, Contrecœur remained in Canada and tended to his very large seigneury (estate) and was appointed to the legislative council in 1775. However, his legislative career was cut short by his death after having attended only one meeting. He died in 1775 at the age of seventy.[2]

Cresap, Thomas (c. 1702–c. 1790)

Born in Skipton, Yorkshire, England, Cresap emigrated to Maryland when he was about fifteen and settled at the mouth of the Susquehanna

Epilogue

River at the head of Chesapeake Bay, Maryland, where he started work as a boat builder. Cresap married Hannah Johnson (1705–1774) about 1727, and dabbled in several enterprises including ferry boat operator, fur trader, merchandiser, and rudimentary surveyor. He was also an agent for Charles Calvert, 5th Lord Baltimore, which in reality meant that he was Calvert's hired enforcer. The Calverts' practice was not to purchase land from the Indians; they instead would appropriate the Indians' land by force. Settlers who moved onto Calvert lands were considered as squatters and trespassers, and Cresap was the person who evicted them by whatever forceful means was necessary. Cresap was notorious in following those orders in the lower Susquehanna region, and his actions made him a wanted criminal in Pennsylvania, although Marylanders looked upon him as a local hero.

In 1736, the Pennsylvanians captured Cresap and his wife, and imprisoned Cresap for a period of three years. During Cresap's imprisonment, his wife and three children lived with his cousin in a home they had evicted a German family from on Codorus Creek, in Pennsylvania.

When Cresap was released, he moved his family to Antietam Creek, and later to Old Town, the site of the old Shawnee village Opessa's Town, at present Oldtown, Maryland. He lived a rough-and-tumble existence, and even his wife Hannah as well as his three sons and two daughters were quick to take offence, and often proved they were capable of effectively handling weapons if necessary. During the French and Indian War, Cresap formed a ranger company and was involved in several skirmishes. Also, during the war, Cresap was elected to the Maryland legislature.

In 1782, when Cresap was eighty years old, he married a second time, to Margaret Millburn, and he died about 1790.

Croghan, George (c. 1718–1782)

With the start of hostilities in 1754, Croghan's successful trading enterprise in the Ohio territory was ruined and his employees in the Ohio territory were either killed or driven back over of the mountains. Croghan moved his trading operation to Aughwick, and after Tanacharison, Queen Aliquippa, and several other Indians who were friendly to the British sought refuge there, Croghan fortified his post and called it Fort Shirley. During the war, he built another three forts along the frontier. Croghan served as captain of scouts during the Braddock

Epilogue

expedition and also assisted Washington's efforts to defend the Virginia frontier. In 1756, Croghan relocated to the New York frontier and was appointed by Sir William Johnson to be his Deputy Superintendent for Indian Affairs. Croghan accompanied General John Forbes's expedition to capture Fort Duquesne in 1758. Interestingly, Forbes assigned Croghan and Montour the perilous job of bringing the intractable Delaware Indians into the English fold. Croghan succeeded, which was something that even Sir William Johnson had been unable to accomplish. In 1760, Croghan went with Colonel Bouquet to occupy Detroit, where he conducted negotiations with the tribes who had supported the French. In 1764, he traveled to England to lobby for a strong Indian department, and upon his return, Johnson sent him on a mission to open the Illinois territory, which was still occupied by the French. In 1768 he played an important role in the Treaty of Fort Stanwix, which designated Indian lands that essentially encompassed the area west and southwest of Fort Stanwix and north of the Ohio River. It was hoped that implementation of the treaty provisions would ease the bloody and costly Indian wars by promising the Indians a permanent homeland that was free from white encroachment. Over the years, Croghan had amassed several thousand acres of land, and throughout his life he continued in land speculation. His greatest rival in land ownership was George Washington, who occasionally challenged Croghan's land titles when they conflicted with his own. He was associated with William Trent in the "Indiana" and "Vandalia" land speculation projects, investing heavily in trying to establish the "fourteenth" English colony. Benjamin Franklin and his son William were also involved in that land deal to a lesser extent. However, British policy prohibited Crown agents from being involved in such ventures, so Croghan resigned his government post in 1772 in order to continue with his land speculation. Lord Dunmore's War, which was fought in 1774, was a war between the colony of Virginia and primarily the Shawnee and Mingo Indians in the Ohio territory. That war and the outbreak of the Revolutionary War in 1775 destroyed all prospects of the "Indiana" and "Vandalia" ventures, and Croghan was wiped out financially. To make matters worse, he was unjustly accused of being a Tory even though he had served the patriot cause as chairman of the Pittsburgh Committee of Correspondence. He was finally able to clear his name in a trial held in November 1778. Croghan spent his final years in poverty, and died at Passyunk, near Philadelphia, on Saturday, August 31, 1782. He was buried in the churchyard at St. Peter's Church in Philadelphia, but by that time he was so unknown that his death was not even reported in the newspapers. He was sixty-four years old when he died.

Dinwiddie, Robert (1693–1770)

Virginia Lieutenant-Governor Dinwiddie refused to release the French captives taken in the fight with Jumonville, and as a result, Robert Stobo and Jacob Van Braam remained hostages of the French until Stobo escaped from Québec in 1759 and Van Braam was released in 1760. After the defeat of Braddock, Dinwiddie criticized the fallen general for splitting his force and advancing with only about half of his army. Dinwiddie maintained that Braddock should have marched to the forks in strength rather than leave Dunbar and half his total force some forty miles to the rear.

Dinwiddie waged a constant struggle with his own Virginia assembly over ways to generate funds to raise troops with which to defend the frontier. In desperation he appealed for intercolonial cooperation, and even suggested that the British Parliament impose a land tax and a poll tax to finance the war. All of these exertions took a toll on his health, and on Tuesday, March 22, 1757, Dinwiddie requested a leave of absence for a recuperative visit to Bath, England. He left Virginia on Sunday, January 8, 1758, and was succeeded by Francis Fauquier as lieutenant-governor. Dinwiddie never returned to America. He died at Clifton, Bristol, England, on Friday, July 27, 1770. He was seventy-seven years old.

Duquesne de Menneville, Michel-Ange (c. 1700–1778)

After the Battle of Fort Necessity in 1754, Duquesne was satisfied with Villiers's success, but the governor-general had reservations concerning the clause in the capitulation that barred the English from returning to the Ohio territory for only one year. His concerns were proven correct when he received intelligence that the British were preparing for a massive retaliation under Braddock.

Duquesne was aware of the steep odds of winning a war against England, so he chose to quit on a high note. He requested to be recalled in October 1754 and was replaced as governor-general by Pierre de Rigaud de Vaudreuil de Cavagnial on June 24, 1755. Back in France, Duquesne was rewarded for his service in Canada and was often consulted on matters pertaining to New France. He resumed his naval career, and in 1756 was named inspector general of the coasts of France. In 1757, he assumed command of the fleet at Toulon and took part in minor actions until 1758 when he was defeated in an engagement with a British squadron and taken prisoner. Upon his return to France, he was granted a pension of 3,000 livres, and in 1763 the king made him a "Commander of the Order of St. Louis." He finally retired in 1776 and spent his last days at his residences in Paris and Antony. He died in September 1778 at the age of seventy-eight.

Forbes, John (1707–1758)

During the march toward Fort Duquesne in 1758, Forbes became severely ill and was transported on a litter for most of the way. During that time, he relied on Colonel Henry Bouquet, who commanded the advance guard.

Unlike many of his predecessor British officers, Forbes believed in building and maintaining a good relationship with the Indians and was able to gain their support.

After the capture of the ruins of Fort Duquesne, Forbes ordered construction of the much larger and more formidable Fort Pitt at the Forks of the Ohio, but during the fort's construction Forbes's health deteriorated rapidly. His illness was described as "wasting disease," but was most likely stomach cancer, combined with dysentery. In December of 1758, he left Colonel Hugh Mercer in command of Fort Pitt and returned to Philadelphia, where he died on Sunday, March 11, 1759, at the age of fifty.

Fraser, John (1721–1773)

After the fight at Great Meadows, John Fraser was unable to maintain his trading venture at either the Venango or Turtle Creek locations. He moved farther east to present Bedford County, Pennsylvania, and in 1754 he married Jane McClain, nee Jane Bell. He continued in the military service both as a militia officer and as a lieutenant in the British army, serving in Braddock's ill-fated expedition. On Wednesday, October 1, 1755, Fraser's wife Jane was returning home from the trading post at Will's Creek, several miles away, when she was captured by

Epilogue

Indians and taken over three hundred miles to an Indian village near present Dayton, Ohio. Jane remained a captive of the Indians for over eighteen months, but she eventually escaped and somehow made her way back home. However, after his wife disappeared, Fraser assumed she was dead, so he remarried. When Jane finally made her way back home, she found that her husband had taken another wife. To rectify the situation, Fraser welcomed his wife back and returned his second wife to her father.

In 1758 Fraser accompanied the successful Forbes expedition against Fort Duquesne. When he returned, he began to petition the government for restitution of his losses caused by the war, and in 1766 he was granted three hundred acres along Forbes Road near present Latrobe, Pennsylvania. As a side note, in 1790 his three hundred acres were sold to Father Theodore Bouwers O. F. M, and in 1846, St. Vincent College and Archabbey were established. It is now the oldest Benedictine monastery in the United States. Fraser continued to speculate in land, and in 1769 he purchased the land that encompassed the Braddock battlefield where he built a cabin. Fraser's widow sold the land in 1774 for living expenses and to satisfy debts. In 1771, Governor Penn appointed John Fraser the justice of the peace for the newly formed Bedford County. John Fraser died suddenly two years later on April 16, 1773. He was fifty-two years old.

Gist, Anne "Nancy" (1734–1795)

Christopher and Sarah Gist's daughter Anne was regularly called "Nancy," which was a diminutive form for Ann or Anne. In some sources, Anne or Nancy Gist is also shown as "Annette." In 1746, when Anne was about twelve years old, her only sister Violetta married William Cromwell, and then her mother passed away about 1757. She was the youngest Gist child, and her brothers by that time were beginning to strike out on their own, so Anne was invited to live with the William Fairfax family whose Belvoir Plantation lay a short distance from George Washington's Mount Vernon home.

It was rumored that Anne (Nancy) Gist was uncommonly attractive, and during her two-year residence at Belvoir Plantation, she was courted by young George Washington, and the two exchanged several romantic letters.

After the French and Indian War, Anne lived for an undetermined period of time with her brother Thomas at his home on the old Ohio Company Gist Settlement tract in western Pennsylvania.

Sources indicate that she married a Nathaniel Hart and moved with her husband to present Clark County, Kentucky, where she died in 1795 at about age sixty-one.

Gist, Nathaniel (1733–1796)

Son of Christopher and Sarah. In 1760, after Forbes's successful expedition, Nathaniel accompanied Daniel Boone on a trek to Wolf Hill (present Abingdon, Virginia) where the two parted company, and Nathaniel went through the Cumberland Gap. Persistent legends relate that during that trip, Nathaniel stayed among the Cherokee, and through a liaison with a native woman, sired *Sequoyah*, the famous inventor of the Cherokee alphabet.

In 1775 Nathaniel Gist was living among the Overhill Cherokee, and during the Revolutionary War, he was suspected of being a British spy; however, he was able to convince Governor Patrick Henry of Virginia and General Washington of his loyalty, and Washington appointed Nathaniel as colonel in command of Gist's Additional Continental Regiment. During the war, Gist recruited five hundred Indians who served as guides and scouts, and also worked to bring the various Indian tribes over to the American cause.

Washington and Nathaniel grew to be close friends, and that relationship continued through Washington's lifetime. In May of 1780, Nathaniel Gist was captured by the British during the siege of Charleston. In 1783, after the war, he was awarded seven thousand acres in Kentucky for his military service, and he moved there in 1783. He died at his home in Kentucky in 1812.

Gist, Richard (1729–1780)

Richard Gist is considered the first-born child of Christopher and Sarah Gist, although there is some indication that they had a daughter named Bell who died in her infancy. At the end of the French and Indian War, Richard joined his brothers in petitioning for a claim to bounty lands for military veterans under the Proclamation of 1763. They were granted land in the old Ohio Company tract that was

Epilogue

settled earlier by his father. In the ensuing years, both Nathaniel and Richard turned their tracts over to their younger brother Thomas, who lived there until the land was sold to several different owners around 1790.

Richard was relatively active in colonial affairs, and during the American Revolution, he enlisted in the American militia. On Saturday, October 7, 1780, he was killed in the Battle of Kings Mountain, near present Blacksburg, South Carolina.

Gist, Thomas (1735–1788)

Son of the frontiersman Christopher Gist and his wife Sarah. According to some sources, Thomas was sometimes referred to as Benjamin.

Thomas was captured by Wyandot Indians during Grant's raid on Fort Duquesne in 1758 and adopted by a Huron family near Fort Detroit, where he was well treated. He lived there through the rest of 1758 and into September of 1759. He escaped after about a year living with the Indians, and later wrote an engaging account of his captivity and escape.

Thomas reclaimed the old Gist Plantation, and by acquiring some of his brothers' land, his holdings totaled about 2,750 acres on which he built a house where his sister Anne (Nancy) lived with him for a time. In 1770 and also again in 1784, he was visited by George Washington, who made complimentary references to Gist's land in his diary. There is no record of Thomas having served as an officer in the army during the Revolution, but he may have served as an enlisted man. He did, however, serve as justice of the peace of three counties in western Pennsylvania. He died at the Gist homestead in 1788.

Gist–Cromwell, Violetta (1731–1768)

Christopher and Sarah Gist's eldest daughter and her husband William Cromwell were married about 1746 when she was about age fifteen. The two became residents of Gist's Ohio Company settlement on the west side of the Allegheny Mountains when her parents established their homestead there in 1752. After the abandonment of the settlement in the face of Contrecœur's army in 1754, not much is known of Violetta's activities other than she and her husband William had four children. Violetta passed away at the age of thirty-seven.

Epilogue

Gist, Nathaniel (c. 1707–c. 1788)

Christopher Gist and his brother Nathaniel were close in their early years, having been in business together. Nathaniel married Mary Howard in 1729, while Mary Howard's sisters, Sarah and Violetta, married Nathaniel's brothers Christopher in 1725 and William in 1737, respectively.

At the time the Gist family fortunes were in collapse, both Nathaniel and his brother Christopher moved from Maryland likely to escape creditors. Around 1750, Christopher relocated to Virginia and then to the Yadkin River in North Carolina, while Nathaniel first moved to Lunenburg County Virginia, and then, before 1754, to the Dan River area in Rowan County, North Carolina. In Rowan County he served as a captain in the militia, and after his wife Mary died about 1755, he returned to Virginia.

Sources indicate that Nathaniel was living with his son Joshua in 1784, and in 1787, both he and Joshua were among those who signed the petition for the formation of the "State of Franklin," also known as "The Free Republic of Franklin" and "State of Frankland." The scheme was to create a state in what is today Eastern Tennessee, which in effect lasted about four-and-a-half years before North Carolina reassumed control of the area. Nathaniel died about 1788.

Gist's Settlement in Pennsylvania

Gist's Settlement, which is also variously referred to as Gist's Plantation, Monongahela, or Mount Braddock, was destroyed by Contrecœur's army in 1754 but latter reclaimed by Gist's children and remained in the family until the latter part of the eighteenth century. Supposedly, it was his son Thomas who gave it the name "Mount Braddock" in 1765 after the French and Indian War, and perhaps it was there that the grievously wounded Braddock was taken after his disastrous battle, and where he spent the night of Thursday, July 10, 1755, and part of Friday, July 11, 1755, while waiting for wagons and medical supplies. Christopher and Sarah Gist's son Thomas settled on a 433-acre tract of land there adjacent to his father's old home site and lived there with his sister Anne (Nancy). Later, Thomas acquired some of his brother's land there, and at one time owned 2,750 acres. In 1788–1789, a good portion of the land passed to Colonel Isaac Meason (1743–1818), one of the first, if not the first, ironmaster in western Pennsylvania.

Epilogue

That came about because Gist's old settlement was put up for sale to satisfy a debt of £9, and Meason bought a four-hundred-acre parcel for £30. The following spring, he bid £31 on the remaining 620 and one-half acres. The Gist heirs took Meason to court, and about five years later, Meason agreed to pay the Gist descendants £1,200 for the 1,020 and one-half acres. In 1802, Isaac Meason built a large, fine stone mansion a short distance from the site of where Christopher Gist had his home. The balance of the tract was then sold off to other buyers in the 1790s.

George Washington visited Thomas Gist and Anne there in 1770 and again in 1784, writing, "When we came down the Hill to the Plantation of Mr. Thomas Gist, the Ld. [Land] appeared charming; that which lay level being as rich and black as anything could possibly be."[3]

Joncaire, Philippe-Thomas Chabert de (c. 1707–c. 1766)

After his meeting with Washington and Gist at Fort Machault in 1753, Joncaire continued to cultivate friendship between the French and the Indians along the Allegheny and the Ohio River frontier. His greatest challenge was maintaining the delicate diplomatic relations with the Iroquois, who opposed the French army's invasion and construction of forts in western Pennsylvania.

In 1755, Joncaire moved from Fort Machault to Fort Niagara, where he worked to keep the mighty Iroquois from siding with the British. If he couldn't sway them to support the French cause, he wanted their commitment to remain neutral. He went so far as to warn them that if they should side with the British, their village would be laid waste by the French army and their Indian allies. The French destruction of Fort Oswego, or what the French called *Chouaguen*, in 1756 lent weight to Joncaire's threat.

However, by 1758, the Indians could see that the tide was turning in favor of the British, and the following year, Joncaire was nearly captured at his trading post by a party of Mohawks. However, the following year, 1759, Joncaire was captured by the British when they captured Fort Niagara.

After the war, Joncaire returned to France where he was made a knight of the order of Saint-Louis. There is some question whether he remained in France or returned to Canada, because Guy Carlton, the

Epilogue

British governor of Canada, wrote a letter announcing Joncaire's death in 1766.

LaForce, René-Hippolyte (1728–1802)

It's unclear what role the enigmatic LaForce played in the French army during the time of Washington and Gist's encounters with him. Robert Stobo, who was a hostage of the French and in a good position to gather information about LaForce, said that it appeared that LaForce was an important personage in the French military. Dinwiddie released LaForce in 1756, and upon his return to Canada, LaForce was given command of a frigate on Lake Ontario. That same year, he was involved in a skirmish against the British near Fort Oswego. In 1758, he was stationed at Fort Niagara until it fell to the British in 1759. After the fall of Québec in 1759, LaForce moved to Kamouraska, about eighty-two miles northeast of Québec City, where he remained until 1767 when he moved to Québec City. There he started a shipping company that dealt primarily with the West Indies trade, and LaForce captained one of his company's ships.

The start of the American Revolution halted LaForce's shipping venture. Governor Guy Carleton initially appointed LaForce as captain of the city's artillery company, but a few days later LaForce was ordered to take command of a British warship that was patrolling the St. Lawrence River. In 1776, he was appointed captain of the armed schooner *Seneca*, which became his flagship when he was later appointed as commander of the British fleet operating on Lake Ontario. In 1778, he was given control of the shipyard at Pointe au Baril, and then named master and commander of "His Majesty's Naval Armament upon the Rivers and Lakes within the Province." In 1780, he was promoted to Commodore of the Fleet. In 1784, after the war, LaForce retired on half-pay and resumed his trading venture between Québec and the West Indies. In 1788, he sold his share of the business, but in 1794, he was appointed lieutenant colonel of militia of Québec. He died in 1802, just two months after his seventy-third birthday.[4]

Legardeur, Jacques de Saint-Pierre (1701–1755)

Shortly after receiving Washington at Fort Le Bœuf, Legardeur requested to be relieved as commander on the Ohio, ostensibly for

Epilogue

health reasons. Turning over his command to Claude-Pierre Pécaudy de Contrecœur, Legardeur returned to Montréal for convalescence. In 1755, in response to the British thrust led by William Johnson to capture Fort St. Frédéric at Crown Point, Legardeur led a large contingent of Canadian militia and Indians south to engage Johnson's army and to defend Lac St. Sacrement and Lake Champlain. On September 8, 1755, Jacques Legardeur de Saint-Pierre was killed in the Battle of Lake George. He was fifty-four years old.

Montour, Andrew (c. 1720–1772)

Montour's native names were *Sattelihu* and *Eghnisara*, and his father was *Carondawanna*, an Oneida war chief. His mother was the well-known Madam Montour with mixed French and Algonquin heritage. Like his mother, Andrew had a gift for languages and was able to converse fluently in English, French, Lenape, Shawnee, and most of the Iroquois dialects.

Montour remained active as an interpreter during the French and Indian War, at which time he received a captain's commission. He was considered so effective that the French actually placed a bounty on his head. He next worked with Sir William Johnson's Indian Department of the Northern District and was active on the side of the British during Pontiac's Rebellion of 1763–1766. For his efforts, he was given a sizable land grant in present Mifflin County and Montour's Island near Pittsburgh.

In 1772, Montour was killed at his own home by a Seneca Indian whom he had entertained for several days. According to legend, Montour was killed during a drunken argument. He was about fifty-two years old when he died.

Nemacolin (c. 1715–c. 1767)

A Lenape chief of the Unami branch of the Lenape (Delaware) nation. He was born in the original Lenape homeland along the Delaware River. With the loss of their homeland, the Lenape were forced to move west, and Nemacolin spent many of his early years near present Shamokin, Pennsylvania. As an adult, he established his village on the Monongahela at present Brownsville, Pennsylvania. In 1749–1750, Nemacolin and his two sons were hired by Thomas Cresap to map the

Epilogue

ancient trail from Will's Creek across the Allegheny Mountains to the Ohio Company storehouse at Redstone Creek, near Nemacolin's village.

A few years later, Nemacolin relocated his village to present Blennerhassett Island in the Ohio River, opposite present Belpre, Ohio. Nemacolin died there around 1767, at about age fifty-two, and soon afterward European settlers occupied the Island.

Ohio Company of Virginia (1748–1776)

The Ohio Company of Virginia did not survive the war it helped to start. When the French and Indian War ended in 1763, the shareholders of the Ohio Company petitioned the king to restore their land grant, and indeed the company began to formulate plans for development and settlement in their old area that had been wrested from France. However, King George III issued the Royal Proclamation of 1763, which proclaimed all land west of the Appalachian Mountains as an Indian Reserve and forbade all white settlement in that area.

In 1768, the Treaty of Fort Stanwix modified the Royal Proclamation by opening the lands south of the Ohio River to white settlement. However, the area north of the Ohio River and western Pennsylvania remained part of the Indian Reserve, and that is where the old Ohio Company land grant and Christopher Gist's settlement had been located.

With their old land grant gone, the Ohio Company reorganized into the "Grand Ohio Company" and petitioned the king for a new land grant. They were awarded a large tract along the south side of the Ohio River from present Pittsburgh to the mouth of the Scioto River, which included most of present West Virginia and a portion of eastern Kentucky. The company's plan was to establish a new colony called "Vandalia."

However, the outbreak of the American Revolutionary War disrupted the planned colonization and development of Vandalia, and in 1776, the company, now based in London, permanently ceased operations.

Pearis, Richard (1725–1794)

Born in Ireland, Pearis and his family emigrated to the Shenandoah Valley around 1735. The family was quite wealthy, and when Richard married, he and his family owned about twelve hundred acres near Winchester, Virginia.

Epilogue

In 1770, Pearis was involved in a land fraud scheme, in which he and one Jacob Hite forged letters purporting to be from Cherokee leaders declaring the Cherokees willingness to cede land to the Colony of Virginia. They also submitted a forged, fraudulent deed purporting to show the transfer of twelve square miles of land near present Greenville, South Carolina. Pearis also presented questionable deeds from the Indians, claiming they were parcels of land given to him in exchange for cancellation of Indians' trading debts. An Indian interpreter named John Watts wrote to John Stuart, the Indian superintendent, concerning Richard Pearis, "I take him to be a very dangerous fellow who will breed great disturbances if he is let alone, for he will tell the Indians any lies to please them."[5]

In 1772, Pearis was prosecuted under a 1739 statute that forbade British citizens from owning Indian land, and in November of 1773, he was found guilty and surrendered his deed. However, the following month, he presented another deed to Indian land that was in the name of his son George, whom Pearis had fathered with an Indian woman. Later, George conveniently transferred the land back to Pearis.

In the 1770s, Pearis cleared one hundred acres of land in the heart of present Greenville, where Pearis built a substantial plantation home and farm. In 1775, he sought the position of patriot commissioner to the Indians, and when the position was given to another man, Pearis became a captain in the Loyalist militia.

In December 1775 his house and farm building were burned by Patriot opponents, and Pearis was captured and imprisoned in Charleston for nine months. When he was released, he rejoined the Loyalist forces until June of 1781, when he was recaptured after the fall of Augusta to the Patriots. The Patriot militia members wanted to kill Pearis, but his life was saved by General Andrew Pickens. However, his lands were confiscated by the state of South Carolina.

He spent the rest of his life as a farmer in the Bahamas, and ironically received compensation from the British government for his confiscated lands, even though he never legally owned them. He died in the Bahamas in 1794, at the age of sixty-nine.

Scarouady (?–c. 1757 or 1758)

Scarouady traveled with Tanacharison to Aughwick in 1754, and he succeeded Tanacharison as the principal half-king after Tanacharison's death in October 1754. Frustrated with their life in Aughwick, most of the Indians who accompanied the half-kings there abandoned Scarouady and returned to Fort Duquesne where they made peace with the French. Scarouady, on the other hand, joined Braddock's expedition. During Braddock's march, Scarouady's son was shot and killed by a nervous sentry who mistook him for a hostile Indian. In spite of his loss, Scarouady stayed with the expedition and survived the devastating defeat on the Monongahela. In 1756, documents indicate that Scarouady attended councils in which he gave speeches that advocated peaceful measures. After 1756 there is no record of his activities. Some sources indicate he died in 1757 or 1758. Scarouady's age when he died is not known.

Sharpe, Horatio (1781–1790)

Maryland's twenty-second proprietary governor from 1753 to 1768 came from a military background, and indeed, prior to the arrival of General Braddock, had been appointed by the king as commander-in-chief of British and colonial forces for Virginia and adjoining colonies.

He was a capable civil and military administrator who enjoyed dabbling in farming at Whitehall, his estate in Annapolis. Sharpe returned to England in 1773 and remained there until his death in 1790 at the age of seventy-two.

St. Clair, John (fl. 1755–1767)

Little of St. Clair's life prior to Braddock's campaign is known, other than that he inherited a Scottish baronetcy. After St. Clair's arrival in Virginia in 1755, Lieutenant-Governor Dinwiddie introduced St. Clair to Lord Fairfax as "a man of great knowledge in military affairs."

Apparently, he also had some unusual ideas. He was appointed Braddock's deputy quartermaster, and to make the Potomac River navigable for barges capable of transporting troops and supplies, St. Clair recommended blowing up the Great Falls.

During the Battle of the Monongahela on Wednesday, July 9, 1755, St. Clair was shot in the chest and severely wounded.

In August 1756, he was appointed lieutenant colonel of the Fourth Battalion of the 60th Regiment of Foot. In a March 1757 letter to Sir

Epilogue

William Johnson, the Reverend John Ogilvie commented that St. Clair's services were more appreciated at home than in the colonies, but he possessed "a perfect knowledge of French and German." In April 1757, St. Clair was still troubled by the wounds he received with Braddock and was convalescing in New Brunswick, New Jersey. Later that year, he was with General John Stanwix working to defend the Pennsylvania frontier.

After Forbes's successful campaign against Fort Duquesne, St. Clair made Philadelphia his headquarters, where he continued as quartermaster general. It was rumored that St. Clair profited by selling passes for trade to merchants. In a letter to Sir William Johnson, Richard Huckburgh wrote in 1761, "General Monkton with Major Gates is arrived from Philadelphia; by the latter I understand that the passes for trade for two years were obtained from the Quarter-Master General, Sir John Sinclair [St. Clair], who made a great many gold cobs[6] by them; now they are issued by the governor."

Though St. Clair lost his shady income from selling trade passes, by 1761 he secured sufficient "gold cobs" to purchase an estate he named "Bellville" near Elizabeth Town, New Jersey, and he wooed and married Miss Betsy Moland, the daughter of an eminent barrister. When the war ended in 1763, his position as quartermaster general saved him from demobilization and a half-pay salary.

St. Clair returned to England for a while, and in 1765 he was reappointed to his old position as quartermaster general. In March 1766, he was appointed lieutenant-colonel of the 28th Foot, stationed in New Jersey, where his health began to fail. He died at Bellville on Thursday, November 26, 1767.

Stephen, Adam (1718–1791)

Adam Stephen continued to serve with his friend George Washington during the French and Indian War. Stephen remained a major of the Virginia Regiment and was part of Braddock's expedition during the disastrous march to the Monongahela in 1755. In 1758, Stephen was promoted to lieutenant colonel, and in that year was involved in actions against the Creek Indians. During the French and Indian War, he was also active in the defense of the Virginia frontier. He was promoted to colonel, and at war's end, Stephen took over command of the Virginia Regiment from Washington. As commander of the Virginia Regiment, Stephen fought in Pontiac's Rebellion in 1763. When the Revolutionary

Epilogue

War broke out, Stephen again offered his services to his friend George Washington, who was now Commander-in-Chief of the American Army. Stephen was appointed major general and served in the campaigns of 1776–1777 including commanding a division during the defense of Philadelphia in September 1777. During the Saturday, October 4, 1777, Battle of Germantown, Stephen's force advanced through heavy fog and came up on Anthony Wayne's troops ahead. Thinking they were the enemy, Stephen's men fired repeated volleys into the backs of Wayne's Division causing several casualties. The court martial that resulted from that incident found that Stephen was drunk at the time, and he was stripped of his command and cashiered out of the army. He returned home, and in 1778 laid out the plan for Martinsburg in what is now West Virginia, naming it after his friend Colonel Thomas Martin. He later became the sheriff of Berkeley County, and in 1788 was elected to the Virginia convention that ratified the U.S. Constitution. Stephen died in Martinsburg in 1791 at the age of seventy-three.

Stobo, Robert (1726–1770)

As hostages after the surrender of Fort Necessity, Captains Robert Stobo and Jacob Van Braam were kept at Fort Duquesne for about a year. Shortly after Braddock's defeat on Wednesday July 9, 1755, the French discovered a detailed map of Fort Duquesne among Braddock's captured documents. While Van Braam fully enjoyed a comradely association with French officers in drinking, carousing, and card playing, Stobo was learning French. At the same time, Stobo was painstakingly collecting every available bit of military intelligence that he incorporated on his secretly hand-drawn map of the French fortifications. Somehow, he was able to smuggle the map out of Fort Duquesne by way of a friendly Indian, and it eventually came into the procession of Lieutenant-Governor Dinwiddie. Dinwiddie subsequently gave the map to Major General Braddock to assist him in the expedition against Fort Duquesne; however, in an incredible breech of military intelligence, neither Dinwiddie nor Braddock redacted Stobo's name from the incriminating document. Worse yet, Braddock carried the original to the Monongahela, and after the battle, the French captured his papers that included Stobo's map. When the French examined Braddock's captured documents, they found the detailed map with Stobo's name on it. Both Stobo and Van Braam were accused of violating their parole by spying for the British, and they were sent to Montréal for trial. After a two-and-a-half-week trial, Van Braam was acquitted, but Stobo, who admitted making the map, was sentenced to death by beheading. He was sent to Québec to await confirmation of the death sentence by the king. That confirmation never came. The court at Versailles secretly decided to do nothing because they were not certain of the technical legality of executing someone for spying during a time when war was not officially declared. In Stobo's favor was the fact that he had an endearing Scottish personality, and he was someone whom everyone seemed to genuinely like. He was given a fair amount of freedom in his personal movements, which he used to attempt escape. During two of his attempted escapes he was recaptured, but his third and most daring attempt in May 1759 was successful. He led a group of escapees consisting of four men and a woman with her three children by canoe down the St. Lawrence River. They subsequently captured a French schooner, and with its crew as captives, they sailed all the way to British-held Fort Louisbourg, arriving there thirty-six days after leaving Québec. At Louisbourg, Stobo joined General Wolfe's staff, and according to Stobo's memoirs, he showed Wolfe the hidden pathway from Anse au Foulon up to the Plains of Abraham, which made possible Wolfe's capture of Québec in September 1759. Stobo remained in the British army and was wounded in the head during a fight against the Spanish. He seemed to have made a full recovery, but later, he frequently became depressed, and his behavior was somewhat erratic, possibly due to his head injury. On Tuesday, June 19, 1770, Stobo killed himself with his pistol in the military barracks at Chatham, England.[7] He was not quite forty-four years old when he died.

Tanacharison (c. 1700–1754)

After he left Great Meadows just prior to the July 3 battle, Tanacharison took no further part in the French and Indian War, and he never saw Washington or Gist again. He, along with his family and most of the Indians at Great Meadows, went to Will's Creek and then to Aughwick, Pennsylvania, where George Croghan had established his trading post. In August 1754, Tanacharison traveled to John Harris's Ferry (present Harrisburg, Pennsylvania) to meet with Conrad Weiser. The half-king had learned that Virginians were blaming the defeat at Great Meadows on the supposed treachery of the Indians, claiming they had secretly aided the French. Tanacharison protested this injustice, and publicly criticized Washington's performance and unwillingness to take the Indians' advice as the primary cause of the defeat. Weiser accompanied the half-king back to Aughwick because the old chief had summoned Delaware and Shawnee leaders for a conference that was held on September 4–6, 1754. The conference was another attempt to gain the Ohio Indians' support for the British. The meeting was a failure because the Indians did not want to leave their homes in Ohio, and they knew that the British could not protect them there.

After the conference, Tanacharison became increasingly ill, and he returned to the trading house of John Harris where he was treated by an Indian healer. The medicine man stated that the half-king had been bewitched by the French in revenge for the great blow he had struck against them in the death of Jumonville. Perhaps not surprisingly, all the Indian acquaintances of the old chief concurred with the medicine man's assessment. However, based on what is known of his symptoms, it is believed that Tanacharison had contracted pneumonia. Tanacharison died at Harris's Ferry on Friday, October 4, 1754. He was about fifty-four years old.

Trent, William (1715–1787)

Captain Trent and John Fraser stood trial for leaving their post when the French captured the Forks, but they both were exonerated. In 1758, Trent took part in Forbes's successful expedition to recapture the Forks of the Ohio. Since 1749, he had been in a trading partnership with John Croghan, but the venture suffered heavy losses during the war. About 1760, he joined another trading firm called Simon, Trent, Levy & Franks out of Fort Pitt, but they also suffered heavy losses as a result of Pontiac's War in 1763. During Pontiac's War, Trent was supposedly the originator of an idea of giving smallpox-infected blankets to the Indians to decimate their numbers.

Trent and his partners spent several years trying to get restitution for their losses that were incurred as a result of the wars. At the Treaty of Fort Stanwix in 1768, he was one of the people awarded compensation in the form of a vast tract of land southwest of Fort Pitt, which became known as "Indiana." It should not be confused with the state of Indiana. The awarded tract was southwest of Fort Pitt between the Monongahela and the Ohio rivers, stopping short of the Kanawha River. Trent tried to merge his land grant with the larger "Vandalia" land speculation project, which abutted his "Indiana" tract on three sides. However, Trent and his partners were unable to receive royal authorization for title to the land, and the project stalled out. They continued to press their claim, but the Revolutionary War overtook their efforts. Trent then tried to obtain recognition of his claim from the American Congress both during and after the Revolution, but he was unsuccessful. Unable to receive authorization of any kind, his land speculation venture failed. In 1784, William Trent moved to Philadelphia where he died in 1787 at the age of seventy-two.

Van Braam, Jacob (1727–?)

As hostages of the French at Fort Duquesne, Van Braam and Captain Robert Stobo, were accused of spying because of the detailed map Stobo had smuggled out of the French fort to the British. They were sent to Montréal for trial, and Van Braam was found not guilty, but he remained a hostage in Montréal. As he did at Fort Duquesne, Van Braam availed himself of French hospitality to the maximum. He was quartered in the home of Lieutenant Louis Herbin, a distinguished French officer and a Knight of St. Louis, who was at the time being held as a prisoner of war in England. Lieutenant Herbin's wife and daughter remained in the home and during the time Van Braam lived there, Herbin's daughter became pregnant. Van Braam was accused of being responsible but asserted that he could not have been the father because at the time he was engaged in an affair with Madame Herbin, the girl's mother. Shortly thereafter, in September 1760, Van Braam was released, and he returned to Williamsburg where despite his earlier censure regarding the Fort Necessity capitulation agreement, he was cordially welcomed. The burgesses voted to give him his back pay and also an added compensation of £500 for his "sufferings." He joined the British regular army as a captain in the Royal American Regiment and served until the end of the war, after which he was placed on half pay. He spent the next years trying to get back on active duty and was called up at the outbreak of the American Revolution. He was promoted to major and served at St. Augustine where he spent a good deal of his time unsuccessfully trying to convince the Royal Governor of Florida to give him a land grant. He resigned his commission in 1779 at the age of fifty and settled in France. His subsequent history is unknown.

Epilogue

Villiers, Louis Coulon de (1710–1757)

After defeating Washington in the Battle of Great Meadows, Villiers continued in the service of the French king. In 1755, Villiers was actively involved in the partisan warfare that raged along the Pennsylvania and western New York frontiers. He gained renown as part of Montcalm's force that captured Fort Oswego on Sunday, August 15, 1756, and Fort William Henry on Tuesday, August 9, 1757. As a result of his distinguished and valorous service to the king, he was awarded the prestigious Cross of Saint-Louis. Villiers went to Québec to receive the coveted award and there he contracted smallpox. "Les Grande" Villiers died of the disease on Wednesday, November 2, 1757, a few days after receiving his award. He was forty-seven years old.

Ward, Edward (fl. 1754–?)

In 1757, according to records in the Pennsylvania archives, Ward was promoted to captain in the 1st Battalion of the Pennsylvania Regiment, and in 1759, he was subsequently promoted to major. There is very little other information regarding his activities during the remainder of the French and Indian War. In 1775, Ward was appointed a justice for the district of West Augusta, Pennsylvania, and records indicate that he served at least into 1776. His son John Ward served as a lieutenant under Washington during the Revolutionary War.

Washington, George (1732–1799)

After the capture of Fort Duquesne, Washington returned to Virginia and resumed the defense of the Virginia frontier from his headquarters at Fort Loudoun in Winchester. On Saturday, January 6, 1759, Washington married the wealthy widow Martha Dandridge Custis, and later that year he was elected a burgess. When he arrived in Williamsburg for the legislative session, the assembly thanked him for his meritorious military service. He spent the ensuing fifteen years until the start of the Revolutionary War as a gentleman farmer and also involved himself in mundane legislative activities. Washington later stated that they were the most enjoyable years of his life.

On Thursday, April 30, 1789, Washington was inaugurated as the

Epilogue

first president of the United States, and he served in that office until Saturday, March 4, 1797. At the end of his presidency, Washington returned to Mount Vernon where he resumed his life as a farmer and planter. Washington died at his Mount Vernon home on Saturday, December 14, 1799, at the age of sixty-seven.

Chapter Notes

Preface

1. At the time, the earth's population was about eight hundred million.

Chapter 1

1. A study of skeletal remains by Richard Steckel, PhD, at Ohio State University indicates that the average male's height during the seventeenth and eighteenth centuries was 173.4 centimeters (68.27 inches), or five feet, eight and one-quarter inches. Richard, H. Steckel, *Heights and Human Welfare: Recent Developments and New Directions* (Cambridge: National Bureau of Economic Research, 2008), http://www.nber.org/papers/w14536.

2. One stone is equivalent to fourteen pounds.

3. At the time, Baltimore County was the northwest frontier of the Province of Maryland, and it included present Baltimore City and Cecil and Hartford counties as well as parts of Carroll, Anne Arundel, Frederick, Howard, and Kent counties.

4. Some records indicate that Edith Cromwell Gist died in 1696.

5. Wilson Gee, *The Gist Family of South Carolina and Its Maryland Antecedents* (Charlottesville: Jarmans, 1934), p. 1.

6. Lawrence A. Orrill, *Christopher Gist and His Sons* (Pittsburgh: Historical Society of Western Pennsylvania, 1932), p. 194, https://journals.psu.edu/wph/article/view/1590/1438.

7. Joshua Howard (1689–1736), Joanna O'Carroll (1683–1764). Christopher married Sarah (1711–1726), Nathaniel married Mary (1712–1755), and William married Violetta (1716–1783).

8. Donna C. Moore, *Genealogy Report: Some Descendants of Christopher Gist* [Updated 1 Jan. 2001], https://www.genealogy.com/ftm/m/o/o/Donna-C-Moore/GENE18-0003.html.

9. Lot 56 was located at or near present 210 E. Redwood Street, Baltimore, Maryland.

10. J. Thomas Scharf, *History of Baltimore City and County from the Earliest Period to the Present Day: Including Biographical Sketches of Their Representative Men* (Philadelphia: L.H. Everts, 1881), p. 53.

11. Paul R. Misencik and Sally E. Misencik, *American Indians of the Ohio Country in the 18th Century* (Jefferson, NC: McFarland, 2020), pp. 10–11.

12. Jean Muir Dorsey and Maxwell Jay Dorsey, *Christopher Gist of Maryland and Some of His Descendants* (Chicago: John S. Swift, 1958), p. 11.

13. A sloop is a single-masted sailing vessel with fore and aft rigging. During the eighteenth century, they normally were rigged with a mainsail, topsail, and one or more head sails.

14. Ship weight is generally calculated according to Archimedes' principle by the amount of water it displaces when fully loaded.

15. Alan Powell, *Christopher Gist Frontier Scout* (Shippensburg, PA: Burd Street Press, 1992), p. 4.

16. Kenneth P. Bailey, *Christopher Gist: Colonial Frontiersman, Explorer, and Indian Agent* (Hamden, CT: Archon Books, 1976), pp. 22–23.

Notes—Chapter 2

17. One pound (£) = twenty shillings (s), one guinea = twenty-one shillings, one shilling = twelve pence (d). There were also halfpennies (pronounced *hay-penny*) and a fourth of a penny, originally called "fourth-ing" and later "farthing."
18. Bailey, *Christopher Gist: Colonial Frontiersman*, pp. 22–23.
19. Dorsey and Dorsey, p. 12.
20. Orrill, p. 196.
21. Dorsey and Dorsey, p. 12.
22. Orrill, p. 196.
23. Robert Millward and Kathleen Millward, "Making History in the Wilderness: Christopher Gist's Explorations into Western Pennsylvania," *Western Pennsylvania History* (Summer 2008): p. 24.
24. Orrill, p. 196.
25. Around 1752, when Daniel Boone was about eighteen years of age, his father invested in land close to the Yadkin River, about eight miles from the site of present Wilkesboro, North Carolina.
26. Joshua Fry (1699–1754) was a surveyor, mapmaker, soldier, adventurer, and member of the Virginia House of Burgesses.
27. Peter Jefferson (1708–1757), father of Thomas Jefferson. Peter was a surveyor and cartographer who worked with Joshua Fry on a map that accurately depicted the Allegheny Mountain region from northern Pennsylvania to the Yadkin River area of North Carolina.
28. Henry Mouzon, Jr. (1741–1807). Mapmaker, civil engineer. Mouzon also served as an American officer during the Revolutionary War.

Chapter 2

1. The Treaty of Ryswick (Rijswijk) (1697) concluded the War of the Grand Alliance, (1688–1697), known in North America as King William's War, Father Baudoin's War, and War of the League of Augsburg.
2. The Treaty of Utrecht (1713) concluded the War of the Spanish Succession (1702–1713) or Queen Anne's War.
3. The Treaty of Aix-la-Chapelle (1748) concluded the War of the Austrian Succession, or in North America, King George's War.
4. Paul R. Misencik, *George Washington and the Half-King Chief Tanacharison: An Alliance That Began the French and Indian War* (Jefferson, NC: McFarland, 2014), pp. 11–13.
5. Venetian Zuan Chabotto, or more popularly as Giovanni Caboto, was an Italian navigator and explorer.
6. Commissioners for Trade and Plantations was an administrative body to promote trade and improve the plantations of the British colonies. They provided their advice to the king through the Privy Council.
7. The Privy Council was a body that advised the king. The word *privy* implies "private" or "secret"; thus, a privy council was originally a committee of the king's closest advisors to provide advice regarding state affairs.
8. Present Cumberland, Maryland.
9. Richard Henry Lee later was a delegate to the Second Continental Congress when the Declaration of Independence was adopted and was president of the Confederation Congress and one of Virginia's first two senators under the Constitution.
10. Father of John Chapman (1774–1845), better known as Johnny Appleseed.
11. Present Stafford, Virginia.
12. The Falls of the Ohio were a long stretch of rapids caused by a twenty-six-foot drop of the Ohio River, which extended a little more than a mile in length near present Louisville, Kentucky.
13. The measuring of geometric magnitudes, lengths, areas, and volumes.
14. Christopher Gist, *Christopher Gist's Journals; With Historical, Geographical and Ethnological Notes and Biographies of His Contemporaries by William M. Darlington* (Pittsburgh: J. R. Weldin, 1893), pp. 31–32.
15. A factor is a business agent or a merchant who buys and sells on commission.
16. Alfred P. James, *The Ohio Company: Its Inner History* (Pittsburgh: University of Pittsburg Press, 1959), p. 40.

Notes—Chapter 3

Chapter 3

1. Gist, *Christopher Gist's Journals*, p. 32.
2. Ibid., p. 34.
3. The Forks of the Ohio are where the Allegheny and the Monongahela rivers join to form the Ohio River.
4. In 1758, it was the route General Forbes took from Carlisle, Pennsylvania, for his successful assault on Fort Duquesne.
5. Gist, *Christopher Gist's Journals*, p. 33.
6. Ibid., p. 35.
7. Lenape (the people) or Lenni Lenape (the real people) are the Native American Nation commonly referred to as the Delaware.
8. The actual distance was about fifty-two miles.
9. Sweat lodge is a Native American custom where individuals enter a small, dome-shaped construction to experience a sauna-like environment. Rocks heated by fire are placed in a shallow depression inside and water is sprinkled on them to produce steam.
10. Gist, *Christopher Gist's Journals*, p. 33.
11. Ibid., p. 34.
12. A *pole* is an old English measure of distance equal to 16.5 feet or 5.029 meters. It is more commonly referred to as a *rod* and occasionally as a *perch pole*.
13. Gist, *Christopher Gist's Journals*, p. 34.
14. Ibid.
15. Misencik and Misencik, *American Indians of the Ohio Country*, p. 31.
16. Gist, *Christopher Gist's Journals*, pp. 34–35.
17. Ibid., p. 35.
18. Ibid., p. 36.
19. Mingo is a corruption of the Lenape word *Mingwe*, which translates to "stealthy" or "treacherous." They were expatriate Iroquois, mostly Seneca and Cayuga, with a smattering of other members of the Iroquois Confederacy, who settled in western Pennsylvania and Ohio. In time, they considered themselves a separate and independent culture from the Iroquois.
20. Also known in some sources as the "Kuskuskies."
21. Gist, *Christopher Gist's Journals*, p. 36.
22. Fort Laurens was built in December 1778 and abandoned in August 1779.
23. Misencik and Misencik, *American Indians of the Ohio Country*, p. 198.
24. Ibid., p. 109.
25. The term "Little Mingo" does not make sense, since the Wyandot are essentially western Huron, or as they refer to themselves, Wendat. Mingo, on the other hand, refers to expatriate Iroquois who have migrated from their traditional homeland around the Finger Lakes area of New York.
26. This is a reference to the Miami Indian town of Pickawillany at present Piqua, Ohio.
27. Gist, *Christopher Gist's Journals*, p. 37.
28. Misencik and Misencik, *American Indians of the Ohio Country*, pp. 17–18.
29. Not to be confused with the British Fort Sandusky (1761–1763) that was built at present Sandusky, Ohio.
30. The portage, named after French Lt. Joseph G. Chaussegros DeLery, who described it in his journal, allowed canoes to and from Fort Detroit to avoid the longer, more treacherous route around the peninsula.
31. The name did not literally mean "good man," since that is *room-wae-ta-wagh-stee*, in the Wyandot language. Some sources indicate it means "speaker of the truth," but I have been unable to verify that.
32. Gist, *Christopher Gist's Journals*, p. 38.
33. Ibid., p. 39.
34. Ibid., p. 41.
35. Misencik and Misencik, *American Indians of the Ohio Country*, pp. 152–154.
36. Ibid., p. 153.
37. Gist, *Christopher Gist's Journals*, p. 41.
38. Misencik and Misencik, *American Indians of the Ohio Country*, p. 153.
39. In the nineteenth century, romanticized and lurid legends sprang up about the White Woman of Coshocton County.

Notes—Chapters 4 and 5

The most persistent account claims that Mary grew jealous of her husband's infatuation with a white captive, so she killed her husband and blamed his death on the white woman captive. The legend had been completely debunked, yet it can still be found in local "historical" publications.

40. The Scioto Trail was the major north-south thoroughfare, which crossed Ohio from Sandusky Bay in the north generally following the Sandusky, the Olentangy, and the Scioto rivers to Lower Shawnee Town (present Portsmouth, Ohio) in the south.

41. The Mekoche, also *Mequachake, Maccachee, Maguck,* and *Mackachack,* were one of the five septs, or branches, of the Shawnee. The others were the Chalahgawatha, Hathawekela, Kispokotha, and Pekuwe.

42. Gist, *Christopher Gist's Journals,* p. 42.

43. Licking Reservoir map, Ohio History Connection, https://ohiomemory.org/digital/collection/p267401coll32/id/26660/.

44. Misencik and Misencik, *American Indians of the Ohio Country,* p. 215.

45. Gist, *Christopher Gist's Journals,* p. 42.

46. Misencik and Misencik, *American Indians of the Ohio Country,* pp. 245–248.

47. Ibid., p. 246.

48. Gist, *Christopher Gist's Journals,* p. 43.

49. In some sources, also written as *Wandochale, Windaughala, Wanduxales,* and others. Wanduchale was the father of the noted war chief Buckongahelas.

50. It was also identified in some sources as Chillicothe, Sonionto, Sinhioto, Chalahgawatha, St. Yotoc, Scioto Town, and Old Lower Shawnee Town.

51. Samuel Prescott Hildreth, *Ohio Valley and the Early Settlement of the Northwest Territory* (Cincinnati: H. W. Derby, 1848), pp. 31–32.

52. Misencik and Misencik, *American Indians of the Ohio Country,* pp. 15–16.

53. Other than Kallandar's name, no other information regarding him can be found.

54. Gist, *Christopher Gist's Journals,* p. 47.

55. Ibid., p. 51.

56. Ibid., p. 53.

57. Ibid., p. 55.

58. Ibid., p. 56.

59. Ibid.

Chapter 4

1. The site is now called Big Bone Lick State Park, Boone County, Kentucky. Many Pleistocene megafauna fossils were found there, including mammoths that were drawn to the salt lick around the springs.

2. Gist, *Christopher Gist's Journals,* pp. 57–58.

3. Ibid.

4. According to Darlington, there was a salt lick at that location.

5. Gist, *Christopher Gist's Journals,* p. 58.

6. Ibid.

7. Ibid., p. 60.

8. Ibid.

9. Pinnacle Rock near Bramwell, Mercer County, West Virginia, is a sandstone "pinnacle" atop a 3,700-foot mountain.

10. Gist was referring to the New River, which flows north and joins the Gauley River to form the Kanawha River.

11. Gist, *Christopher Gist's Journals,* p. 64.

12. Ibid., p. 65.

13. Mountain Lake Hotel was the site of much of the filming of the 1987 movie *Dirty Dancing* starring Patrick Swayze and Jennifer Grey.

14. Gist, *Christopher Gist's Journals,* p. 65

15. Ibid., p. 66.

16. Ibid.

Chapter 5

1. James, pp. 52–53.

2. Christopher Gist, *Instructions Given Mr. Christopher Gist by the Committee of the Ohio Company the 11th day of September 1750 and July 16th 1751. Also the Daily Record of Christopher Gist*

Notes—Chapters 6 and 7

Containing an Account of his Travels Discoveries, Transactions with the Indians (n.p.: Franklin Classics, 2018), p. 28.

Chapter 6

1. David. B. McCoy, *Christopher Gist* (Massillon, OH: Spare Change Press, 2019), p. 36.
2. Ibid., p. 36.
3. Gist, *Christopher Gist's Journals*, p. 137.
4. The storehouse was constructed on Redstone Creek, which got its name from the predominantly reddish sandstone in the area.
5. Gist, *Christopher Gist's Journals*, p. 68.
6. Ibid.
7. Ibid.
8. The Indians called the area near present Confluence, Pennsylvania, the Turkeyfoot because they believed the junction of the Casselman River and Laurel Hill Creek with the Youghiogheny River resembled a bird's foot.
9. The full moon fell on the night of Saturday, May 16, 1752.
10. Gist, *Christopher Gist's Journals*, p. 69.
11. Ibid., pp. 69–70.
12. Ibid., p. 70.
13. Ibid., p. 71.
14. Ibid.
15. Present Beaver, Pennsylvania.
16. Gist, *Christopher Gist's Journals*, p. 72.
17. Ibid.
18. Ibid., p. 73.
19. Ibid.
20. The inscription on the stone had effaced over time, and reportedly it had been broken up by industrial operations in the area.
21. Gist, *Christopher Gist's Journals*, p. 74.
22. Ibid., p. 75.
23. Ibid., p. 76.
24. Ibid., p. 77.
25. Ibid., p. 78.
26. Beaver is the English name of Tamaqua (c. 1710–c. 1770), who is also referred to as King Beaver.
27. No biographical information about Oppamylucah can be found. Quite possibly, the Indian may have been referring to *Shingas* (fl. 1740–c. 1764), who was the brother of Tamaqua (c. 1710–c. 1770).
28. Gist, *Christopher Gist's Journals*, p. 78.
29. Ibid.
30. Ibid., p. 79.
31. Ibid.

Chapter 7

1. Lois Mulkearn, "Why the Treaty of Logstown, 1752," *Virginia Magazine of History and Biography* 59, no. 1 (January 1951): 3–20, http://www.jstor.org/stable/4245750.
2. The term "half-king" was essentially an English appellation applied to leaders or headmen who represented the Iroquois council. The half-kings supervised the subjugated tribes that were under the domination of the Iroquois and also the expatriate Iroquois known as Mingo. The British often found it easier to deal with a local half-king than with the Iroquois Grand Council at Onondaga (present Syracuse, New York). The French also used the term *le demi-roi*, or half-king, in the same context.
3. James Patton was a Scots-Irish immigrant to Virginia around the 1739, when he settled in the Shenandoah Valley. Between the years 1744 to his death in 1755, he was at one time or another the Augusta County Justice of the Peace, Colonel of Militia, President of the Court, Sheriff, Augusta Parish Vestry, and member of the Virginia House of Burgesses. Patton was killed by Indians in July 1755.
4. Joshua Fry was a surveyor, adventurer, mapmaker, soldier, and member of the Virginia House of Burgesses. He is best known for collaborating with Peter Jefferson, the father of Thomas Jefferson, in making a detailed map of Virginia in 1752. In 1754, he was appointed Commander-in-Chief of Virginia Forces, with George Washington as his second-in-command. En route to join Washington near present Cumberland,

Notes—Chapters 8, 9 and 10

Maryland, he fell from his horse and was fatally injured, which elevated Washington to command of the Virginia Regiment.

5. Lunsford Lomax from Portobago on the south side of the Rappahannock River near present Port Royal, Virginia. Lomax was a member of the Virginia House of Burgesses from 1742 until 1756.

6. Mulkearn, "Why the Treaty of Logstown," 1951.

7. Ibid.

8. William Trent, soldier, Indian trader, and land speculator.

9. Order of the Council referring the humble petition of the Ohio Company, April 2, 1754, P. R. O. Colonial Office Papers, 5:1328, 153–159, 164, Memorial of the Ohio Company, November 20, 1778, Virginia State Library.

Chapter 8

1. As near as can be determined, the Gist cabin was located approximately at 39.943703 latitude, -79.651128 longitude.

2. Cherokee people who lived on the western side of the Appalachian Mountains.

3. Also known as Chote, Echota, Istati, and other variations.

4. David B. Trimble, "Christopher Gist and Settlement on the Monongahela, 1752–1754," *Virginia Magazine of History and Biography* 63, no. 1 (January 1955): 15–27, http://www.jstor.org/stable/4246087.

5. Ibid.

6. James, p. 74.

7. Kenneth P. Bailey, "Christopher Gist and the Trans-Allegheny Frontier: A Phase of the Westward Movement," *Pacific Historical Review* 14, no. 1 (1945): 45–56, https://doi.org/10.2307/3634512.

8. The Acts of Toleration from Monday, May 24, 1689, granted freedom of worship to Nonconformist religions, as long as they accepted certain oaths of allegiance. It allowed people the freedom not to conform to or support the Church of England, but the act did not apply to Roman Catholics, nontrinitarians, and atheists.

9. Lois Mulkearn, ed., *George Mercer Papers Relating to the Ohio Company of Virginia* (Pittsburgh: University of Pittsburgh Press, 1954), pp. 147–148.

10. A quit-rent is a tax on occupants of a freehold.

11. James, pp. 77–78.

12. Mulkearn, *George Mercer Papers*, pp. 147–148.

13. Ibid., p. 148.

14. A measuring wheel, also known as a surveyor's wheel, clickwheel, hodometer, waywiser, trundle wheel, or perambulator, is a device for measuring distance. To measure distance, the surveyor places the wheel at the starting point and pushes or pulls it along to the end point.

Chapter 9

1. La Chine, or Lachine, was a small community south of the city of Montréal but was incorporated into Montréal in 2002.

2. Misencik, *George Washington and the Half-King Chief Tanacharison*, p. 53.

3. Ibid., p. 54.

4. Ibid., p. 55.

5. Ibid.

6. A two-story stone house, built about 1749 by Sir William Johnson in present Fort Johnson, New York. He lived there until 1763 before moving eight and one-half miles northwest to Johnson Hall, in present Johnstown, New York.

7. Misencik, *George Washington and the Half-King Chief Tanacharison*, pp. 49–50.

8. A type of dysentery, with symptoms of extreme bloody diarrhea, fever, and abdominal pain.

9. Misencik, *George Washington and the Half-King Chief Tanacharison*, p. 60.

Chapter 10

1. Ibid., p. 61.

2. Ibid., pp. 61–62.

3. Gist, *Christopher Gist's Journals*, p. 80

4. Ibid.

5. Ibid.

Notes—Chapters 11 and 12

6. Misencik, *George Washington and the Half-King Chief Tanacharison*, p. 64.

7. Shingas (c. 1740–1763) was an Ohio Delaware chief who tried to remain neutral but eventually sided with the French during the French and Indian War. He became known as "Shingas the Terrible" because of his devastating raids against Anglo-American settlements. The colonial governments of Virginia and Pennsylvania offered a reward for his death. Though he was a very effective warrior, he was also a mild-mannered orator who was never known to treat prisoners with cruelty. He adopted several young white captives as his sons, and according to them, they were accorded equal treatment with his own offspring. It is assumed that he died in the winter of 1763–1764, possibly from smallpox-infected blankets that were given to the Indians during Pontiac's War.

8. William A. Hunter, *Forts on the Pennsylvania Frontier, 1753–1758* (Lewisburg, PA: Wennawoods, 1999), p. 27.

9. Gist, *Christopher Gist's Journals*, p. 81.

10. *Dictionary of Canadian Biography Online*, s.v. Legardeur de Saint-Pierre, Jacques, http://www.biographi.ca/en/bio.php?&id_nbr=1474.

11. Hugh Cleland, *George Washington in the Ohio Valley* (University of Pittsburgh Press, 1955), p. 20.

12. Cleland, p. 21.

13. Ibid., pp. 31–32.

Chapter 11

1. Gist, *Christopher Gist's Journals*, p. 84.
2. Ibid.
3. Cleland, p. 25.
4. Gist, *Christopher Gist's Journals*, p. 84.
5. Cleland, p. 26.
6. Gist, *Christopher Gist's Journals*, p. 84.
7. Some sources indicate that the Indians referred to Gist as *Annosanah*, which supposedly means "speaker of the truth," but there is no scholarly documentation to support that.
8. Gist, *Christopher Gist's Journals*, p. 84.
9. Ibid., p. 85.
10. Ibid., pp. 85–86.
11. Ibid., p. 86.
12. Cleland, pp. 26–27.
13. The island was later named Wainwrights Island, but it no longer exists.
14. Cleland, p. 27.
15. Queen Aliquippa, born sometime between 1670 and the early 1700s, was a leader of a Mingo community near the Forks of the Ohio. She died at Aughwick on December 23, 1754.
16. Gist, *Christopher Gist's Journals*, p. 86.
17. James, p. 97.
18. Ibid.
19. Ibid.
20. Bailey, *Christopher Gist: Colonial Frontiersman*, p. 85.
21. Walter O'Meara, *Guns at the Forks* (University of Pittsburg Press, 1965), pp. 41–42.
22. Joseph L. Peyser, *Jacques Legardeur De Saint-Pierre—Officer, Gentleman, Entrepreneur* (East Lansing: Michigan State University Press, 1996), p. 192.
23. O'Meara, p. 43.
24. Ibid.
25. Cleland, p. 61.
26. Ibid., p. 63.
27. George Washington, "Letter from George Washington to Robert Dinwiddie, March 9, 1754," Virginia Historical Society, Richmond, E312.72 1962 v.1 p. 73.
28. Charles H. Ambler, *George Washington and the West* (Chapel Hill: University of North Carolina Press, 1936), p. 58.

Chapter 12

1. Ward was also the half-brother of trader George Croghan. No other information regarding Ward's birth or death has been located.
2. O'Meara, pp. 47–49.
3. Misencik, *George Washington and the Half-King Chief Tanacharison*, p. 90.
4. O'Meara, pp. 49–50.
5. Linsey-woolsey was a coarse twill used on the frontier that was composed

of linen and wool or sometimes of cotton and wool.

6. Adam Stephen, Scottish-born physician, c. 1718–1791. Graduated from King's College in Aberdeen and studied medicine in Edinburg. He served in the Royal Navy as a medical doctor and emigrated to Virginia in the late 1730s or early 1740s.

7. A discussion or conference, particularly between opposing sides, to discuss terms of a truce or other matters. From the French word *parler*, which means "to speak," or specifically from *parlez*, meaning "you speak."

8. *Minutes of the Provincial Council of Pennsylvania, Vol. VI* (Harrisburg: Published by the State [Pennsylvania]—Theo. Fenn, 1851), pp. 29–30

9. O'Meara, p. 52.

10. William W. Fowler, Jr., *Empires at War* (New York: Walker, 2005), p. 37.

11. Ibid. Fowler states that "Contrecœur offered rations for the tools, and the next morning as the Virginian's were leaving, the French were already busy with their newly acquired hammers and saws."

12. Gist, *Christopher Gist's Journals*, p. 276.

13. J.C.B., *Travels in New France*, ed. Sylvester K. Stevens, Donald H. Kent, and Emma E. Woods (Harrisburg: Pennsylvania Historical Commission, 1941), p. 56.

Chapter 13

1. J.M. Toner, ed., *Journal of George Washington, Commanding a Detachment of Virginia Troops* (Albany: Joel Munsell's Sons, 1893), pp. 50–51.

2. Ambler, p. 62.

3. Toner, p. 63.

4. It's unclear what rank LaForce held at the time. Some sources indicate he was an ensign, while other sources list him as a lieutenant.

5. George Washington, *The Papers of George Washington: 1748–August 1755*, ed. W.W. Abbot (Charlottesville: University of Virginia Press, 1983), p. 105.

6. Toner, p. 74.

7. *Ye* is an older spelling of the definite article *the*. The *y* in *ye* was pronounced "th." In Old English and Middle English, the sound "th" was represented by the letter "thorn" (þ). When English printing presses were first established in the 1470s, the type came from Continental Europe, where the letter "thorn" was not in use. Instead, typesetters used the letter *y* for þ, because in the handwriting of the day, the two were similar. This practice was carried over into handwritten documents. The modern revival of the archaic spelling of *the* has not been accompanied with an understanding of how it was pronounced, with the result that the usual pronunciation is "yee."

8. Robert Dinwiddie, *The Official Records of Robert Dinwiddie, Lieutenant-Governor of the Colony of Virginia 1751–1758*, ed. R.A. Brock (Richmond: Virginia Historical Society, 1883), p. 175.

9. No other information regarding "Silverheels" has been found.

10. Toner, p. 88.

11. J.C.B., pp. 57–58.

12. Ibid., p. 58.

13. Ambler, p. 65.

14. Fred Anderson, *Crucible of War* (New York: Vintage Books, 2001), p. 6.

Chapter 14

1. Toner, p. 98.

2. Bailey, *Christopher Gist: Colonial Frontiersman*, p. 98.

3. Ibid., p. 101.

4. O'Meara, p. 93.

5. It is difficult to determine the precise size of Villiers's force. His own journal states that Contrecœur detailed five hundred French and eleven hundred Indians. Historians generally agree that this is a gross overestimation of the Indian force. Other sources list the French and Canadian force as around 500–650 men, plus anywhere from 100 to 300 Indians. J.C.B., who accompanied the expedition, does not give a number of French troops other than to say it was originally intended to be one hundred men; however, he says it was

Notes—Chapters 15, 16, 17 and 18

"augmented by 300 savages." In any case, it is safe to say that the force greatly outnumbered Washington's defenders.
  6. Trimble, 15–27.
  7. Misencik, *George Washington and the Half-King Chief Tanacharison*, pp. 144–145.

Chapter 15

  1. Bailey, "Christopher Gist and the Trans-Allegheny Frontier," pp. 45–56.
  2. Stanislaus M. Hamilton, *Letters to Washington and Accompanying Papers*, Vol. II (Boston: Houghton, Mifflin, 1898–1902), p. 148.
  3. Bailey, *Christopher Gist: Colonial Frontiersman, Explorer*, p. 171.
  4. Bailey, "Christopher Gist and the Trans-Allegheny Frontier," pp. 45–56.
  5. George Washington to William Fitzhugh, November 15, 1754, in *Papers of George Washington*, Colonial Series, Vol. I, W. W. Abbot, ed. (Charlottesville: University of Virginia Press, 1983), pp. 225–227.
  6. George II was the last British monarch to actually lead troops in battle.
  7. Misencik, *George Washington and the Half-King Chief Tanacharison*, p. 176.
  8. Thomas E. Crocker, *Braddock's March: How the Man Sent to Seize a Continent Changed American History* (Yardley, PA: Westholme, 2009), p. 72.
  9. Ibid., p. 75.
  10. Ibid.
  11. Winthrop Sargent, ed., *The History of an Expedition Against Fort Du Quesne in 1755* (Philadelphia: Lippencott, Grambo, 1855), p. 349.
  12. McCoy, p. 49.
  13. Dinwiddie, Official Records, 2:26, 76, 77 (Richmond: Virginia Historical Society, Collections, Vol. 4, 1884); Daniel Dulany, "Military and Political Affairs in the Middle Colonies in 1755," *Pennsylvania Magazine of History and Biography* 3, no. 19 (1879): 11–31.
  14. Crocker, pp. 117–118.
  15. Ibid., p. 118.
  16. Crocker, p. 146.
  17. Scarouaday ("side of the sky") (?–1757). Also referred to as Monacatuatha, Monakaduto, Monacatootha, Monacatoocha, etc. ("great arrow"). He was an Oneida Iroquois and like Tanacharison, was also a "half-king." He was recognized by the Iroquois to provide oversight of the Shawnee in the Ohio territory. He was also known as a famous warrior and chief who participated in thirty-one battles, killed seven warriors, and took eleven captives. He sided with the British and attempted to sway the Delaware Indians to the British cause. He died in Lancaster, Pennsylvania, in 1757 while attending a treaty.
  18. Crocker, p. 140.

Chapter 16

  1. In some sources it's spelled "Spendelow."
  2. Bailey, *Christopher Gist: Colonial Frontiersman*, p. 92.

Chapter 17

  1. Often called "canister"; was a closed metal cylinder filled with round lead or iron balls, sometimes scrap metal, packed with sawdust for solidity, which upon firing from a cannon quickly spread out as an effective, short-range anti-personnel weapon.
  2. Bailey, *Christopher Gist: Colonial Frontiersman*, p. 94.
  3. George Washington, *George Washington Papers, Series 2, Letterbooks 1754–1799: Letterbook 2, March 2–Dec. 6, 1755*, 1755, Manuscript/Mixed Material, Library of Congress, Washington, D.C., https://www.loc.gov/item/mgw2.002/.

Chapter 18

  1. Twenty shillings (20s) equals one pound (£1).
  2. Bailey, *Christopher Gist: Colonial Frontiersman*, p. 108.
  3. Hamilton, *Letters to Washington*, pp. 129–130.
  4. John C. Fitzpatrick, ed., *The Writings*

Notes—Chapters 19, 20 and Epilogue

of George Washington from the Original Manuscript Sources 1745–1799 (Washington, D.C.: U.S. Government Printing Office, 1931), p. 382.

5. Ibid., p. 420.
6. Bailey, *Christopher Gist: Colonial Frontiersman*, p. 110.
7. Ibid., p. 111.
8. The northern cornerstone of a chain of forts built by Virginia to protect frontier settlers from Indian forays during the French and Indian War, Fort Maidstone was built on the south side of the Potomac River opposite present Williamsport, Maryland. During the fall of 1755 and spring of 1756, it served as an outpost and depot for the Virginia Regiment.
9. Fitzpatrick, *The Writings of George Washington*, p. 40.
10. Ibid., p. 41.
11. Ibid., pp. 43–44.
12. Trimble, "Christopher Gist and the Indian Service in Virginia," p. 148.

Chapter 19

1. Also Abercromby.
2. Trimble, "Christopher Gist and the Indian Service in Virginia," p. 158
3. Ibid.
4. Charles R. Hildeburn, "Sir John St. Clair, Baronet, Quarter-Master General in America, 1755–1767," *Pennsylvania Magazine of History and Biography* 9, no. 1 (1885), https://archive.org/stream/-jstor-20084686/20084686_djvu.txt.
5. S.K. Stevens, D.H. Kent, and A.L. Leonard, eds., *The Papers of Henry Bouquet, Vol II: The Forbes Expedition* (Harrisburg: Pennsylvania Historical and Museum Commission, 1951), p. 15.
6. Ibid., p. 181.
7. Ibid., p. 205.
8. Ibid., pp. 210–211.
9. Ibid., p. 217.
10. Ibid., p. 356.
11. Fitzpatrick, *The Writings of George Washington*, p. 201.
12. Thomas Gist was captured by Wyandot Indians during the fight and taken to a Wyandot town near Fort Detroit, where he was adopted by a Wyandot family and well treated. He escaped after a year in captivity and made his way back to Virginia.

Chapter 20

1. Bailey, *Christopher Gist: Colonial Frontiersman*, p. 148.
2. Leake was not yet aware that Gist died of smallpox eleven day earlier on Sunday, July 25, 1759.
3. Stevens, Kent, and Leonard, p. 7.
4. Ibid., p. 217.
5. D.H. Kent, L. Waddell, and A.L. Leonard, eds., *The Papers of Henry Bouquet, Vol III, January 1, 1759–August 31, 1759* (Harrisburg: Pennsylvania Historical Commission, 1976), p. 544.

Epilogue

1. Robert Hilliard, "Queen Aliquippa; A History," *Milestones* 21, no. 3 (Autumn 1996), https://www.bcpahistory.org/beavercounty/BeaverCountyTopical/NativeAmerican/QueenAliquippMA96.html
2. *Dictionary of Canadian Biography Online*, s.v. "Pécaudy de Contrecœr, Claude-Pierre," http://www.biographi.ca/en/bio/pecaudy_de_contrecoeur_claude_pierre_4E.html
3. J.C. Fitzpatrick, ed., *The Diaries of George Washington, 1748–1799, Vol. I* (Boston: Houghton, Mifflin, 1925), p. 407.
4. Pierre Pouchot, *Memoirs on The Late War in North America Between France and England*, trans. Michael Cardy (Roxbury, 1866), pp. 141–238.
5. Archie V. Huff, Jr., *The History of the City and County in the South Carolina Piedmont* (Columbia: University of South Carolina Press, 1995), pp. 14–15
6. Gold cobs was a name for the Spanish gold escudos or doubloons, and in common vernacular denoted coins of considerable value.
7. For the full biography of Stobo, see Robert C. Alberts, *The Most Extraordinary Adventures of Major Robert Stobo* (Cambridge: Riverside Press, 1965).

Bibliography

Albert, G.D. *Report of the Commission to Locate the Site of the Frontier Forts of Pennsylvania: The Frontier Forts of Western Pennsylvania.* Harrisburg: Wm. Stanley Ray, 1916.

Alberts, Robert C. *A Charming Field for an Encounter.* Washington, D.C.: National Park Service, 1975.

Alberts, Robert C. *The Most Extraordinary Adventures of Major Robert Stobo.* Cambridge: Riverside Press, 1965.

Ambler, Charles H. *George Washington and the West.* Chapel Hill: University of North Carolina Press, 1936.

Anderson, Fred. *Crucible of War.* New York: Vintage Books, 2001.

Anonymous. *Hazards Register of Pennsylvania (Volume 4).* Ann Arbor: University of Michigan Library, 1831.

Anonymous. *The Militia-Man: Containing Necessary Rules for Both Officer and Soldier With an Explaination of the Manual Exercise of the Foot.* Schenectady, NY: United States Historical Research, 1995. First published ca. 1740.

Axelrod, Alan. *Blooding at Great Meadows.* Philadelphia: Running Press, 2007.

Bailey, Kenneth P. "Christopher Gist and the Trans-Allegheny Frontier: A Phase of the Westward Movement." *Pacific Historical Review* 14, no. 1 (1945): 45–56. https://doi.org/10.2307/3634512.

Bailey, Kenneth P. *Christopher Gist: Colonial Frontiersman, Explorer, and Indian Agent.* Hamden, CT: Archon Books, 1976.

Baker, Norman L. *Fort Loudon: Washington's Fort in Virginia.* Winchester, VA: French and Indian War Foundation, 2006.

Baker-Crothers, Hayes. *Virginia and the French and Indian War.* Chicago: University of Chicago Press, 1928.

Cave, Alfred A. *The French and Indian War.* Westport, CT: Greenwood Press, 2004.

Chartarand, René. *Monongahela 1754–55, Washington's Defeat, Braddock's Disaster.* Oxford: Osprey, 2004.

Cleland, Hugh. *George Washington in the Ohio Valley.* Pittsburgh: University of Pittsburgh Press, 1955.

Corzier, William Armstrong, ed. *Virginia Colonial Muster: 1651–1776.* New York: Genealogical Association, 1905.

Crocker, Thomas E. *Braddock's March: How the Man Sent to Seize a Continent Changed American History.* Yardley, PA: Westholme, 2009.

Dale, Ronald J. *The Fall of New France.* Toronto: James Lorimer, 2004.

Dinwiddie, Official Records, 2:26, 76, 77. Virginia Historical Society, Collections, Vol. 4, Richmond, 1884.

Dinwiddie, Robert. *The Official Records of Robert Dinwiddie, Lieutenant-Governor of the Colony of Virginia 1751–1758.* Edited by R.A. Brock. Richmond: Virginia Historical Society, 1883.

Dorsey, Jean Muir, and Maxwell Jay Dorsey. *Christopher Gist of Maryland and Some of His Descendants.* Chicago: John S. Swift, 1958.

Dulany, Daniel. "Military and Political Affairs in the Middle Colonies in 1755." *Pennsylvania Magazine of History and Biography* 3, no. 19 (1879): 11–31.

Everts, L. H. *History of Allegheny County, Pennsylvania.* Philadelphia: L. H. Everts, 1876.

Bibliography

Fitzpatrick, John C., ed. *The Diaries of George Washington, 1748–1799, Vol. I.* Boston: Houghton, Mifflin, 1925.

Fitzpatrick, John C., ed. *The Writings of George Washington from the Original Manuscript Sources 1745–1799.* Washington, D.C.: U.S. Government Printing Office, 1931.

Fowler, William W., Jr. *Empires at War.* New York: Walker, 2005.

Gee, Wilson. *The Gist Family of South Carolina and Its Maryland Antecedents.* Charlottesville: Jarmans, 1934.

Gillman, Carolyn. *Where Two Worlds Meet: The Great Lakes Fur Trade.* St. Paul: Minnesota Historical Society, 1982.

Gipson, Lawrence Henry. *The British Empire Before the American Revolution.* New York: Alfred A. Knopf, 1858–70.

Gist, Christopher. *Christopher Gist's Journals; With Historical, Geographical and Ethnological Notes and Biographies of His Contemporaries by William M. Darlington.* Pittsburgh: J. R. Weldin, 1893.

Gist, Christopher. *Instructions Given Mr. Cristopher Gist by the Committee of the Ohio Company the 11th day of September 1750 and July 16th 1751; Also the Daily Record of Christopher Gist Containing an Account of his Travels Discoveries, Transactions With the Indians.* N.p.: Franklin Classics, 2018.

Goodman, Alfred T., ed. *Journal of Captain William Trent from Logstown to Pickawillany, A.D. 1752.* Cincinnati: Robert Clarke, 1871.

Hamilton, Stanislaus M., ed. *Letters to Washington and Accompanying Papers, Vol I, 1752–1756.* Boston: Houghton, Mifflin, 1898.

Hamilton, Stanislaus M., ed. *Letters to Washington and Accompanying Papers, Vol II.* Boston: Houghton, Mifflin, 1898–1902.

Hildeburn, Charles R. "Sir John St. Clair, Baronet, Quarter-Master General in America, 1755–1767." *Pennsylvania Magazine of History and Biography* 9, no. 1 (1885). https://archive.org/stream/jstor-20084686/20084686_djvu.txt.

Hildreth, Samuel Prescott. *Ohio Valley and the Early Settlement of the Northwest Territory.* Cincinnati: H. W. Derby, 1848.

Hilliard, Robert. "Queen Aliquippa; A History." *Milestones* 21, no. 3 (Autumn 1996). https://www.bcpahistory.org/beavercounty/BeaverCountyTopical/NativeAmerican/QueenAliquippMA96.html.

Huff, Archie V., Jr. *The History of the City and County in the South Carolina Piedmont.* Columbia: University of South Carolina Press, 1995.

Hunter, William A. *Forts on the Pennsylvania Frontier, 1753–1758.* Lewisburg, PA: Wennawoods, 1999.

J.C.B. *Travels in New France.* Edited by Sylvester K. Stevens, Donald H. Kent, and Emma E. Woods. Harrisburg: Pennsylvania Historical Commission, 1941.

Jacobs, Wilbur R. *Diplomacy and Indian Gifts, Anglo-French Rivalry Along the Ohio and Northwest Frontiers, 1748–1763.* Lewisburg, PA: Wennawoods, 2001.

James, Alfred P. *The Ohio Company: Its Inner History.* University of Pittsburg Press, 1959.

Jennings, Francis. *Empire of Fortune.* New York: W. W. Norton, 1988.

Joncaire to Marin, undated. Archives du Séminaire de Québec, V-V, 5:60:2.

Kent, D. H., L. Waddell, and A. L. Leonard, eds. *The Papers of Henry Bouquet, Vol III, January 1, 1759–August 31, 1759.* Harrisburg: Pennsylvania Historical Commission, 1976.

Kent, Donald D. *The French Invasion of Western Pennsylvania 1753.* Harrisburg: Pennsylvania Historical and Museum Commission 1954.

Knepper, George W. *Ohio and its People.* Kent State University Press, 1989.

Leach, Douglas Edward. *Arms for Empire.* New York: MacMillan, 1973.

Leach, Douglas Edward. *Roots of Conflict: A Military History of the British Armed Forces and Colonial Americans, 1677–1763.* Chapel Hill: University of North Carolina Press, 1986.

Lowdermilk, Will H. *History of Cumber-*

Bibliography

land County (Maryland). Washington, D.C.: Clearfield, 1878.

McCardell, Lee. *Ill-Starred General: Braddock of the Coldstream Guards*. University of Pittsburgh Press, 1958.

McCoy, David. B. *Christopher Gist*. Massillon, OH: Spare Change Press, 2019.

Millward, Robert, and Kathleen Millward. "Making History in the Wilderness: Christopher Gist's Explorations into Western Pennsylvania." *Western Pennsylvania History* (Summer 2008).

Minutes of the Provincial Council of Pennsylvania, Vol. VI. Harrisburg: Published by the State [Pennsylvania]—Theo. Fenn & Co. Printer, 1851.

Misencik, Paul R. *George Washington and the Half-King Chief Tanacharison: An Alliance That Began the French and Indian War*. Jefferson, NC: McFarland, 2014.

Misencik, Paul R., and Sally E. Misencik. *American Indians of the Ohio Country in the 18th Century*. Jefferson, NC: McFarland, 2020.

Moore, Donna C. *Genealogy Report: Some Descendants of Christopher Gist [Updated 1 Jan. 2001]*. https://www.genealogy.com/ftm/m/o/o/Donna-C-Moore/GENE10-0003.html.

Mulkearn, Lois. "Why the Treaty of Logstown, 1752." *Virginia Magazine of History and Biography* 59, no. 1 (January 1951): 3–20. http://www.jstor.org/stable/4245750.

Mulkearn, Lois, ed., *George Mercer Papers Relating to the Ohio Company of Virginia*. University of Pittsburgh Press, 1954.

Ohio History Connection. *Map of the Licking Reservoir*. Circa 1894–1900. https://ohiomemory.org/digital/collection/p267401coll32/id/26660/

O'Meara, Walter. *Guns at the Forks*. University of Pittsburgh Press, 1965.

Order of the Council referring the humble petition of the Ohio Company, April 2, 1754. P. R. O. Colonial Office Papers, 5:1328, 153–159. 164; Memorial of the Ohio Company, November 20, 1778, Virginia State Library.

Orrill, Lawrence A. *Christopher Gist and His Sons*. Pittsburgh: Historical Society of Western Pennsylvania, 1932.

Peyser, Joseph L. *Jacques Legardeur De Saint-Pierre—Officer, Gentleman, Entrepreneur*. East Lansing: Michigan State University Press, 1996.

Pouchot, Pierre. *Memoirs On The Late War In North America Between France And England*. Translated by Michael Cardy. Roxbury, 1866.

Powell, Alan. *Christopher Gist Frontier Scout*. Shippensburg, PA: Burd Street Press, 1992.

Rupp, Israel Daniel. *Early History of Western Pennsylvania and of the West, and of Western Expeditions and Campaigns from MDCCLIV to MDCCCXXXIIII*. Pittsburgh: Daniel W. Kauffman, 1846.

Sargent, Winthrop, ed. *The History of an Expedition Against Fort Du Quesne in 1755*. Philadelphia: Lippencott, Grambo, 1855.

Scharf, J. Thomas. *History of Baltimore City and County from the Earliest Period to the Present Day: Including Biographical Sketches of Their Representative Men*. Philadelphia: L. H. Everts, 1881.

Steckel, Richard H. *Heights and Human Welfare: Recent Developments and New Directions*. Cambridge, MA: National Bureau of Economic Research, 2008. http://www.nber.org/papers/w14536.

Stevens, S. K., D. H. Kent, and A. L. Leonard, eds. *The Papers of Henry Bouquet, Vol II: The Forbes Expedition*. Harrisburg: Pennsylvania Historical and Museum Commission, 1951.

Stotz, Charles Morris. *Point of Empire: Conflict at the Forks of the Ohio*. Pittsburgh: Historical Society of Western Pennsylvania, 1970.

Toner, J. M., ed. *Journal of George Washington, Commanding a Detachment of Virginia Troops*. Albany: Joel Munsell's Sons, 1893.

Trimble, David B. "Christopher Gist and Settlement on the Monongahela, 1752–1754." *Virginia Magazine of History and Biography* 63, no. 1 (1955): 15–27. http://www.jstor.org/stable/4246087.

Trimble, David B. "Christopher Gist and the Indian Service in Virginia,

Bibliography

1757–1759." *Virginia Magazine of History and Biography* 64, no. 2 (April 1956): 148–165.

Vincens, Simone. *Madame Montour and the Fur Trade (1667–1752)*. Translated and edited by Ruth Bernstein. Bloomington, IN: Xlibris, 2011.

Washington, George. *George Washington Papers, Series 2, Letterbooks 1754–1799: Letterbook 2, March 2–Dec. 6, 1755*. 1755. Manuscript/Mixed Material. Washington, D.C.: Library of Congress. https://www.loc.gov/item/mgw2.002/.

Washington, George. *Journal of Colonel George Washington Commanding a Detachment of Virginia Troops*. Edited by J. M. Toner. Albany: Joel Munsell's Sons, 1893.

Washington, George. "Letter from George Washington to Robert Dinwiddie, March 9, 1754." Virginia Historical Society, E312.72, 1962, Vol. 1, p. 73.

Washington, George. *The Papers of George Washington: 7 July 1748–14 August 1755*. Edited by W.W. Abbot. Charlottesville: University of Virginia Press, 1983.

Washington, George. *The Papers of George Washington*. Colonial Series, Vol I. Edited by W.W. Abbot. Charlottesville: University of Virginia Press, 1983.

Index

Abercrombie, James 164–165, 167
Abingdon, Virginia 184
Abraham 81, 165–166, 195
Acts of Toleration 69, 206
Addison, Pennsylvania 55, 118
Adventure (land parcel) 7
Africa 1
agent 2, 10–11, 56, 74, 139, 141, 143, 155, 159–161, 163–164, 166, 173, 179–180, 201–202, 211
aide-de-camp 140, 146
Alexandria, Virginia 110, 112, 141
Algonquin 25, 189
Aliquippa 100, 127, 175, 179, 207, 210, 212
Allegheny Mountains 1, 5, 8, 16–17, 63, 141, 155, 185, 190, 202, 206, 209, 211
Allegheny Path 23
Allegheny River 1–2, 25, 65, 71, 73, 75–77, 79, 81–82, 87, 89–91, 97–103, 105–106, 109–110, 112–113, 151, 187, 203
Anglican 44719
Annapolis, Maryland 163, 192
Anne Arundel 7, 201
Annosanah 32, 207
Antietam Creek 179
Appalachian Mountains 13, 177, 190, 206
artillery 102, 109–110, 112–113, 115–118, 130, 133–134, 142, 147–148, 150–152, 154, 170, 188
Ashland, Wisconsin 93
assassin, assassination 134–136
Atkin, Edmund 158–162, 165, 171
Attakullakulla (also Little Carpenter) 169–170
Aughwick, Pennsylvania 176, 179, 191, 195–196, 207
Augusta County, Virginia 70, 102, 205

Bahamas 191
Baltimore 5–11, 13, 179, 201
Baltimore Gazette 11
batteau, batteaux 94, 104
Battle of Dettington 140
Battle of Kings Mountain 185

Battle of Lake George 189
Battle of Saratoga 142
Beauharnois, Charles de la Boische, Marquis de 93
Beaujeu, Daniel Liénaqrd de 152
Beautiful River 25, 113–114; *see also* La Belle Rivière; Ohio River
Beaver 30, 205; *see also* King Beaver; Tamaqua
Beaver, Pennsylvania 28, 205
Beaver River 28, 58, 89–90
Beaver Town 30; *see also* King Beaver Town; Shingas's Town The Tuscarawas
Beaver Wars 8; *see also* Iroquois Wars
Bedford, Pennsylvania 22–23; *see also* Rays Town
La Belle Rivière 25, 104, 124, 135; *see also* Beautiful River; Ohio River
Belpre Trail 35
belt 80, 90, 95
Belvoir 183
Big Bone Lick 46, 204
Big Hannaona 38
Big Knife 30
Big Lick 49; *see also* Roanoke, Virginia
Big Pond *or* Big Swamp 35
Big Spoon 20; *see also* Cresap, Thomas
bivouac 104, 122–123
Black Mountain 37
Blacksburg, Virginia 48
blacksmith 32, 43, 158
Blair, John 70, 165
Blakistone, Richard 10
Blennerhasset Island 190
bloody flux 83
Blue Licks 46, 176
Blunder Camp 150
Board of Trade 70, 158
Bolivar, Ohio 30
bonus 106, 156
Boone, Daniel 2, 5, 13, 142, 176, 184, 202
Boone, Israel 176
Boone, Jemima 176
Boone's Trace 176

215

Index

Bootleg 9
borax 47
Bosomworth, Abraham 165–167, 171, 177
bounty 25, 32, 106, 162, 172, 184, 189
Bouquet, Henry 165–168, 170, 174–175, 177, 180, 182, 210, 212
Braddock, Edward 2, 71, 140–155, 160, 168, 174, 178–179, 181–183, 186, 192–194, 209
Braddock, Pennsylvania 89
Braddock Road 71, 164
Bradstreet, Anne 84
Brandt, Joseph 81l *see also* Thayendanegea
Brandt, Molly 81
Brandywine Creek 57
British Fur Company 10, 155
Brown Bess 154
Brownsville, Pennsylvania 54, 57, 189
Buchanan County, Virginia 47
buckskin 110
buffalo 15, 42, 44, 47
burgesses 18, 106, 137, 159, 197, 202, 205–206
Burney, Thomas 32
Butler, Scot 34
Byrd, James 170
Byrd, William 169

Cabot, John 16, 202
Callowhill, Hannah 56
Calmes, Maquis 70
Calvert family 6–9, 179
camp-followers 154
campmaster general 139
Canada 30, 33–34, 80, 86, 94, 113–114, 151, 170, 178, 181, 187–188
cancer 182
cannon 94, 110, 113, 116, 134, 150–152, 209; *see also* artillery
canoe 38, 45, 89, 94, 96–97, 112, 117, 195, 203
Captain Jacob 136, 172
Carlisle, Pennsylvania 164, 168–169, 203
Carlton, Guy 187
Carlton, Pennsylvania 92
Carlyle, John 128–129
Cartier, Jacques 16
Casselman River 55, 205
Catawba 14, 38, 161, 163, 167–168, 171–173
Catholic 5–7, 206
Céloron de Blaineville 24, 76, 91, 103, 177–178
Chagouamigon 93
Chalahgawatha 38–39, 204
Champlain, Samuel 16, 189
Chapman, Nathaniel 20–21
Charleston, South Carolina 158, 184, 191
Charlevois, Fr. Pierre-François Xavier de 16
Charlottesville, Virginia 108

Chartiers Creek 74, 89, 101
Chatakoin Portage 78
Chauvignerie, Michel Maray de La 105
Checochinican 57
Chenango 104; *see also* Chiningué; Logs Town; Logstown; Shenango
Cherokee 14, 68, 87, 142, 144, 160–161, 163, 166–171, 184, 191, 206
Chesapeake Bay 179
Chestnut Ridge 54, 120, 130–131, 148
Chief of Scouts 141
Chillicothe 38–39, 204
La Chine 77, 206
Chiningué 24, 104; *see also* Chenango; Logs Town; Logstown; Shenango
Chippewa 30; *see also* Ojibwe
Chota 68, 206
Chouaguen 187; *see also* Fort Oswego
church 69, 157, 180, 206
Cincinnati, Ohio 45, 204
Circleville, Ohio 37
Clark, George Rogers 2, 176
Clinton, George (also Corlear) 79, 92
Clinton County, Ohio 41
coal 47
Codorus Creek 179
Columbus, Ohio 34
commissary 92, 128,-129, 139, 143–144, 172
Commissioners for Trade and Plantations 16–17, 202
compass 24, 51
Conawago Creek 78
Conchaké 31–35, 41
Confluence, Pennsylvania 55, 205
Connellsville, Pennsylvania 56, 68
Conococheague 87, 143, 157
Conotocarious (Taker of Towns) 118
consumption 24, 67; *see also* tuberculosis
Contrecœur, Claud-Pierre Pećaudy 103–105, 113–117, 119–120, 123–124, 137, 151–152, 178, 185–186, 189, 208
Conway, Virginia 47
Coonce, Mark 30
coroner 10
Cosfort family 13
Coshocton 28, 31, 34–35, 203
court-martial 110, 194
Coyacolline 38
Crawford, Hugh 45
Crawford, William 69
credit, creditors 11, 13, 69, 129, 186
Cresap family 3, 18–20, 22–23, 51, 54, 57, 64, 68, 74, 117, 143–144, 173, 178–179, 189
Crescentia 6
Crocker, Thomas 141
Crockett, Davy 5
Croghan, George 25–28, 31–33, 35, 37–38,

216

Index

40–41, 43–44, 69, 81–82, 101, 1103, 128, 142, 144, 148, 161, 173, 176, 179–180, 195–196, 207
Cromwell, Edith 5, 7, 201; *see also* Gist, Edith Cromwell
Cromwell, Oliver 7
Cromwell, William 11, 68–69, 71, 183, 185
Cross Creeks 60
Crowfoot 15
Crown Point, New York 189
Cumberland, Maryland 202, 205
Cumberland Gap 176, 184
Curran, Barnaby 87, 96–97
Curran, Barney 24
Cussewago 92–93
Custaloga's Town 92
Cynthiana, Ohio 41

Darcy, Robert 84–85
Darlington, William 55, 58–59, 204
Davidson, John 89–90, 97, 120
Dayton, Ohio 183
debtor's prison 13
Deer Creek 92
Deerfield, Massachusetts 33–34
Delaware Indians 1, 24, 35, 37, 61, 79, 189, 203, 207, 209; *see also* Lenni Lenape
Delaware River 56, 189
DeLery 203
DeLery Portage 32, 203
La Demoiselle 39; *see also* Memeski; Old Briton
depot 101, 168, 210
deputy superintendent 158, 160, 171, 180
desert, desertion, deserter 32, 119–120, 130–131, 139, 157, 170–171
Dinwiddie, Robert 2, 18, 41, 63–68, 76–77, 81, 84–86, 90, 92–95, 97, 101–107, 110, 115, 118–119, 121–122, 127, 129, 138–142, 144, 154–163, 172–173, 175, 181, 188, 192, 194, 207
Dorsey 10
Dresden, Ohio 34
Drouillon de Mace, Pierre Jacques 120–121
Dumas, Jean 152
Dunbar, Thomas 148, 153, 181
Dungannon, Ohio 28
Duquesne, Michel-Ange Duquesne de Menneville Marquis 77, 81, 83, 94, 103–105, 178, 181
dysentary 182, 206

ecclesiastic courts 69
education 8
Eghnisara 25, 189; *see also* Montour, Andrew; Sattrelihu
Elizabeth, West Virginia 59
elk 42, 47, 55 58

Elk's Eye 28–31; *see also* Muskingum
Elledges Folly 11
England 1, 5–7, 16, 34, 51, 59, 126, 129, 133, 140, 158, 160, 178, 180–181, 192–193, 195, 197; *see also* Britain; Great Britain
English 77, 79–82, 84, 87, 89, 95–96, 100, 102–105, 107, 109–110, 112–117, 119–120, 123–124, 126–127, 130–136, 145–146, 149, 151–152, 154, 158, 180–181, 189, 203, 205; *see also* British
Erie, Pennsylvania 77, 82
Erie Indians 9, 16
Etna, Pennsylvania 81
Eucyer, Simon 177
Europe 1, 8–9, 55, 131–132, 190, 208
Evans, Lewis 37, 71–73
Evans City, Pennsylvania 91
expatriate 25, 203, 205

factor 21, 53, 202
Fairfax, William 129, 138, 157, 173, 175, 183, 192
Fairfield County, Ohio 35
Falls of the Ohio 20, 44–47, 49, 202
Farmington, Pennsylvania 120
farthing 70, 129, 202
Fauquier, Francis 163, 169, 172, 181
fee 70
Fendall, Josias 6
Fish Creek 58
Fishing Creek 60; *see also* Nawmissipia
fleur-de-lis 109
Florida 177, 197
Floyd's Fork 46
Floydsburg, Kentucky 46
flying column 148, 151
Forbes, John 2, 164–171, 174, 180, 182–184, 193, 196, 203
Forks of the Muskingum 34, 41, 57
Forks of the Ohio 1, 15, 22–25, 58, 65, 75–79, 85, 89, 97–99, 101–107, 109–110, 112–113, 115–117, 119–120, 164, 170, 172, 181–182, 196, 203, 207
Fort Bedford 170
Fort Carillon 164
Fort Cumberland 18, 53, 137, 143–144, 147, 154, 157, 166, 168
Fort de Chiningué 25; *see also* Shenango
Fort de la Presqu' Île 77, 79, 81–82, 104–105; *see also* Fort Presque Isle
Fort de la Rivière au Bœuf 76–77, 79, 82–83, 92–95, 97, 104–105, 151, 188; *see* Fort la Bœuf
Fort des Miamis 40, 42, 50, 66, 76
Fort Detroit 32, 40, 50, 76, 105, 172, 177, 180, 185, 203, 210
Fort du Portage 78, 88
Fort Duquesne 104, 117, 119, 124, 135, 137,

217

Index

140–143, 147–151, 164, 167–171, 178, 180, 182–183, 185, 192–194, 197–198, 203
Fort Johnson 81, 206
Fort Laurens 30, 203
Fort Ligonier 3, 24, 111, 169–171
Fort Loudoun 157, 166, 171, 198
Fort Machault 82–83, 90–92, 96–97, 104–105, 187
Fort Maidstone 157, 210
Fort Mount Pleasant 139, 143; see also Fort Cumberland
Fort Necessity 86, 127–128, 130, 133, 134, 137, 148, 181, 194, 197
Fort Niagara 76, 103, 187–188
Fort Oswego 187–188, 198; see also Chouaguen
Fort Pitt 71, 177, 182, 196
Fort Presque Isle 77, 79, 82, 104, 105
Fort Prince George 102, 105, 110, 112–113, 117
Fort St. Frédéric 189
Fort St. Phillipe 40
Fort Sandoské, Fort Sandoski 32
Fort Shirley 179
Fort Stanwix 180, 190, 196
Fort Ticonderoga 164
Fort Wayne, Indiana 39
Fort William Henry 198
Fortress Louisbourg 195
Frankfort, Kentucky 47, 176
Franklin, Benjamin 142, 144, 173, 180
Franklin, Pennsylvania 83
Fraser, John 82, 89, 100, 109–110, 113, 115, 151, 182–183, 196
Frederick, Maryland 142–143
Frederick the Great 137, 147
Fredericksburg, Virginia 87
Free Republic of Franklin 186
Fremont, Ohio 34, 41
French and Indian War 3, 34, 177, 179, 183–184, 186, 189–190, 193, 196, 198, 207, 210; see also Seven Years' War
French & Indian War Foundation 3, 211
French Creek 79, 82, 92–93, 96, 104
frostbite 58, 61
Frostburg, Maryland 54
Fry, Joshua 12, 14, 64, 66, 71–72, 74, 107–109, 112, 117–118, 122, 127–128, 138, 202, 205
Fur Trade 8–9, 25, 76, 212, 214

Gage, Thomas 152–153
Galissonière, Roland-Michel Barrin de la 77
garrison 10–11, 93–94, 105, 110, 113, 115, 117, 120, 134, 142, 151, 169–170
Garrison Road 10
geography 10

George, Richard 70
Georgia 13
German 69, 179, 193
Gest 7; see also Gist
le Gest 7; see also Gist
Geyste 7; see also Gist
Ghest 7; see also Gist
gifts 43, 51, 64–66, 95, 145, 160–163, 165, 167–168, 170, 212; see also presents
Giles, Jacob 11
Giles County, Virginia 48
Gist, Anne or Nancy (Christopher's daughter) 8
Gist, Bell (Christopher's daughter) 8, 184
Gist, Christopher (Christopher's grandfather) 5, 7
Gist, Christopher (death) 172–173
Gist, Edith (Christopher's sister) 7
Gist, Edith (née Edith Cromwell) 5, 7, 201
Gist, Jemima (Christopher's sister) 7
Gist, John (Christopher's brother) 8
Gist, Nathaniel (Christopher's brother) 7–8, 9, 186, 201
Gist, Nathaniel (Christopher's son) 5, 11, 53, 68, 87, 142, 155, 160, 162, 184–185
Gist, Richard (Christopher's father) 7, 10–11
Gist, Richard (Christopher's son) 8, 11, 53, 68, 184–185
Gist, Ruth (Christopher's sister) 7
Gist, Sarah (Christopher's sister) 8
Gist, Sarah (Christopher's wife) 3, 8, 11, 15, 22, 49, 53, 68, 84, 89, 138, 175, 183–186, 201; see also Howard, Sarah
Gist, Thomas (Christopher's brother) 7
Gist, Thomas or Benjamin (Christopher's son) 8, 11, 68–69, 72, 142, 162, 170, 172, 184–187, 210
Gist, Violetta (Christopher's daughter) 8, 11, 68–69, 183, 185–186, 201
Gist, William (Christopher's brother) 8, 186, 201
Gist, Zippora (née Murray; Christopher's mother) 7
Gist's Limepits 11
Gist's Meadows 11
Gist's Plantation 72, 82, 84, 120–121, 129, 131, 137–138, 148, 185–186
Gist's Rest 7
Gist's Settlement 69–74, 77, 82, 89, 100–101, 109, 129, 131, 137, 141, 184–187, 190
Glen, James 107
Gooch, William 15–16, 18
Goochland County, Virginia 108
Governor-General 81, 83, 93–94, 103–105, 177–178, 181
Governor of Fort Cumberland 143
Grand Jury 7

218

Index

Le Grand Villiers 130
Grant, James 169–170
Grantsville, Maryland 55
Great Crossing 55, 118, 120, 148
Great Dismal Swamp 48
Great Falls 192
Great Meadow Run 120
Great Meadows 120
Great Miami River 40, 42, 45, 50
Great Trail 28
Great Wagon Road 49, 138
Green Spring Traverse 7
Green Spring Valley 11
Greene, Thomas 6
Greene County, Ohio 41
Gregorian Caledar 59
Guest 7, 71; *see also* Gist
guide 2, 97–98, 141, 149–150, 153, 161, 184
Gunn, James 173
gunsmith 158
Guyasuta (Hunter) 90, 97

Half-King 64–66, 89–90, 97, 102, 109, 112, 116, 118, 121–122, 126–127, 145, 149, 174, 176, 191–192, 195–196, 202, 205
Halkett, James 152
Halkett, Peter 148, 152
Hall, Richard 48–49
Hamilton, James 81–82, 106
Hampton, Virginia 140, 143
Harmony, Pennsylvania 91
Harris, John 195–196
Harris, Mary 33–34
Harrisburg, Pennsylvania 22, 195
Harriskintom Town (also Hurricane Tom's Town) 37
Harrison, Thomas 11
Hart, Nathaniel 184
Hendrick 81; *see also* King Hendrick; Tiyanoga
Hendrick, Caroline 81
Henrietta Maria 6
Henry, Patrick 184
Herbin, Louis 197
Hero of the Monongahela 153
Hockhocking River 35, 44
Hocking River 35, 44
holy experiment 55
Honors of war 133–134
Hose, Michael 3
hostage, hostages 135–136, 172, 181, 188, 194, 197
Howard, Joanna O'Carroll 8, 201
Howard, Joshua 8, 138
Howard, Sarah 8, 138; *see also* Gist, Sarah
Huckburgh, Richard 193
Huron 9, 185, 203; *see also* Wyandot, Wendat

Hurricane Tom's Town (*also* Harrickintom Town) 37

independent companies 106, 119, 128, 132, 139
India 1
Indian Affairs 138, 158–161, 165, 167, 171, 173, 180
Indian agent 2, 139, 141, 155, 159–160, 163–164, 166, 173, 180
Indian fighter 2
Indian Run 120
Indiana 39, 180, 196–197
Industrial Revolution 40
injure, injured 47–48, 127, 206
Innes, James 127–128, 138–139, 143
interpreter 26, 28, 32, 38, 53, 57, 64, 89, 90, 114, 120, 126, 160–161, 163, 189, 191
Iroquois 8–9, 16, 30, 55–56, 63–66, 77, 79–82, 84–85, 90, 92, 114, 141, 145, 187, 189, 203, 205, 20
Iroquois Wars (*also* Beaver Wars) 8

Jackson County West Virginia 60
Jacobs, Captain (Indian) 172
James River 161
Jefferson, Peter 12, 14, 71, 74, 108, 202, 205
Jefferson, Thomas 108, 202, 205
Jenkins, William 87, 96–97
Jeskekake 90
Johnson, Hannah 179
Johnson Hall 206
Johnson, William 81, 158, 161, 179–180, 189, 193, 206
Joliet, Louis 16
Joncaire, Phillipe-Thomas Chabert de 91.92, 96, 98, 187–188, 212
Jonquiére, Jacques-Pierre de Taffanel de la 77, 177
Joshua's Lot 8
Julian Calendar 59
Jumonville, Joseph Coulon de Villiers de 119–121, 123–124, 126, 130–131, 135–136, 181, 196
Jumonville Glen 123, 125
Juniata River 22
Junqueindundeh 34, 41

Kaghswaghtaniunt (White Thunder) 90, 97
Kallandar, Robert 41, 204
Kamouraska, Québec 188
Kanawha River 15, 18, 48, 50–51, 59–60, 65, 196, 204
Kanawha Trail 37–38
Katchinodiagon (*also* Paille Coupe) 78
Kekionga 39
Kellog, Joseph 33
Kenton, Simon 2, 5

219

Index

Kentucky 1–3, 5, 44, 46–47, 142, 173, 176, 184, 190, 202, 204
Kentucky River 47
Kernstown, Virginia 137
Killbuck Creek 33
King Beaver 30, 205; see also Beaver; Tamaqua
King Beaver Town 30; see also Beaver Town; Shingas's Town; The Tuscarawas
King Charles I 6
King George I 6
King George II 84, 102, 140, 143
King George III 102, 190
King George's War 92, 202
King Hendrick 81; see also Tiyanoga, Hendrick
King Henry VII 16
King William III, William of Orange 6
king's house 31
Kitchin, Thomas 71–72
Kittanning 28
Kuskusky 28

LaForce, René-Hippolyte 92, 96, 107, 119–121, 123, 188, 208
Lake Chautauqua 78
Lake Drummond 48
Lake Erie 13, 32, 40, 73, 78, 104
Lake George 189
Lancaster, Ohio 35–36
Lancaster, Pennsylvania 63–65, 75, 209
land grant 16, 18, 63, 66–67, 70, 76–77, 141, 189–190, 196–197
Langlade, Charles Michel de de 66
Latrobe, Penssylvania 183
Layparewah 38
lead plates 24, 76
Leake, Robert 172, 210
Lee, Richard Henry 20, 202
Lee, Thomas 15–16, 18, 20, 24, 49–50
Legardeur, Jacques de St. Pierre 92–95, 101–104, 118, 188–189
legislature 18, 70, 85, 106, 178–179, 198
Lehigh River 56
Lenni Lenape 1, 24–25, 28, 30, 33, 35, 37, 54–58, 60–61, 64, 79, 82, 87, 89, 91–92, 129–130, 169, 189, 203; see also Delaware
Leon, West Virginia 60
Lewis, Andrew 70, 112
Lexington, Kentucky 47
Licking County, Ohio 35
Licking River (Kentucky) 45–46
Licking River (Ohio) 35, 37, 204
Ligonier, Pennsylvania 24; see also Fort Ligonier
limepits 11
Lincoln Highway 164
linen 110, 208

linsey-woolsey 110, 207
Little Carpenter 169–171; see also Attakullakulla
Little Cuttaway 47; see also Kentucky River
Little Kanawha River 59
Little Meadow Mountain 55
Little Miami River 44, 50
Logstown 25–28, 37–38, 43, 51, 55, 57–58, 63–67, 73, 79, 89, 91, 104, 108, 205; see also Chiningué; Loggs Town; Shenango
Lomax, Lunsford 64, 66, 206
London 11, 18, 74, 84, 190
long knives 30; see also Mechanschican
Longueuil, Charles Le Moyne de 77
Lord Dunmore's War 180
Louisville, Kentucky 44, 202
Lower Shawnee Town 13, 24, 35, 38–39, 41–42, 44, 204
Loyalhanna 24, 170

Macé, Pierre Jacques Drouillon de 120–121
Mad River 44
Maguck 35–37, 204
Mahican 9
mammoth 45, 204
Manitoulin Island 30
Margaret's Creek 30–31
Marin, Paul de la Malgue 77, 79–83, 90, 92–93, 103, 105
Markleysburg, Pennsylvania 118
Marquette, Fr. Jacques 16
Marshall County, West Virginia 58
Martin, Thomas 194
Martinsburg, West Virginia 194
Maryland Rangers 9, 20
Mason, George 18, 20, 50, 67, 173, 175
Mason County, West Virginia 60
Massachusetts 6, 33
McClain, Jane Bell 182–183
McGuire, John 87, 96–97
McKee's Rocks, Pennsylvania 58, 73, 100
McKeesport, Pennsylvania 58, 100, 150
McNeil, John 157
Meadville, Pennsylvania 92
Meason, Isaac 186–187
measuring wheel 75, 206
Mechanschican 30; see also long knives
Mekocke Shawnee 34, 204
Memeskia 39–40, 42–43, 66; see also La Demoiselle; Old Briton
mercantile 10, 15
mercenary 87, 177
Mercer, George 67, 157, 172, 173
Mercer, Hugh 182
Mercier, François-Marc-Antoine Le 104–105, 113–115, 133
Métis 25
Miami 37, 39,-43, 66, 177, 203

220

Index

Middlebourne, West Virginia 59
Mihtohseeniaki 39
Military Order of Saint Louis 83, 178, 182, 187, 197–198
militia 9, 20, 30, 76, 85–86, 104–105, 107, 111, 143, 148–149, 151–153, 155, 170, 176, 182, 185–186, 188–189, 191, 205, 211
Millburn, Margaret 179
Mingo 1, 25, 28, 31, 34, 44, 60, 129–130, 180, 203, 205, 207
Mingo Junction, Ohio 60; see also Mingo Town
Mingo Town 60; see also Mingo Junction, Ohio
Mississippi River 20
Mitchell, John 37
Mohawk 81, 187
Moland, Betsy 193
Monacatuca 149, 209
Monkton, Robert 193
Monongahela River 1, 15, 18, 50, 51, 54, 56–58, 61, 67–69, 71–72, 75–77, 82, 89, 100, 130, 141, 147–148, 150–151, 153, 155, 172, 186, 189, 192–194, 196, 203, 206
Montcalm, Louis-Joseph de 198
Montour, Andrew 25–28, 31–33, 35, 37–38, 41, 43–44, 51, 64–65, 68, 129, 180, 189
Montour, Madam 26, 30, 189
Montour, Margaret 30
Montréal 40, 80, 83, 104, 114, 178, 189, 195, 197, 206
Morgan, Daniel 142
Moundsville, West Virginia 58
Mount Pleasant 35–36; see also Standing Stone
Mount Vernon 141, 183, 199
Mountain Lake 48
Mouzon, Henry 13–14, 202
Muddy Creek 93
Mulberry Field 13
Murdering Town or Murthering Town 91, 98
Muse, George 128, 132
Museum of American History 3
Museum of the American Indian 3
Muskingum 24, 28–29, 31, 33–35, 41; see also Elk's Eye

National Library for the Study of George Washington 3
National Road 54
Nawmissipia 60; see also Fishing Creek
Negro Mountain 55
Nemacolin 54, 57, 189
Nemacolin Path 54–55, 57, 72, 164, 189–190
Neucheconneh 38

Neutral Indians 9
New Castle, Pennsylvania 28
New England 34
New France 16–17, 76–77, 82, 113, 18
New Martinsville, West Virginia 59
New River 48, 204
new settlement 89, 100
New York 79, 85, 92, 106, 119, 158, 180, 198, 205–206
Newport, Virginia 48
Niagara Portage 65, 104
Nicholas 31; see also Orontony
Nicollet, Jean 16
North, Robert 11
North Carolina 3, 11, 13–14, 20, 40, 49, 74, 107–108, 114, 128, 138–139, 161, 186, 202
Northern Department 158, 161, 189
Nottoway 167

Ogilvie, John 193
Ohio 1–2, 13, 16, 18, 23, 25–26, 28, 31, 32–41, 44, 50–51, 60, 65–66, 68–69, 71, 79–80, 82, 84–85, 88–94, 101, 103, 105–106, 118, 129, 145, 159, 171, 173, 176–181, 183, 190, 196, 204, 207, 209
Ohio Company of Virginia 1, 3, 5, 15–16, 18, 20–22, 24, 26, 28–30, 33, 37, 42, 44, 47–48, 50–51, 53–55, 57–60, 62–77, 84–86, 101, 106–107, 109, 137–139, 141, 144, 155, 159, 165, 175, 184–185, 190, 202, 206
Ohio History Connection 3, 35
Ohio River 1–2, 17–18, 20, 22–24, 25, 28, 38–39, 43, 45–46, 51, 58–61, 64–65, 73–74, 76–78, 81, 85, 87, 94, 97, 100–101, 103–107, 119–120, 164, 170, 172, 180, 182, 187–188, 190, 196, 202–203, 207; see also Beautiful River; Belle Rivière
Ohio-Standing Stone Trail 35
Ojibwe 30; see also Chippewa
Old Briton 39–42, 66; see also La Demoiselle; Memeskia
Old Town, Oldtown, MD 19, 22–23, 117, 179
Onas 79; see also Sharpe, Horatio
Oneida 25, 89, 145, 149, 189, 209
Onondaga 205
Ontario 20, 188
Opequon Creek 137–138
Opessa, Straight Tail Meaurroway 19
Opessa's Town 19, 179
Oppaymolleah 58
Oregonia, Ohio 44
Orme, Robert 140–141
Orontony 31, 40–41; see also Nicholas
Ottawa 30, 66, 99, 177
Overhill Cherokee 68, 184

Index

Paille Coupe (also Katchinodiagon) 78
Painted Post 28
palisade 112–113, 127, 129
panther 59
Paris 40, 182
Parish Fork 59
Parker, Hugh 18, 20–21, 53
parley 113
Passyunk, Pennsylvania 180
Patapsco River 7
patronage 85
Patton, James 64, 66, 205
Paxtang 22
Péan, Michel-Jean-Hughes 105
Pearis, Richard 68, 142, 160, 163, 167, 171, 190–191
Penn, John 56, 183
Penn, Thomas 56
Penn, William 56–57
Penn, William (son) 56
Pensacola, Florida 177
pension 178, 182
Perry County, Ohio 35
Peters, Richard 69
Peyronie, William La 133–134
Philadelphia, Pennsylvania 57, 101, 138, 180, 182, 193–194, 197
Philadelphia Wagon Road 138
Philippines 1
Piankashaw Miami 39–40
Pickaway Plains 37
Pickawillany 24, 33, 40–45, 50, 66, 76, 177, 203
Pickawillany Trail 38, 41, 44
Pickens, Andrew 191
pickets 122, 131, 144, 146, 170
pictograph 47
Pike County, Ohio 41
Pinnacle Rock 48, 204
Piqua, Ohio 40, 203
pistoles 156
Pittsburgh 1, 15, 22, 180, 189–190, 201
Plains of Abraham 195
plantation 11, 16–17, 72, 82, 84, 120–121, 129, 131, 137–138, 148, 184–187, 191, 202
Plenty Coups 63
Pointe au Baril, Ontario 188
Poke, Charles 57
Pontiac 66, 177, 193, 196, 207
Port Clinton, Ohio 32
portage 32, 65, 96, 104–105, 203
Portsmouth, Ohio 13, 38, 204
posts 18–20, 22–23, 31, 50, 71, 73, 76, 82, 89, 93, 109, 115, 117, 119, 144, 158, 161–163, 176, 179, 182, 187, 195, 210
Potawatomie 30
Potomac River (also Potomack) 18, 22, 25, 53–54, 61–62, 67, 137–138, 157, 161, 163, 192
pound sterling 11, 21, 103, 155–156, 160, 202, 209
presents 33, 42, 142, 149, 162, 166, 168, 170, 173; *see also* gifts
Prince William Augustus, Duke of Cumberland 143
Privy Council 17, 202
prohibition 9, 145, 180
proprietor, proprietary governor 6, 56–57, 79, 192
protest 56, 79, 195
Protestant Revolution 6
Puritan 6

Quaker 6, 144
Québec City 40, 54, 103–104, 181, 188, 195, 198
Queen Aliquippa 100, 127, 175, 179, 207, 210, 212; *see also* Aliquippa
Queen Anne's War 33
Quiskakon 39–40, 42–43
quit-rent 70, 206

Radford, Virginia 48
Radisson, Pierre-Espirit 16
raft 42, 61, 82, 99–100
raid 8–10, 33, 49, 160–162, 171–172, 185, 207
Raleigh, Walter 49
ranger 2, 9–10, 20, 58, 172, 179
rattlesnake colonel 20
Raven, Simon 5
Ray, John 23
Rays Town 23, 168–170; *see also* Bedford, Pennsylvania; Raystown
Raystown 23–24; *see also* Bedford, Pennsylvania; Rays Town
recruit 21, 68, 74, 85, 101–102, 106–107, 111–112, 117, 142, 156–157, 160, 162, 171–172, 184
Red River 47
Reddies River 13
Redstone Creek 54, 57, 102, 190
Redstone Old Fort 101
Redstone Storehouse 57, 102, 205
regiment 97, 106–107, 110–111, 118, 126, 128, 138–140, 148, 151, 153, 155–157, 160, 162, 169, 172–173, 182, 193, 197, 206, 210
regulars 104, 106, 117, 119, 121, 123, 128, 151–152, 154, 170
reinforcements 102, 104–105, 107, 109, 111, 117, 120, 122, 127, 130, 169
religious liberty 69
Revolutionary War 30, 142, 176, 180, 184–185, 188, 190, 193, 197–198, 202

222

Index

Riviére au Bœuf *or* La Bœuf Creek 76–77, 93, 95
Riviére des Blanches Femmes *see* Walhonding River, White Woman's Creek 33
Roanoke 49, 161
Roanoke River 161
Robinson, John 159
Rowan County, North Carolina 49, 186
Royal American Regiment 173, 197
royal charter 6
Royal Colony 6
Russell, William 70
Rutherford, Thomas 165

sailors 147
St. Augustine, Florida 197
St. Clair, John 143, 147, 166–167, 192–193
St. Lawrence River 195
St. Vincent College 183
Salisbury, North Carolina 49
Salt Creek 37
Salt Lick 35, 45, 204
Salt Lick Creek 37, 46
Salt Lick Town 34
salt springs 35
Sandusky Bay 31–32, 40, 204
Sandusky River 41
Sandy Creek 30
Sattrelihu 25; *see also* Eghnisara, Montour Andrew
Sauconk 28, 58
Saw Mill Creek 13
scalp 32, 80, 126, 131, 148–149, 153, 162
Scalping Camp 148
Scarouady 82, 89, 118, 145–146, 149, 174, 191–192, 209
school 8, 89, 132
Scioto River 34–38, 41, 190, 204
Scioto Trail 13, 34, 37–38, 204
Scott, Rev. James 20, 50
Scottsville, Virginia 108
scout 2, 47, 110, 119. 121, 130–131, 141–142, 146, 148–151, 153, 155, 157, 159, 161–163, 165, 169, 171, 179, 184
Seneca 1, 28, 188, 213
sept (clan) 38, 204
Sequoyah 184
Seven Years' War 1; *see also* French and Indian War
Shamokin, Pennsylvania 189
Shannopin's Town 24–25, 99–100, 113
Sharpe, Horatio 79, 81, 128–129, 139, 142, 157, 160, 163, 167, 192; *see also* Onas
Shaw, John 126
Shawnee 1, 13, 18–19, 24–25, 34–35, 37–39, 41–42, 44–45, 64, 79, 92, 118, 129, 176, 179–180, 189, 196, 204, 209
Shawnee-Miami Trail 37

Shenandoah Valley 63, 190, 205
Shenango 25; *see also* Chiningué; Logs Town; Logstown
Shertees Creek 74; *see also* Chartier's Creek
Shilling 11, 110, 149–150, 155–156, 159, 202, 209
Shingas 30, 89, 205, 207
Shingas's Town 30, 89; *see also* Beaver Town; King Beaver Town; The Tuscarawas
Silverheels 122, 208
Simon, Trent. Levy & Franks 196
Six Nations of Iroquois 30, 81; *see also* Iroquois
slave 11, 24
sloop 10–11, 201
smallpox 31, 172–173, 177, 196, 198, 207, 210
Smith, Richard 161
Smith, Robert 45–46
Smith's Creek 60
Smithsonian Institution 3
snowshoe 104
South America 1
South Carolina 40, 106–107, 128, 132, 158–159, 161, 165, 167–168, 185, 191, 201
Southern Department 158–161, 165
Spanish 156, 176, 195, 202, 210
speech belt 90, 95; *see also* wampum
Spendlow, Charles 147, 209
spy, spies 112, 129, 146, 184, 195, 197
Stafford Court House, Virginia 20, 202
Standing Stone 35–36, 44, 59; *see also* Mount Pleasant
Standingstone Creek 59
Stanwix, John 173, 193
State of Franklin 186
Stephen, Adam 111, 124, 156, 160, 166, 193–194, 208
Stewart, Henry 87, 96–97
Stobo, Robert 112, 117, 128, 135–136, 181, 188, 194–195
stockade 103, 112, 127, 131
Stone, William 6
storehouse 18, 31, 51, 53–54, 57, 62, 64–65, 69, 81, 85, 87, 101–102, 109, 137–138, 143–144, 157, 166, 190, 205
stronghouse 85, 103
Suffield, Connecticut 33
Sugar Creek 31
sulphur 47
Sun Tsu 154
superintendent 158, 160, 166–167, 171, 180, 191
surrender 113, 115, 117, 127, 133–134, 148, 155
survey 7–8, 10, 18, 20, 26, 66–67, 70, 75, 131, 133, 143, 172, 179, 205–206
Susquehanna River 178–179

223

Index

Susquehannock 9
sweat-house 24, 47, 203
Swiss 177
swivel-gun 110–111, 116, 131, 133

Tamaqua 30, 58, 61, 205; see also Beaver; King Beaver
Tanacharison 64–66, 79–80, 84, 89–90, 95, 97, 102–103, 109–110, 112–113, 115–118, 120–124, 126–127, 129, 145, 174–175, 179, 191, 195–196
Tasker, Benjamin 11
taxes 69, 181, 206
Tecumseh 19
Terra Mariae (Mary Land) 6
Thayendanegea 81; see also Brandt, Joseph
Three Fires Confederacy 30
Thucydides 127
Tiyanoga 81; see also Hendrick; King Hendrick
tobacco 7, 10, 43, 105
tomahawk 126, 149
tools 11, 101–102, 115, 208
tory 180
trading post 10, 18, 20, 23, 31, 38, 40, 66, 73, 82, 101, 109, 119, 158, 176, 179, 182, 187, 195–196
Trans-Allegheny 1, 5, 8, 16–17, 82, 141, 155
Transylvania 176
Treat of Logstown 58, 66
treaties 1, 16, 56, 64, 66, 86, 90, 95, 113, 135, 155, 158, 180, 190, 196, 202, 209
Treaty of Aix-la-Chapelle 16, 84, 202
Treaty of Fort Stanwix 180, 190, 196
Treaty of Lancaster 63–65, 75
Treaty of Ryswick (Rijswijk) 16, 84, 202
Treaty of Utrecht 84, 202
Trent, Willam 66, 74–75, 101
Trenton, New Jersey 101
Trent's Fort 102–103, 105, 107, 109–113, 115, 177, 180, 196–197, 206
tuberculosis 24, 67; see also consumption
Tulleken, John 173
Turkey Cock Hall 7
Turkeyfoot 55, 205
Turkeyfoot Path 55
Turtle Creek 82, 89, 100, 109, 115, 150, 182
Tuscarawas 30; see also Beaver Town; King Beaver Town; Shingas's Town
Tuscarawas River 28–31
Tuscarora 166–167
Twightwee 39, 43, 44
Two Brothers sloop 10, 11

Uniontown, Pennsylvania 56, 68
U.S. Library of Congress 3, 12–13, 71–73, 91
Upper Sandusky, Ohio 41

Van Braam, Jacob 87, 94, 97–98, 133–136, 181, 194–195, 197
Vandalia 180, 190, 196
Vaudreuil, Pierre de Rigaud de Cavagnial 181
Venago 79, 82–83, 90–91, 96, 98, 182
Venango Path 91
Vérendrye, Pierre Gaultier de la 16
Villiers, Louis Coulon de 130–134, 137, 139, 148, 181, 198, 208
Virginia Council 18, 21, 162, 169
Virginia Regiment 107, 128, 139, 155, 157, 160, 161–162, 169, 172–173, 193, 206
Virginia Supreme Court 18
Vonore, Tennessee 68

Wabash River 43
Wakatomika 34
Walhonding River 28, 31, 33–34; see also Riviére des Blanche Femmes; White Woman's Creek
Walking Purchase 56
Walpole, Horace 117
wampum 33, 43, 48, 65, 80, 90, 118
Wanduchale 37, 204; see also Windaughala
Wapsid Lenape (White People) 30
Ward, Edward 69, 110, 112–113, 115, 117, 119, 198, 207
Ward, John 198
warehouse 10–11, 69, 155
Warren County, Ohio 44
Warriors Path (*also known as* Great Indian Warpath) 13, 15, 38, 47, 49
Washington, Augustine 18
Washington, George 2–3, 18, 24, 69, 86–102, 105–107, 109–112, 117–143, 146, 148, 151, 153–162, 165, 167–171, 173, 175, 180, 183–185, 187, 193–197, 199, 206, 209
Washington, John 146
Washington, Lawrence 18, 24, 50, 67, 86–87
Washington, Martha Dandridge Custis 198
Waterford, Pennsylvania 82
Watts, John 161, 191
Weisenberg, Catherine 81
Weiser, Conrad 56, 195–196
Wellsburg, West Virginia 60
Wendat 203; see also Wyandot, Huron
Wenro 9
West Virginia 2–3, 48, 54, 58–60, 173, 190, 194
Wheeling Creek 60; see also Scalp Creek
White Eagle 53
White Woman 33–34, 203–204
White Woman's Creek 33–34; see also Riviére des Blanche Femmes; Walhonding River
Wilderness Road 176

224

Index

Wilkesboro, North Carolina
William and Mary 67, 75, 108
Williamsburg, Virginia 20, 50–51, 67–68, 86–87, 93, 95, 101, 106, 109, 112, 136, 138, 140, 157–158, 165, 172–173, 197
Williamsport, Maryland 87, 157, 201
Will's Creek 51, 53–54, 57, 61–62, 65, 75, 87–88, 97, 100–101, 109, 112, 115, 117, 120, 127, 130, 136–139, 141–148, 151, 154, 182, 190, 195
Winchester, Kentucky 47
Winchester, Virginia 66, 85, 111, 122, 128, 137–139, 143, 157, 160–163, 165–173, 198
Windaughala 37, 204; *see also* Wanduchale
Winstone, William 70
Wirth County, West Virginia 60

Wolf Hill 184
Wolfe, James 195
Wyandot 31, 40–41, 64, 92, 129, 172, 185, 203, 210; *see also* Huron, Wendat
Wyandot Old Town 31

Yadkin River 3, 13, 16, 22, 49–50, 53, 61, 63, 67, 72, 176, 186, 202
yellow-fever 177
York Town, Pennsylvania 156
Youghiogheny River 55–56, 61, 67, 69, 100, 118, 120, 205

Zanesville, Ohio 35
zoology 8

www.ingramcontent.com/pod-product-compliance
Lightning Source LLC
Chambersburg PA
CBHW052059300426
44117CB00013B/2202